T0270933

Prices and Quantities

Fundamentals of Microeconomics

Rakesh V. Vohra offers a unique approach to studying and understanding intermediate microeconomics by reversing the conventional order of treatment, starting with the topics that are mathematically simpler and progressing to the more complex. The book begins with monopoly, which requires single-variable rather than multivariable calculus and allows students to focus very clearly on the fundamental trade-off at the heart of economics: margin vs. volume. Imperfect competition and the contrast with monopoly follows, introducing the notion of Nash equilibrium. Perfect competition is addressed toward the end of the book, where it is framed as a model of non-strategic behavior by firms and agents. The last chapter is devoted to externalities, with an emphasis on how one might design competitive markets to price externalities and linking the difficulties to the problem of efficient provision of public goods. Real-life examples and anecdotes engage the reader while encouraging them to think critically about the interplay between model and reality.

Rakesh V. Vohra is the George A. Weiss and Lydia Bravo Weiss University Professor at the University of Pennsylvania. He is the author of *Principles of Pricing: An Analytical Approach* with Lakshman Krishnamurthi (2012) and *Mechanism Design: A Linear Programming Approach* (2011).

Prices and Quantities

Fundamentals of Microeconomics

RAKESH V. VOHRA
University of Pennsylvania

CAMBRIDGE
UNIVERSITY PRESS

CAMBRIDGE
UNIVERSITY PRESS

University Printing House, Cambridge CB2 8BS, United Kingdom

One Liberty Plaza, 20th Floor, New York, NY 10006, USA

477 Williamstown Road, Port Melbourne, VIC 3207, Australia

314–321, 3rd Floor, Plot 3, Splendor Forum, Jasola District Centre, New Delhi – 110025, India

79 Anson Road, #06-04/06, Singapore 079906

Cambridge University Press is part of the University of Cambridge.

It furthers the University's mission by disseminating knowledge in the pursuit of education, learning, and research at the highest international levels of excellence.

www.cambridge.org
Information on this title: www.cambridge.org/9781108488938
DOI: 10.1017/9781108773218

© Rakesh V. Vohra 2020

This publication is in copyright. Subject to statutory exception and to the provisions of relevant collective licensing agreements, no reproduction of any part may take place without the written permission of Cambridge University Press.

First published 2020

A catalogue record for this publication is available from the British Library.

ISBN 978-1-108-48893-8 Hardback
ISBN 978-1-108-71569-0 Paperback

Additional resources for this publication at www.cambridge.org/vohra

Cambridge University Press has no responsibility for the persistence or accuracy of URLs for external or third-party internet websites referred to in this publication and does not guarantee that any content on such websites is, or will remain, accurate or appropriate.

Lead, Kindly Light, amidst th'encircling gloom,
Lead Thou me on!
The night is dark, and I am far from home,
Lead Thou me on!
Keep Thou my feet; I do not ask to see
The distant scene; one step enough for me.

John Henry Newman

Stones are hard, water is wet and objects unsupported fall towards the earth's center.

George Orwell

Brief Contents

Contents

Preface

I am a late in life convert to economics. I did not come to it in a rush but slowly, reluctantly. Impelled by curiosity, repelled by the subject's apparent disconnect from reality. The experience of that long courtship informs this book. I understand, I think, why outsiders find the subject forbidding or treat it with skepticism or both. This is the audience I have written for.

This book exists because I made an impolitic remark about intermediate microeconomics in public. "It was remarkable," I said, "that the nature of the course had not changed in half a century." I went on to list the changes that I thought were needed. My chair obliged by giving me a chance to put the world to rights. Cornered, I could not demur.

Intermediate microeconomics is the gateway course into the economics major at most US universities. It differs from the more widely consumed "principles" course in the level of mathematics expected of students. At the University of Pennsylvania, students are required to have taken a course in multivariable calculus before or concurrently with intermediate microeconomics. This requirement is not intended to limit entry into the major, but is essential for understanding if one is interested in how multiple economic variables interact with each other. The demand for various goods, for example, is influenced by both their price and the buyer's budget. Intermediate courses that do not presume a knowledge of multivariable calculus risk becoming a pastiche of pidgin calculus and cursory economic analysis.

This book assumes the reader is familiar with the relevant mathematics.[1] It does not assume the reader is an undergraduate. The intended audience is anyone equipped with modest mathematical fluency, an appetite for close reasoning, and a curiosity about how markets work.

The use of mathematics in economics is often criticized as either physics envy or a conspiracy to maintain the status quo. I understand the criticisms. In my salad days, I believed them. They are wrong. For this reason the book emphasizes why mathematics is essential by using examples where words and intuition alone are insufficient to resolve the question at hand. Mathematics forces one to be both precise and explicit about the assumptions made. Students often recoil at the need for assumptions. In their minds it makes the subject less definitive. Other subjects also make assumptions, but conceal them. In economics, one holds them up to catch the light.

---

[1] Appendix A contains an *aide memoire* on the relevant mathematics.

Main Features of the Book

This book differs from other intermediate micro books in the following ways.

Less is more: It is Lilliputian in comparison to current intermediate micro textbooks. It favors a "less is more" approach. I prefer the student to come away with a solid understanding of a small and important set of topics rather than a nodding acquaintance with a larger set. Adverse selection, for example, is not covered because an honest treatment requires students to have an understanding of probability, which is usually not a prerequisite for intermediate microeconomics. That some topics are not covered in the book does not mean that students are not exposed to them. They find their way into homework problems that both challenge and intrigue the students.

My experience suggests that students prefer the sense of having gone deeper into the material. Informal feedback from colleagues who teach follow-on courses suggests that students appear better prepared than they did before.

A more student-friendly order of topics: The book reverses the conventional order of topics. It begins with monopoly, followed by imperfect competition, consumer theory, perfect competition, and closes with externalities. In short, from the concrete to the abstract rather than the reverse.

Why begin with monopoly? It requires single-variable calculus rather than multivariable, allowing the students to "warm up." It allows one to focus very clearly on the fundamental trade-off at the heart of economics: margin and volume. Also, students enter thinking that firms "do things" like set prices. The conventional sequence assumes a world where no one does anything. Undergraduates are not yet, like the white queen, willing to believe six impossible things before breakfast.

The conventional sequence begins with the abstraction of preference orderings, which, early in the course, students find dry, dull, and pointless. Some may ask how one can begin without such a discussion, but quasi-linear preferences suffice. They are easy to convey, understand, and, up to a point, plausible. Astute students will ask about budget constraints and the plausibility of preferences being denominated in a common monetary scale. Excellent questions. Ones whose answers come later in the book. In this way the abstraction of preferences is teed up to be an answer to a problem that the students have. Following the conventional order is like asking the students to read the manual for their mobile phone before using it.

Imperfect competition follows naturally from the monopoly case. At this stage, the students themselves are curious about what happens if a firm's demand depends not just on own price but a rival's price as well. The notion of Nash equilibrium will be new to them, but the underlying mathematics is familiar as it is a sequence of monopoly pricing problems holding rivals' actions fixed.

The subject of perfect competition comes towards the end of the book where it is properly framed as a model of non-strategic behavior by firms and agents. Importantly, the students, having been exposed to imperfect competition first, can now clearly see what the price-taking assumption entails. No less important is to convey what a full general equilibrium model can deliver that a partial equilibrium model of imperfect competition cannot. Trying to understand the effect of automation on an economy is a powerful way to highlight this difference.

The last chapter, as with many books, is devoted to externalities. The novelty here is a greater focus on how one might design competitive markets to price externalities (auctioning off the right not to be vaccinated, perhaps), and linking the difficulties to the problem of efficient provision of public goods.

Substantive examples: I offer substantive examples that emphasize the interplay between model and reality. They begin with behavior that appears puzzling, then show how economic modeling can shed light on the puzzle. Many are specific to the book, as are the anecdotes used to motivate each chapter. For example, Amazon and Hachette's struggle over e-book pricing models is used to illustrate the concepts of margin, volume, and elasticity of demand. Details of Mylan's pricing of the EpiPen is used as a vehicle to discuss price discrimination. Real-life examples such as these are incorporated into each chapter to anchor the mathematical models in stories that will engage readers and encourage them to think critically about the distance between model and reality.

Practice problems with solutions: These are designed to help students learn modeling rather than simply practice algebra.

There are other differences whose virtues I could extoll. But the proof is in the "reading."

Acknowledgments

Many thanks are due to the generations of students who have had to digest (or not) the material within these pages. Some of it is based on an earlier book called *Principles of Pricing* written with Lakshman Krishnamurthi, that was inspired by my experience of teaching managers. From them I learnt what was important and from my undergraduates I learnt what was hard.

1 Introduction

Within the pages of Herodotus is a passage that begins

Beyond the Pillars of Hercules there is a race of men . . .

The Pillars are a pair of mountains that flank the entrance to the Straits of Gibraltar. According to Plato, the lost city of Atlantis was to be found beyond this point. The race of men were the Carthaginians, who were frequent visitors to this unnamed country lying beyond Gibraltar:

. . . where they no sooner arrive but forthwith they unlade their wares, and, having disposed them after an orderly fashion along the beach, leave them, and, returning aboard their ships, raise a great smoke. The natives, when they see the smoke, come down to the shore, and, laying out to view so much gold as they think the worth of the wares, withdraw to a distance. The Carthaginians upon this come ashore and look. If they think the gold enough, they take it and go their way; but if it does not seem to them sufficient, they go aboard ship once more, and wait patiently. Then the others approach and add to their gold, till the Carthaginians are content. Neither party deals unfairly by the other: for they themselves never touch the gold till it comes up to the worth of their goods, nor do the natives ever carry off the goods till the gold is taken away.

Dumb barter; trade with neither sight nor sound of the other. Could it be true? Herodotus is known to have told some whoppers in his time. His account of gold-digging ants bigger than foxes but smaller than dogs beggars belief.

From the fourteenth century, the explorer Ibn Battuta sends us an account from the Volga River of a land of darkness, 40 days journey hence where those

who go there do not know whom they are trading with or whether they be jinn or men, for they never see anyone.

A century later, the prelate Paulus Jovius reports that dumb barter was common among the Lapps, writing

They bargain in simple faith with absent and unknown men.

These accounts, taken at face value, raise at least three questions:

1. If trade is anonymous, why doesn't one party steal the goods offered by the other?
2. If trade was mutually profitable and longstanding wouldn't this be an inducement to communication?

3. How do the parties decide the location of the "trading post" in the absence of communication?

If you find these questions of interest, then the study of economics is for you.

What is economics? The essayist Thomas Carlyle damned it as the *dismal science*. The art critic and social reformer John Ruskin called it the *bastard science*, which for him was a mild reproof.[1] The poet Matthew Arnold referred to economists as a *one-eyed race*.[2] In those days cyclopean economists were concerned with the causes of wealth and the exchange of material things. In 1932 Lionel Robbins[3] changed the conception of the subject. "Economics," he wrote, "is the science which studies human behavior as a relationship between ends and scarce means which have alternative uses."[4] And so, economics was elevated from mere catallactics to the study of all human behavior. It is not for nothing that economics is called the imperial science!

The goal of this book is more modest. It is to show how the economist's perspective is useful for thinking about the trade-offs associated with setting the terms of trade. Note the use of the word "perspective" in this paragraph's second sentence. This book is not a laundry list of facts or "take aways." It is about a particular way of approaching problems.

A remark about method is in order. Natural scientists can, and do, run randomized controlled trials to determine whether A causes B as well as the precise quantitative nature of the relationship. Economists rarely enjoy this luxury.[5] However, they can and do run controlled *thought* experiments called models. These are caricatures of reality in which the superfluous or complicated is stripped away. In this artificially constrained environment it is possible to deduce exactly what a rational agent will do and its consequences. Like the Chorus in *Henry V*, one asks that you "piece out our imperfections with your thoughts."

At the end of the exercise, one can conclude that there is a combination of circumstances in which A causes B. The actual quantitative nature of that relationship will be elusive, as it depends intimately on the specifications of the model. The usefulness of such *qualitative* conclusions depends on two things. First, would you ever have imagined that A could cause B? Second, are the circumstances under which A causes B reasonable?

---

[1] Of the painter James Whistler, Ruskin wrote "I have seen, and heard, much of Cockney impudence before now; but never expected to hear a coxcomb ask two hundred guineas for flinging a pot of paint in the public's face." Whistler sued Ruskin for libel, and won a farthing and no costs.

[2] Wandering between two worlds, one dead
The other powerless to be born, . . .

[3] Later Lord Robbins of Clare Market (1898–1984). Famous in the larger world as the author of the Robbins Report that instituted some of the most sweeping reforms of British higher education ever seen.

[4] Robbins, L. (1932). *An Essay on the Nature and Significance of Economic Science*, 2nd edn, London, Macmillan.

[5] It is now very much the rage among some economists to run controlled trials. Like all fashions, this too will pass.

Now, some advice. Reading economics is *not* like reading fiction. One is not a spectator to be entertained while waiting to die. Instead, one must engage with the text. Wrestle with its arguments. Find flaws in the logic. Discuss them with others.

1.1   Is Economics a Science?

It's a bad question. Comparisons made to arrive at a demarcation are problematic. If science were a country, physics might be its capital. If one asks whether history is a science, the customary thing is to measure the proximity of history to science's capital city. Why to the capital and not one of the outlying settlements like geology and archaeology?

Second, the question "is X a science?" is of interest only if we believe that scientific knowledge is privileged in some way. Perhaps it alone is valid and useful while non-scientific knowledge is not. If so, the correct question is not whether X is a science, but whether X produces knowledge that is valid and useful. Now we have something interesting to discuss: what constitutes useful or valid knowledge? Does economics provide this? Read on and judge for yourself.

1.2   Rationality

Economics begins with the assumption that the participants in a trade are rational; suggesting that mad dogs and Englishmen aren't the only ones who run out into the noonday sun. The assumption attracts criticism and deserves discussion. What precisely does it mean to be *rational*?[6]

The economist's conception of rationality has three parts. First, trading agents have *preferences*. Second, their preferences are *consistent* at all times. For example, if on a given day you like oranges, then you should, other things equal, prefer 5 oranges at least as much as 4 oranges. In other words, more of a good thing is never worse and possibly preferred to less of it. If you say you prefer apples to oranges and oranges to cherries then, other things equal, you should prefer apples to cherries. These restrictions do not rule out the possibility that on hot days you prefer ice-cold beer to hot chocolate and the reverse on cold days. Notice the qualifier "other things equal." Under identical conditions, separated in time, one's likes and dislikes are invariant. The trading agent is as

constant as the northern star,
Of whose true-fixed and resting quality
There is no fellow in the firmament.

---

[6] The reader who thinks that rationality does not require a definition should ponder the following: I'll give you a million dollars to do something irrational.

Third, when asked to select from a menu of things, outcomes, or possibilities, one will choose the most preferred item from the menu. This is the assumption of self-interest. Francis Edgeworth (1845–1926) described it thus:

the first principle of Economics is that every agent is actuated only by self-interest.[7]

Given the first two conditions, the third is inevitable. Why wouldn't one choose one's most preferred outcome.

Is the rationality assumption plausible?[8] This book takes the view that the plausibility of the assumption depends on the context. Further, these contexts are neither rare nor exceptional. Less well appreciated is that the rationality assumption is more interesting than the alternatives. When perverse things happen because agents are irrational, this is dull. Why? One can eliminate the perverse outcomes by replacing the agents concerned. When perverse things happen *because* agents are rational, this is interesting because the cause of the perverse outcomes cannot be laid at the agent's feet. One must look, instead, to the environment they inhabit.

Not all economists are wedded to the assumption of rationality. A subset, called behavioral, examines, with gusto (but no brio), the consequences of relaxing the rationality assumption. Invariably charming, they are full of delightful tales about human foibles. Their writings are more properly housed in the self-help sections of book stores, but that is my own prejudice. Should you read what they write, do so with suspicion.[9] To illustrate, consider the following from Daniel Ariely, a celebrated member of the tribe:

If you spend three years in a hospital with 70% of your body covered in burns, you are bound to notice several irrationalities. The one that bothered me in particular was the way my nurses would remove the bandage that wrapped my body. Now, there are two ways to remove a bandage. You can rip it off quickly, causing intense but short-term pain. Or you can remove it slowly, causing less intense pain but for a longer time. My nurses believed in the quick method. It was incredibly painful, and I dreaded the moment of ripping with remarkable intensity. I begged them to find a better way to do this, but they told me that this was the best approach and that they knew the best way for removing bandages. It was their intuition against mine, and they chose theirs. Moreover, they thought it unnecessary to test what appeared (to them) to be intuitively right.

Or, the nurses lied because time is short and they had many patients to care for. Enough of prologue. Down to brass tacks.

1.3   Rational Buyer Model

The simplest transaction to contemplate is that between buyer and seller. To determine a price, the seller must have in mind how the buyer will respond. The model of buyer

---

[7] Edgeworth has been described as "adept at avoiding conversational English." He once asked T. E. Lawrence (of Arabia): "Was it very caliginous in the Metropolis?" Back came the reply: "Somewhat caliginous but not altogether inspissated."

[8] If you disagree, you are welcome to send me twenty dollars and stop reading.

[9] As you should with this book.

behavior used in the first portion of this book will be described here.[10] Called the rational buyer model, it is characterized by three assumptions.

1. **Assumption 1**

   A buyer is able to assign an immutable monetary value to *every* transaction. This value is called their **reservation price** (RP for short). It is the maximum price a buyer is willing to pay for an additional unit of the product (or service).

   Assigning a monetary value to some transactions is difficult. How much for one's grandmother? Argosies of gold, silver, and peacock's eggs? Be careful not to confuse an unwillingness to assign a hard dollar figure to the life of another with the inability to do so. Our actions can betray us, like purchasing a morning coffee rather than donating to Oxfam. Even were it impossible to place a dollar value on everything, this would not invalidate a model based on this assumption. A model can be useful without being universal. What matters is that there be a sufficiently important class of transactions in which such an assumption is plausible.

   If one accepts the assumption, one might wonder about the possibility of determining a buyer's RP. This is challenging but not impossible. There are a host of statistical and econometric tools that have been developed to do just that.

2. **Assumption 2**

   A buyer evaluates a transaction in terms of its **consumer surplus**, which is the difference between her RP and the price she pays. For example, suppose a buyer's RP for a pound of pepper is $5 and we sell it to her for $3. If she buys the pepper from us, she will enjoy a consumer surplus of $5 − $3 = $2. A buyer will never purchase a product that yields negative consumer surplus.

3. **Assumption 3**

   In choosing between transactions, the buyer will choose the transaction which maximizes her consumer surplus. This assumption captures the idea that more money is better than less. For example, suppose our buyer has a choice between a pound of pepper or a pound of salt. For simplicity, assume she will buy one or the other but not both. Let her RP for pepper be $5 and for salt be $4. Pepper is sold at $3 a pound while salt is sold at $3.50 a pound. Which will she acquire? In this case, the consumer surplus on pepper is $2 while on salt it is $0.50. So, she will buy pepper.

   Implicit in this assumption is that a buyer is not cash constrained.

   We incorporate cash constraints in Chapter 5. Until further notice we ignore them. Imaginative sellers find ways around cash constraints, something that even Lenin recognized. When asked how capitalists were to be hanged, there being insufficient rope, he is supposed to have responded "they will sell it to us on credit."

Return to the pepper vs. salt choice. As the seller of salt, how can you induce the buyer to purchase salt instead of pepper? Obviously, by dropping the price, in this case to below $2. At that point the consumer surplus from salt is larger than that from pepper. Alternatively, one can induce the buyer to increase their RP for salt by at least

---

[10] A more general model is described in Chapter 5.

$1.51. Put differently, get them to value salt more highly. This might require making the buyer more aware of the product's usefulness (advertising), or making changes in the product (or service) (i.e. adding value).

If a buyer is interested in more than one unit of the product, we can model this using *incremental* RPs.

Example 1 *Table 1.1 displays the incremental RPs for various amounts of the product Soma.*[11]

Table 1.1 Incremental RPs

Quantity	First unit	Second unit	Third unit	Fourth unit
A's RP	7	5	3	1

This table means that she values the first unit of Soma at $7. She values the second unit of Soma at $5 and so on. Notice that her incremental RPs are declining; she exhibits diminishing marginal returns. You may assume that the RP for the fifth and higher units is zero.

If each unit of Soma was priced at $4, how many units would she buy? She will buy as many units as maximize her consumer surplus. Thus, if she buys one unit, her surplus will be $7 - 4 = 3$. If she buys two units, her surplus will be $7 + 5 - 4 \times 2 = 4$. If she buys three units, her surplus will be $7 + 5 + 3 - 4 \times 3 = 3$. If she buys four units, her surplus will be $7 + 5 + 3 + 1 - 4 \times 4 = 0$. Hence, her surplus is maximized when she buys two units. □

Frequently a buyer will purchase through an agent. Large companies, for example, employ purchasing specialists. In these cases the incentives of the agent and their superiors need not coincide.[12] In what follows we will not consider this possibility.

1.4   Demand Curves

Demand curves summarize how the demand of a single individual, or a collection of them, changes with the price paid (holding the price of other goods and services fixed). To illustrate why they are convenient, imagine a population of a million buyers

---

[11] A possibly fictitious plant whose juice was used in India to produce an intoxicating drug. It appears in Aldous Huxley's *Brave New World* as a narcotic that is distributed by the state to produce social harmony.

[12] In some industrial settings an equipment purchase locks the buyer into the purchase of spare parts and services. If the buyer's agent is evaluated on initial expenditures, the shrewd seller will price the original equipment low and the spare parts high.

each interested in purchasing at most one unit of a particular good. Each buyer is endowed with an RP for the good. At a given price, p say, we would have to count up the number of buyers with an RP of at least p. Sorting the 1 million RPs on file would not be a burden. However, having to store the 1 million RPs would be inconvenient. Instead, we summarize the information needed, the number of buyers at a given price, using an algebraic function.[13] An example of a demand curve is $D(p) = 100 - 2p$. The left-hand side denotes the demand as a function of the unit price p faced by the consumer. The right-hand side is the precise functional form of that demand. In this example, if the unit price p is \$3, demand will be $100 - 2 \times 3 = 94$ units. We interpret a price p at which $D(p) < 0$ to mean demand is zero. The lowest price p at which $D(p) = 0$ is called the **choke price**. Strictly speaking we should express a demand curve as $D(p) = \max\{100 - 2p, 0\}$ to emphasize the fact that for a price above the choke price, demand is zero. We will usually not express demand curves this way with the understanding that one will remember that demand is zero for prices above the choke price.

Demand is a function of the price faced by the buyer *not* the price set by the seller. The two prices are not always identical. For example, suppose a sales tax of 5% is imposed on the price set by the seller. If the seller sets a unit price of p *exclusive* of tax, the price paid by the buyer is $1.05p$.

An important feature of a demand function is that as the price paid by the buyer of the product rises (holding other prices fixed), the demand for it declines. If you sold a good or service for which this relationship was reversed, you should be sitting on a beach somewhere earning 10% instead of reading this book.

1.4.1 Price Sensitivity

Fundamental to understanding how prices are set is the sensitivity of demand to a change in price. This is measured using **elasticity of demand**. It measures the sensitivity of demand to a change in price *holding other prices fixed*. Formally, it is the percentage change in the amount demanded for an infinitesimally small percentage change in the unit price *other things being equal*. Overlooking, for the moment, what an infinitesimally small percentage change in price is, we can express the elasticity of demand as

$$-\left(\frac{\% \text{ change in quantity}}{\% \text{ change in price}} \right).$$

While there is a negative sign in the expression for elasticity of demand, it is a non-negative number between 0 and ∞.[14] This is because a percentage increase in price will result in a percentage decrease in demand, making the numerator negative. The negative sign makes everything positive again. This definition of elasticity,

---

[13] In the case of a single individual, a demand curve summarizes the information contained in the table of incremental RPs (see Example 1).

[14] This is a departure from convention, where the negative sign is absent. This would make elasticity a negative number. However, no one ever refers to an elasticity of -3, for example.

while easy to digest, does not make explicit the fact that the elasticity of demand will vary with the current price. For example, if chocolate cost 1 cent a pound, we would not expect a 50% increase in price to have a significant effect on demand. On the contrary, if it cost 1 dollar a pound, a 50% increase in price might have more of an effect on demand. So, the sensitivity of demand to a change in price doesn't just depend on the magnitude of the change, but the base price from which the change is made.

Now let us turn to the issue of what an infinitesimally small percentage change in price is.

1. Suppose the current unit price is p. Therefore, the current demand is $D(p)$.
2. Increase the price by a small amount, h say, to $p + h$.
3. Demand at the new price is $D(p + h) < D(p)$.
4. % drop in demand is $100 \times \frac{D(p) - D(p+h)}{D(p)}$.
5. % increase in price is $100 \times \frac{(p+h)-p}{p}$.
6. Divide the percentage change in demand by the percentage change in price to get elasticity and let h go to zero. This step can only be executed if $D(p)$ is differentiable.

Step 6 leads to

$$\frac{\frac{D(p)-D(p+h)}{D(p)}}{\frac{(p+h)-p}{p}} = \frac{D(p) - D(p + h)}{D(p)} \times \frac{p}{(p + h) - p}$$

$$= \frac{D(p) - D(p + h)}{D(p)} \times \frac{p}{h} = \frac{p}{D(p)} \times \frac{D(p) - D(p + h)}{h}$$

$$= -\frac{p}{D(p)} \times \frac{D(p + h) - D(p)}{h}. \tag{1.1}$$

Now, let h go to zero. The term to the right of the product sign in (1.1) becomes

$$\lim_{h \to 0} \frac{D(p + h) - D(p)}{h} = \frac{dD(p)}{dp}.$$

Therefore, if $D(p)$ is differentiable, the elasticity of demand is $-[\frac{p}{D(p)}]\frac{dD(p)}{dp}$.

Example 2 *Suppose demand $D(p)$ as a function of unit price p is given by $3 - 0.5p^2$. Then, the elasticity of demand (as a function of p) is*

$$\frac{-p}{3 - 0.5p^2}(-p) = \frac{p^2}{3 - 0.5p^2}. \qquad \square$$

Demand as a function of unit price p, as Example 3 shows, need not be differentiable.

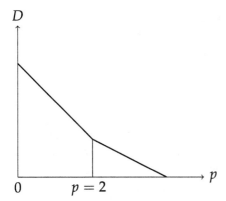

Figure 1.1 Non-differentiable demand

Example 3 *Suppose $D(p) = 3 - p$ for $0 \leq p < 2$ and $D(p) = 2 - 0.5p$ for $2 \leq p \leq 4$. A sketch of the demand curve appears in Figure 1.1.*

When $p < 2$, the derivative of demand with respect to price is -1, however, for $p \geq 2$ the derivative is -0.5. Hence, the slope of the demand curve depends on whether one is to the left of $p = 2$ or to the right of it. For $p < 2$, we use the expression $3 - p$ to compute the elasticity of demand, which comes out to be $\frac{p}{3-p}$. For $p > 2$ we use the expression $2 - 0.5p$ to compute the elasticity of demand, which comes out to be $\frac{0.5p}{2-0.5p}$. Notice, at $p = 2$, the first expression for elasticity yields a value of 2 while the second yields a value of 1. Therefore, the percentage change in demand from a 1% change in the \$2 price will depend on whether one is contemplating a 1% increase or decrease in price.

How might such a demand curve arise? Imagine two distinct markets for a hypothetical good. In market #1, demand as a function of price is given by $D_1(p) = 1 - 0.5p$ and in market #2 it is $D_2(p) = 2 - 0.5p$. The choke price in market #1 is \$2 a unit. For a price p in each market that is at most \$2, total demand will be $D_1(p) + D_2(p) = 1 - 0.5p + 2 - 0.5p = 3 - p$. When the unit price exceeds \$2 a unit, the demand in market #1 falls to zero. Total demand will be $2 - 0.5p$. ☐

1.5 Inverse Demand Curve

While natural to express demand as a function of price, it is frequently convenient to represent this relationship via an **inverse** demand curve. That is, write price as a function of quantity demanded, denoted $p(q)$. For example:

$$p(q) = \max\{7 - 2q, 0\}.$$

As in the case of demand curves, we will write the inverse demand curve as $p(q) = 7 - 2q$, keeping in mind that $p(q) = 0$ when $7 - 2q < 0$. The corresponding demand curve will be $D(p) = \frac{7-p}{2}$. If we were to order buyers by decreasing RP, we can think of $p(q)$ as the RP of the qth buyer in the ordered list. Equivalently, if you sell q units, the RP of every buyer who purchases is at least $p(q)$.

1.6   Relevant Costs

In deciding the profitability of a particular choice, the only costs that matter are those that are relevant to the choice under consideration. Consider the following hypothetical situation. There is a machine capable of making two kinds of widget; red and blue.[15] Red widgets cost \$1 a unit to make and can be sold for \$2 a unit. At that price there are 100 buyers for red widgets. Blue widgets cost \$2 a unit and can be sold to a market of 300 buyers for \$2.50 a unit. The purchase price of the machine is \$X. There are two questions one can ask:

1. Given that you own the machine, which color widget should you make to maximize profit?
2. Should you buy the machine if you don't own it?

The answer to the first question is clearly blue. The blue widgets generate a profit of \$150. More importantly, the purchase price of the machine was irrelevant for deciding this issue. The purchase price of the machine was not a relevant cost in deciding on the color of widgets to make. The machine could have cost a billion dollars or nothing and the answer to the first question would be unchanged.

The answer to the second question is more involved. First, we must decide on how much profit we could make if we owned the machine (answer to the first question) and then we must verify whether that profit is sufficient to cover the purchase of the machine. If the purchase price \$X were smaller than \$150, we would buy the machine, otherwise not. So, for the second question the purchase price of the machine is a relevant cost.

A particular cost can be relevant for one set of choices and irrelevant for another set. We ignore throughout irrelevant costs when deciding on a profit-maximizing option.

1.7   Cost Function/Curve

The technological characteristics of a firm can be summarized by its total **cost function** or curve $C(q)$. The function $C(q)$ denotes the *minimum* total cost needed to

---

[15] The *Oxford English Dictionary* defines a widget to be any gadget or mechanical contrivance. The plastic container at the bottom of some beer cans used to produce a head of beer is called a widget as well.

generate q units of output.[16] We assume that as the volume of output increases, the total cost either stays constant or increases.[17]

Of interest is how the firm's efficiency changes as its output increases. Does it become more or less efficient as its scale (measured by the volume of output) increases? The answer will depend on the way the *slope* or the *derivative* of the cost curve (with respect to q) behaves. The derivative of $C(q)$ with respect to q is called the **marginal cost** of output. Hence, marginal cost is the increase in cost from producing an additional, infinitesimally small, amount of output. Thus, the marginal cost at the tth unit of output is the function $\frac{dC}{dq}$ evaluated at $q = t$. We will sometimes write this as $\frac{dC}{dq}|_{q=t}$.

When contemplating marginal cost it is sometimes useful to have the following approximation of it in mind: the increase in cost from making an additional unit of output.

The increase in cost from producing a *whole* additional unit is an *approximation* to the actual marginal cost. To see why, consider the cost curve $C(q) = q^2$. Suppose you are currently generating two units of output and would like to know the marginal cost at two units of output. The cost of generating two units of output is \$4. Now, increase output to three units. The cost of making three units is \$9. So, the increase in cost is $\$9 - \$4 = \$5$. The approximation would lead one to claim that the marginal cost (at two units of output) is \$5. This is incorrect. Notice, in this case, $\frac{dC}{dq} = 2q$. Hence, $\frac{dC}{dq}|_{q=2} = 2 \times 2 = 4$, that is the marginal cost at two units of output is \$4 and *not* \$5.

By observing how the marginal cost changes as the volume of output increases, we can place the firm into one of three categories.

A firm with cost curve $C(q)$ is said to exhibit **constant returns to scale** if $\frac{dC}{dq}$ is constant. A firm is said to exhibit **increasing returns to scale** if $\frac{dC}{dq}$ is decreasing, so the second derivative is negative: $\frac{d^2C}{dq^2} < 0$. Delivery companies like Federal Express will enjoy increasing returns to scale. As the number of customers they deliver to increases, the incremental cost of serving each additional customer drops. This is because the cost of incorporating a new customer into an existing route is lower than serving them with a dedicated route.

A firm is said to exhibit **decreasing returns to scale** if its marginal cost *increases* as the volume of output increases. Thus, the second derivative of the cost function is positive. Resource extraction industries typically suffer decreasing returns to scale. The incremental cost of extracting oil, for example, increases the deeper one drills.

In reality it is not the case that a firm's technology places it into exactly one of these scale categories. Rather, for small values of q, $C(q)$ might exhibit increasing

---

[16] It assumes that each firm will use its technology in the most efficient way possible. This avoids having to explain why two firms with an identical technology will have different costs. Further, the cost function captures all aspects of a firm's productive capabilities, that is skill, knowledge, as well as machines, etc.

[17] Think about what would happen if this were false.

returns to scale. This can be interpreted as the firm learning and improving production techniques as it ramps up production. At some point the firm will achieve constant returns to scale because it has squeezed every improvement out of the production process it can. Subsequently, the firm may run into capacity constraints or overtime considerations, which will mean that $C(q)$ will exhibit decreasing returns to scale.

Let p be the prevailing per-unit selling price of Soma and to keep things simple, suppose the firm can sell *any* amount at price p per unit. This is, of course, unrealistic and this assumption will be relaxed in the next chapter.

Let $C(q)$ be the total cost to produce q units of Soma. If the firm chooses to produce q units of Soma, its profit will be

$$pq - C(q).$$

The first term, pq, is the total revenue from the sale of x units, assuming it can sell all that it produces. The second term, $C(q)$, is the total cost of producing q units.

If $C(q) = q^2 + 3$ and the unit selling price is \$7, then our mythical firm's profit as a function of the output volume q is

$$7q - (q^2 + 3).$$

To determine the profit-maximizing level of output, that is the value of q that maximizes $7q - (q^2 + 3)$, we can differentiate the profit expression with respect to q and set it to zero:

$$7 - 2q = 0 \Rightarrow q = 3.5.$$

So, $q = 3.5$ is a candidate for the profit-maximizing level of output. To verify that it is indeed a global maximum, we need to check the sign of the second derivative of profit. It is easy to see that it is negative, so we have confirmed that $q = 3.5$ is the profit-maximizing level of output.

More generally, had we differentiated $pq - C(q)$ with respect to q and set it to zero, we would obtain

$$p - \frac{dC}{dq} = 0. \tag{1.2}$$

The value of q that solves equation (1.2) is our candidate for the profit-maximizing level of output. To verify, we need that the second derivative of profit evaluated at this output level be negative $\left(\text{i.e. } -\frac{d^2C}{dq^2} < 0\right)$. This means $\frac{d^2C}{dq^2} > 0$. In words, the technology must exhibit decreasing returns to scale. Assuming the technology satisfies decreasing returns to scale, we have found our profit-maximizing level of output. This simple example shows that the profit-maximizing level of output is determined by two things: the unit selling price and the marginal cost of output.

What if the technology employed by the firm enjoyed increasing returns to scale? Does it mean we cannot determine a profit-maximizing level of output? If the technology enjoys increasing returns to scale, marginal cost goes *down* as the volume of output increases. Thus, if it was profitable to make the first unit, it becomes even more profitable to make the second unit and so on. Eventually the firm generates an infinite amount of output. The conclusion is clearly silly. It is a consequence of the assumption that we can sell all that is produced at price p per unit. As the volume of output increases, we would expect difficulty in moving the product without a price cut. See Section 2.10 for a detailed discussion.

With decreasing returns to scale, as the volume of output rises, the marginal cost increases. Eventually, the marginal cost will bump up against the selling price. When this happens the firm would stop making Soma. Why? Because the increase in cost of the next unit of output would exceed the revenue to be had from that unit. The preceding can be summarized as follows:

Suppose the firm can sell *any* amount at price p per unit. In the presence of decreasing returns to scale, the profit-maximizing level of output is achieved when marginal cost of output equals p.

2 Margin vs. Volume

Should one visit Melbourne, Australia's second city, a stop at the Sky High Observatory in the Dandenong Ranges is obligatory. Looking north from this point one will see the town of Kinglake, named after Alexander Kinglake (1809–1891). He never set foot in Australia. It was upon the strength of his eight-volume history of the Crimean War, published to general approbation, that he was so honored. He is recalled, if at all, for another book, *Eothen*, that records his travels into the Levant. Its novelty lay in its attention to people and impressions rather than places, making it, perhaps, the first modern travel book. Like his history, it was a best seller.

In 1834, Kinglake departed the Austrian border town of Semlin (now in Poland), "the end of this wheel-going Europe," on his way to the "splendour and havoc of the East." Across the river dividing Semlin from the Ottoman Empire was a land gripped by the plague. Preparations for departure resembled those for death:

> . . . they asked if we were perfectly certain that we had wound up all our affairs in Christendom, and whether we had no parting requests to make. . . . No; all our treasures lay safely stowed in the boat, and we were ready to follow them to the ends of the earth.

In Constantinople (now Istanbul), Kinglake visited the grand bazaar (*Kapilcarsi*), where he was moved to wonder how a merchant selects a price:

> Old Moostapha, or Abdallah, or Hadgi Mohamed waddles up from the water's edge with a small packet of merchandise, which he has bought out of a Greek brigantine, and when at last he has reached his nook in the bazaar he puts his goods before the counter, and himself upon it; then laying fire to his tchibouque he 'sits in permanence', and patiently waits to obtain 'the best price that can be got in an open market'. This is his fair right as a seller, but he has no means of finding out what that best price is except by actual experiment.
>
> He cannot know the intensity of the demand, or the abundance of the supply, otherwise than by the offers which may be made for his little bundle of goods; so he begins by asking a perfectly hopeless price, and then descends the ladder until he meets a purchaser, for ever
>
> > Striving to attain, By shadowing out the unattainable.
>
> This is the struggle which creates the continual occasion for debate. The vendor, perceiving that the unfolded merchandise has caught the eye of a possible purchaser, commences his opening speech. He covers his bristling broadcloths and his meagre silks with the golden broidery of Oriental praises, and as he talks, along with the slow and graceful waving of his arms, he lifts his undulating periods, upholds and poises them well, till they have gathered their weight and their strength, and then hurls them bodily forward with grave, momentous swing. The possible purchaser listens to the whole speech with deep and serious attention; but when it is over his

turn arrives. He elaborately endeavors to show why he ought not to buy the things at a price twenty times larger than their value. Bystanders attracted to the debate take a part in it as independent members; the vendor is heard in reply, and coming down with his price, furnishes the materials for a new debate. Sometimes, however, the dealer, if he is a very pious Mussulman, and sufficiently rich to hold back his ware, will take a more dignified part, maintaining a kind of judicial gravity, and receiving the applicants who come to his stall as if they were rather suitors than customers. He will quietly hear to the end some long speech that concludes with an offer, and will answer it all with the one monosyllable 'Yok', which means distinctly 'No'.

Some sellers chaffer while others post a price and don't flinch. Which is best? If one is to post a price, what should it be? These are the questions we now take up. We begin with the strategy of Kinglake's "pious Mussulman," a posted price. A high price means a high margin, but a low likelihood of sale or low volume. A low price means a low margin, but a high chance of sale or a large sales volume. Between the two prices is a "sweet spot" and it is natural to ask what that sweet spot depends on.

So that we may focus on the trade-off between margin and volume, we ignore competition. Therefore, as we change our price, we assume that the competition, if any, does not change their price or offering, or both. The economics shorthand for this assumption is that the firm setting prices is a **monopoly**, from the Greek *monos polein*, meaning "alone to sell." When the monopoly assumption is invoked, we no longer have in mind its literal meaning. When we assume that a firm is a monopoly, we mean that its rivals do not change their prices in response to its price changes. The assumption is restrictive, but it allows us to understand how a buyer will react to the seller's price to the exclusion of other issues. The consequences of dropping this assumption are examined in subsequent chapters.

Why choose to sell via a posted price? When selling to many buyers at the same time, negotiating with each one becomes costly. In this case it is reasonable to adopt a posted price (i.e. make a "take-it-or-leave-it" offer to every buyer).[1] If the seller is selling through an intermediary, a posted price saves on having to offer detailed instructions on when and by how much to change the price on each transaction. A posted price also serves to reduce the possibility of collusion between intermediary and buyer.

Assume a single divisible good (Soma) sold by the monopolist whose qualities are known to all buyers. The monopolist charges the same price per unit for the good to one and all.

The monopoly is characterized by a decreasing returns to scale cost function $C(q)$, where q is the amount produced. Demand is characterized by a downward-sloping, differentiable demand function $D(p)$, which is the amount of Soma demanded at price per unit p. The monopolist's problem is to choose both a price *and* a quantity to produce, so as to maximize profit. Because the demand is known, once you choose a unit price p, you have implicitly chosen the quantity $D(p)$ to produce. The reverse is also true.

---

[1] This argument does not apply if there is only one buyer. We return to this issue later in this chapter.

Thus, one version of the monopolist's problem is to choose the price p at which to sell so as to maximize profit. The algebraic rendition of the monopolist's problem is

$$\max pD(p) - C(D(p))$$
$$\text{s.t. } p, D(p) \geq 0.$$

Here, s.t. is an abbreviation for "subject to." To make progress we must understand how to solve this problem.

Example 4 *Suppose a monopolist has a production cost function $C(q) = q$. This means, for example, that if the monopolist makes five units, the total cost to produce those five units will be \$5. If the monopolist makes six units, the total cost will be \$6. Notice that the marginal cost of each unit is \$1 (constant returns to scale). Let $D(p) = 9 - p$. Once the monopolist chooses a unit price p, that determines the demand. The monopolist will produce to exactly meet that demand. So:*

1. *Choose a price p.*
2. *At the chosen price, demand will be $9 - p$.*
3. *So, the monopolist will produce $9 - p$ units.*
4. *For this quantity choice, their revenue will be $p(9 - p)$.*
5. *The cost of producing this quantity will be $9 - p$.*
6. *Profit will be $(9 - p)p - (9 - p) = -p^2 + 10p - 9$.*
7. *Our goal is to solve*

$$\max -p^2 + 10p - 9$$
$$\text{s.t. } 9 - p \geq 0$$
$$p \geq 0.$$

The first constraint ensures that demand is non-negative and the second ensures that price is non-negative.

8. *We ignore the two constraints (for the moment) and solve the unconstrained maximization problem: $\max_p -p^2 + 10p - 9$.*
9. *We differentiate $-p^2 + 10p - 9$ and set to zero:*

$$-2p + 10 = 0 \Rightarrow p = 5.$$

As the second derivative of profit is negative for all values of p, we know that we have found the optimal solution to the unconstrained maximization problem.

10. *Notice that $p = 5$ satisfies the two omitted constraints, so we have found the solution to the original optimization problem stated in item 7 above.*

Subsequently we omit many of the steps above, trusting the reader to fill them in. □

In Example 4 we chose p as our variable. We could just as well have chosen output q as our variable instead.

Example 5 *Suppose a monopolist has a production cost function $C(q) = q$. Thus, the marginal cost of each unit is \$1. Let $D(p) = 9 - p$. Once the monopolist chooses an output level q, that determines the price to be set so as to sell the entire output. Thus, to sell q units, the monopolist must choose the unit price p so that $q = 9 - p$ (i.e. $p = 9 - q$). The expression $p = 9 - q$ is the inverse demand curve. So:*

1. *Choose a quantity or output q.*
2. *At the chosen quantity, price will be $9 - q$.*
3. *For this quantity choice, their revenue will be $q(9 - q)$.*
4. *The cost of producing this quantity will be q.*
5. *Profit will be $(9 - q)q - q = -q^2 + 8q$.*

To find the value of q that maximizes profit, we differentiate $-q^2 + 8q$ with respect to q and set to zero (i.e. $-2q + 8 = 0 \Rightarrow q = 4$). You should check that the second derivative is negative. □

Thus, given demand and cost functions we can, in principle, determine a profit-maximizing price. However, this calculation does not reveal, at least immediately, what factors determine the appropriate balance between margin and volume.

2.1   Markup Formula

To get a second view of things, rewrite the profit function in Example 4 as

$$(p - 1)(9 - p).$$

The first term in brackets is the profit per unit (margin), while the second bracketed term is the volume sold. The product of the two terms is total profit. As one increases p, two things happen in the expression for profit. First the margin, $p - 1$, increases *but* the volume sold, $9 - p$, declines. If one decreases p, then the margin declines *but* the volume sold increases. The profit-maximizing price is chosen so as to balance these two opposing forces.

If one were to draw the total profit vs. price curve (which you should do) you will see that the profit rises from 0 as p increases from $p = 1$, reaches a peak at $p = 5$, and then declines to zero when $p = 9$. When the price is smaller than \$5, say $p = 2$, the monopolist can increase profit by raising price. This is obvious from the graph. Here is what is going on: as one raises price, margin increases while volume drops. However, the profit per unit is rising faster than the demand is dropping. How do we know this? Compute the elasticity of demand at $p = 2$. You will see that it is less than 1. Thus, if we increase price by 1%, demand drops by *less than* 1%. Taken together, the monopolist winds up better off.

In general, if the elasticity of demand at a particular price is smaller than 1, it is always profitable to increase the unit price of the product. What one loses on volume is made up for by what one gains in per-unit profit.

Notice that the monopolist's profit-maximizing price in the example above, $5, is *larger* than its marginal cost of production of $1. In fact, it is always the case that the monopolist's profit-maximizing price exceeds its marginal cost of production. The magnitude of the excess will depend on how sensitive demand is to a change in price. For example, if the elasticity of demand is high at all prices, we would expect that the monopolist would charge prices close to its marginal cost. This intuition is made precise in the following formula:

$$\frac{(p-c)}{p} = \frac{1}{e(p)}. \tag{2.1}$$

Here p is the profit-maximizing price, c is the constant marginal cost of production, and $e(p)$ the elasticity of demand at price p.[2] The left-hand side of equation (2.1) is the ratio of the profit margin to the price, which is called the **relative markup**.[3] The term on the right-hand side is the reciprocal of the elasticity of demand. At the profit-maximizing price, **the relative markup is the reciprocal of the elasticity of demand**.[4]

The larger the elasticity of demand (at the profit-maximizing price), the smaller the relative markup will be. In plain language, the more sensitive buyers are to price increase, the smaller the markup that the monopolist can sustain. Therefore, the power to sustain a price above marginal cost depends only on elasticity of demand. The elasticity term captures how buyers will respond to a change in the seller's price. This will depend on the value they place on the seller's product, the opportunity costs of using a substitute product, and so on. In this sense the relative markup formula applies to all firms and not just monopolies.

Notice that the left-hand side of equation (2.1) cannot exceed 1. In fact, if $c > 0$, it must be strictly less than 1. Thus, at the *profit-maximizing* price, the elasticity of demand is strictly larger than 1. At the *revenue-maximizing* price, the elasticity of demand will be 0. This can be deduced from the markup formula by setting $c = 0$, because revenue maximization coincides with profit maximization when the marginal cost is zero. Assuming that the elasticity of demand increases with price, it follows that the revenue-maximizing price can never exceed the profit-maximizing price.

Is the elasticity of demand increasing in price? Not always. Recall the expression $e(p) = -(p/D(p))(dD/dp)$. As p increases, demand falls, that is $D(p)$ decreases. Hence $\frac{p}{D(p)}$ must increase. What about the term $-\frac{dD}{dp}$? It is clearly positive, but is it increasing or decreasing? If it is increasing, then obviously $e(p)$ increases with p. Consider, however, $D(p) = \frac{1}{p}$. Then $-\frac{dD}{dp} = \frac{1}{p^2}$, which declines as p increases. In this case $e(p)$ will be a constant (i.e. the elasticity does not change with price). Consider $D(p) = 1 - p + p^2/2$. For $p \in [0, 1]$, demand decreases as p increases. However:

$$e(p) = -\frac{p}{1 - p + p^2/2}(-1 + p).$$

---

[2] Equation (2.1) is valid only at the profit-maximizing price.
[3] Also called the Lerner index.
[4] Later in this chapter you will find a discussion of the markup formula for the case where the firm does not have constant marginal costs.

As the reader can verify by direct calculation, this expression decreases for $p \in [0, 0.5]$. Therefore, while we might think it natural that $e(p)$ should increase with price, it is not a given. Hence, it is something we assume on the grounds that it is natural. It is hard to imagine that buyers would become *less* sensitive to a price increase as we raise the price.

What happens to the relative markup if the elasticity of demand increases (at every price)? The relative markup decreases. As customers become more sensitive to a price change, the margin per customer decreases. This does not automatically imply a decrease in profits though. If the margin decrease is accompanied by a large enough increase in volume, profit will increase.

2.1.1 Derivation of Markup Rule

Here we derive the markup formula for more general cost functions. Suppose we have a monopolist with cost function $C(\cdot)$ and facing a demand curve $D(p)$. If the monopolist sets a price of p per unit, then demand will be $D(p)$. The monopolist will produce to meet this demand and incur a cost of $C(D(p))$. Hence, the monopolist's profit-maximization problem is

$$\max pD(p) - C[D(p)]$$

$$\text{s.t. } p, D(p) \geq 0.$$

The profit-maximizing price must satisfy the relevant first-order condition, that is the derivative of profit with respect to price should be zero:

$$D(p) + p\frac{dD}{dp} - \frac{dD}{dp}C'(D(p)) = 0$$

$$\Rightarrow D(p) + \frac{dD}{dp}[p - C'(D(p))] = 0$$

$$\Rightarrow p - C'(D(p)) = -(D(p)/D'(p))$$

$$\Rightarrow [p - C'(D(p))]/p = 1/e(p),$$

where $e(p) = -(p/D(p))(dD/dp)$ is the elasticity of demand. Recall that the first-order condition is a *necessary* condition for optimality, not a sufficient one. Hence, the profit-maximizing price satisfies the markup rule, but it does not preclude a *non-profit*-maximizing price also satisfying the markup rule. If the price that satisfies the markup formula is unique, it must be profit maximizing. If many prices satisfy the markup formula, one must select from among them the one that maximizes profit.

2.2 Amazon vs. Hachette

Amazon's Kindle arrived in 2007. Though not the first reader on the market, it succeeded in jumpstarting e-book sales. By 2013, e-books constituted 27% of the adult books sold and annual US revenues were about $3 billion. Two-thirds of this market was in Amazon's hands.

Initially, publishers set the list price of an e-book at a few dollars below the print price, and then gave Amazon a 50% discount. For example, an e-book with a list price of $24 would be sold to Amazon at a wholesale price of $12 with the expectation that Amazon would resell the book for about $24. This is called the wholesale model of pricing.

Amazon, however, would sell the e-book for $9.99 or even less. This made publishers unhappy. To force Amazon to raise the price that it set, publishers raised their wholesale price to Amazon. Amazon was undeterred. Publishers then delayed the release of an e-book for several months after its hardcover release. Amazon was unyielding.

In an attempt to force Amazon to raise e-book prices, the biggest publishers (Hachette included) approached Apple and switched from the wholesale price model to an agency model where publishers would set the price of the book to readers and Apple and Amazon would receive 30% of the revenues. Apple required that the price set by a publisher on Apple be no higher than the price set on the book sold through any other channel. In 2012, the US Department of Justice filed an anti-trust law suit against the publishers on the grounds that they had illegally conspired to fix e-book prices. Hachette settled. Apple and some of the other publishers did not, but subsequently lost at trial.

In March 2014, Hachette's contract with Amazon expired. As a condition for renewal, Amazon wanted to set the price of e-books at $9.99. As this was the first of similar negotiations with other publishers, Amazon wanted to set a precedent. They turned the thumbscrews by delaying the shipment of some Hachette titles to customers, as well as reducing the discounts of many Hachette titles. For good measure, Amazon suggested cheaper substitutes to people searching for Hachette titles. Amazon asserted that the sticking point was the pricing of e-books. In July 2014, Amazon published an open letter to Hachette authors:

A key objective is lower e-book prices. Many e-books are being released at $14.99 and even $19.99. That is unjustifiably high for an e-book. With an e-book, there's no printing, no overprinting, no need to forecast, no returns, no lost sales due to out-of-stock, no warehousing costs, no transportation costs, and there is no secondary market – e-books cannot be resold as used books. E-books can be and should be less expensive.

It's also important to understand that e-books are highly price-elastic. This means that when the price goes up, customers buy much less. We've quantified the price elasticity of e-books from repeated measurements across many titles. For every copy an e-book would sell at $14.99, it would sell 1.74 copies if priced at $9.99. So, for example, if customers would buy 100,000 copies of a particular e-book at $14.99, then customers would buy 174,000 copies of that same e-book at $9.99. Total revenue at $14.99 would be $1,499,000. Total revenue at $9.99 is $1,738,000.

The important thing to note here is that at the lower price, total revenue increases 16%. This is good for all the parties involved: The customer is paying 33% less. The author is getting a royalty check 16% larger and being read by an audience that's 74% larger. And that 74% increase in copies sold makes it much more likely that the title will make it onto the national bestseller lists. (Any author who's trying to get on one of the national bestseller lists should insist to their publisher that their e-book be priced at \$9.99 or lower.) Likewise, the higher total revenue generated at \$9.99 is also good for the publisher and the retailer. At \$9.99, even though the customer is paying less, the total pie is bigger and there is more to share amongst the parties.

A drop in price from \$14.99 to \$9.99 is a $\frac{14.99 - 9.99}{14.99} \times 100 = 33\%$ decrease. The reported increase in demand from 100,000 to 174,000 copies is a 74% increase. Hence, the estimated elasticity of demand is $\frac{74}{33} = 2.24$. It is larger than 1.

Authors and Amazon are compensated by percentage of revenue. As the marginal cost of e-books is zero, publishers are also focused on revenue. From the markup formula we know that the revenue-maximizing price should be set at the point where the elasticity of demand is 1. Given Amazon's estimate of the elasticity of demand, the current price of e-books is not revenue maximizing. Does Amazon have a point?

Put yourself in the shoes of an author. Is the elasticity estimate from Amazon an estimate of the elasticity of demand for your book alone or the entire category of e-books? To see why this question matters, recall that elasticity of demand is a measure of how demand changes with price while *holding* other prices fixed. If this elasticity estimate is for your book alone, then, of course, it's a good idea to lower the price of your e-book *holding* the price of other e-books fixed. Is this what Amazon is proposing? Of course not. They want to lower the price of *all* e-books. The aggregate demand for e-books will increase.[5] This is good for Amazon because they care about the total revenue on e-books, not the revenue of your book alone. If aggregate demand increases with a price drop, it does not follow that the demand for your book will increase.

2.3   Marginal Revenue

Marginal revenue is the derivative of revenue with respect to *quantity* or output.[6] Informally, it is the increase in revenue from the production of an additional unit of output. Marginal revenue sounds like the unit selling price; it isn't. To see why, let us consider two examples.

In the first, suppose that you can sell every unit of output for p per unit. Then, one's revenue from q units of output would be $R(q) = pq$. The marginal revenue would be $\frac{dR}{dq} = p$ (i.e. the unit selling price).

In the second, recall Example 4. You face a demand curve $D(p) = 9 - p$. To determine the marginal revenue, you first need to write revenue as a function of output. Why? Recall the definition. It is the derivative of revenue with respect to output. From Example 5, we know how to do this:

$$R(q) = (9 - q)q.$$

---

[5] One should ask where this extra demand is coming from. Is it current readers buying more than they otherwise would, or bringing in new readers who were perhaps playing video games before?

[6] It is *not* the derivative of revenue with respect to price.

Thus

$$\frac{dR}{dq} = 9 - 2q.$$

Notice that marginal revenue depends on output level and is declining with output. Why? To sell more you have to lower the price. This is true more generally. Let $q(p)$ be the inverse demand curve. Then the marginal revenue, $MR(q)$, is given by

$$MR(q) = \frac{dR(q)}{dq} = p(q) + q\frac{dp(q)}{dq}.$$

As q increases, $p(q)$ goes down. As $\frac{dp(q)}{dq} < 0$, it follows that $q\frac{dp(q)}{dq}$ will also decrease as q increases, provided $\frac{dp(q)}{dq}$ also decreases. Formally, the derivative of $MR(q)$ with respect to quantity is

$$\frac{dp(q)}{dq} + \frac{dp(q)}{dq} + q\frac{d^2p(q)}{dq^2} = 2\frac{dp(q)}{dq} + q\frac{d^2p(q)}{dq^2}.$$

For $MR(q)$ to be decreasing, we need

$$2\frac{dp(q)}{dq} + q\frac{d^2p(q)}{dq^2} < 0. \tag{2.2}$$

Given that $\frac{dp(q)}{dq}$ is negative, we can ensure (2.2) if we assume that $\frac{d^2p(q)}{dq^2} < 0$.

If $C(q)$ is the cost curve and $p(q)$ is the inverse demand curve (i.e. the unit price at which q units will be demanded), profit will be

$$qp(q) - C(q).$$

Notice that revenue as a function of output q is $R(q) = qp(q)$. To find the profit-maximizing level of output, we differentiate with respect to q and set to zero:

$$\frac{dR}{dq} - \frac{dC}{dq} = 0 \implies \frac{dR}{dq} = \frac{dC}{dq}.$$

For this to be a maximum we need the second derivative of profit to be negative. You should verify that this is the case when the second derivative of revenue is non-positive and $C(q)$ exhibits decreasing returns to scale, or the second derivative of revenue is negative and $C(q)$ exhibits constant returns to scale. Thus, we arrive at one of the more well-known slogans of economics: profit is maximized when the output is chosen to equalize marginal revenue with marginal cost *provided* the second derivative of revenue with respect to quantity is negative and production costs satisfy decreasing or constant returns to scale.

2.3.1   An Aside on Areas

If $R(q)$ is the total revenue from q units of output, then the marginal revenue $MR(q)$ is given by $MR(q) = \frac{dR(q)}{dq}$. Hence, by the Fundamental Theorem of Calculus:

$$R(q) = \int_0^q \frac{dR(x)}{dx}dx = \int_0^q MR(x)dx.$$

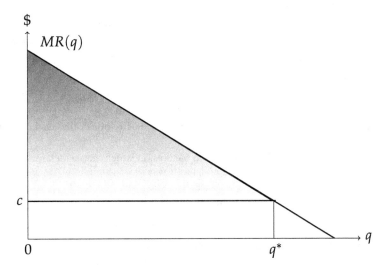

Figure 2.1 Profit and area

Informally, revenue is the area under the marginal revenue curve, $MR(x)$.

Similarly, total cost is the area under the marginal cost curve, $MC(q)$. To see why, suppose $C(q)$ is the total cost to produce q units, then $MC(q) = \frac{dC(q)}{dq}$. Therefore:

$$C(q) = \int_0^q \frac{dC(x)}{dx}dx = \int_0^q MC(x)dx.$$

Hence, profit is the area of the region trapped between the marginal revenue curve and the marginal cost curve. Thus, if q^* is the profit-maximizing level of output, total profit will be

$$\int_0^{q^*} MR(x)dx - \int_0^{q^*} MC(x)dx.$$

In words, the area under the marginal revenue curve less the area under the marginal cost curve. Equivalently, the area above the marginal cost curve but below the marginal revenue curve. This is illustrated in Figure 2.1 for the case of a constant marginal cost c. The shaded area corresponds to the profit.

2.4 Double Marginalization

The 21st Amendment to the US Constitution ended prohibition and gave to American states the power to regulate the sale of alcohol within their borders. Some chose to control all alcohol sales (control states). The rest mandated a state-based middleman between alcohol producers (brewers, distillers, wineries) and retailers (restaurants, grocery stores, liquor stores). These are called three-tier states, where no one is allowed to buy directly from a producer, they must go through a distributor. Frequently, distributors are given exclusive rights to distribute alcohol in a particular region, effectively creating government-enforced monopolies. The restriction was promoted by prohibitionists eager to prevent the establishment of "tied houses," bars owned by liquor producers.

Tied houses existed before prohibition and were criticized for tempting workers with free, but heavily salted, food. This encouraged the purchase of alcohol to slake their thirst. Their popularity attracted the attention of Kipling, the bard of empire:

> ... came upon a bar-room full of bad Salon pictures, in which men with hats on the backs of their heads were wolfing food from a counter. It was the 'institution of the free lunch' I had struck. You paid for a drink and got as much as you wanted to eat. For something less than a rupee a day a man can feed himself sumptuously in San Francisco, even though he be a bankrupt. Remember this if ever you are stranded in these parts.

In England, tied houses were the norm since the age of Queen Victoria. In the mid-1890s, about 90% of the beer sold for consumption on the premises was tied. The twentieth century saw brewers enlarging the size of their tied estates. By 1989, six brewers were responsible for 75% of the UK's beer output and owned 75% of its tied houses. That year, the UK Monopolies and Mergers Commission concluded that "the complex monopoly has enabled brewers with tied estates to frustrate the growth of brewers without tied estates ... and that, over time, the monopoly has served to keep the bigger brewers big and the smaller brewers small." The commission introduced what was known as the "beer order," restricting the number of tied pubs that could be owned by a large brewery. This order was revoked in 2003.

Sale through a tied house is the same as buying directly from the brewer. The three-tier arrangement, in contrast, requires one to purchase through a middleman. Is there a reason, as consumer or brewer, to prefer one arrangement over the other? The question, while easy to pose, is devilishly difficult to answer. No attempt to offer a complete analysis will be made here. Instead, we focus on one aspect only, called **double marginalization**, which arises when a seller does not sell directly to the end user, but through an intermediary.

Suppose a monopoly manufacturer (M) sells to a monopoly retailer (R), who in turn sells into a downstream market. The demand in the downstream market as a function of R's unit price p is $1000 \times (10 - p)$. M's unit cost of production is a constant $1 a unit. M sells the product at a wholesale price of w per unit to R. For simplicity, assume that R incurs no other costs beyond the wholesale price of w per unit.[7] An example of a situation that *resembles* this was discussed earlier, with Hachette playing the role of M and Amazon the role of R.[8]

M will move first and dictate a price w per unit to R. By allowing M to unilaterally set the terms of trade, we have given M bargaining power over M. Now, M will choose w to maximize M's profit. Then, R takes w as given and determines the unit price p in

---

[7] These other costs can be included, but they clutter the analysis without adding insight.

[8] Resembles rather than "identical to" because it would be hard to argue that Hachette and Amazon are monopolists in their respective markets.

the downstream market that maximizes R's profit. Call this scenario #1. Each agent in the chain takes a markup. In scenario #1, what value of w will M choose? What value of p will R choose?

As M "moves" first, one might think that our analysis should begin with M. This poses a difficulty. How M should price depends on R's reaction. Thus, M must anticipate R's behavior, before she can determine what price w to charge R. Therefore, we examine how R chooses p as a function of w first, which is R's unit cost. By the markup formula, R's profit-maximizing price p^* would be set so that

$$\frac{p^* - w}{p^*} = \frac{10 - p^*}{p^*} \Rightarrow p^* = \frac{10 + w}{2}.$$

Therefore, downstream demand will be

$$1000(10 - p^*) = 1000\left(10 - \frac{10 + w}{2}\right) = 1000\left(5 - \frac{w}{2}\right).$$

Since R must order from M, R's demand is also M's demand. This implies, for M, an elasticity of demand of $\frac{w/2}{5-(w/2)}$. The profit-maximizing value of w for M will, by the markup formula, satisfy

$$\frac{w - 1}{w} = \frac{5 - (w/2)}{w/2} \Rightarrow w - 1 = 2 \times \left(5 - \frac{w}{2}\right).$$

Solving for w yields $w = \$5.5$.

If M sets a wholesale price of $w = \$5.5$, then R will set a price equal to $\frac{10+w}{2} = \$7.75$. At this price R will generate a margin of $\$7.75 - \$5.5 = \$2.25$ a unit and demand of $1000 \times (10 - 7.75) = 2250$. Thus, R's profit, denoted Π_R, will be $\$2.25 \times 2250 = \$5062.5$.

Now, M's margin is $\$5.5 - \$1 = \$4.5$. Hence, M makes a profit, denoted Π_M, of $\$4.5 \times 2250 = \$10{,}125$. Therefore, the total profit made by R and M is $\Pi_M + \Pi_R = \$5062.5 + \$10{,}125 = \$15{,}187.5$.

It is instructive to compare this scenario with one where M sells directly downstream into the market. Call this scenario #2; it has three interpretations. First, M simply cuts R out as a middleman and sells directly to the end user. Second, M and R merge into a single firm. Third, M and R agree to coordinate so as to maximize their combined profit. Denote by Π the profit of M in this scenario.

What unit price will M pick to maximize profit? We can determine this using the markup formula. Since demand as a function of price p is $1000 \times (10 - p)$, the elasticity of demand will be $\frac{p}{10-p}$. By the markup formula (with $c = 1$), the profit-maximizing price p^* must satisfy

$$\frac{p^* - 1}{p^*} = \frac{10 - p^*}{p^*}.$$

Solving for p^*, we determine that $p^* = 5.50$. Demand equals $1000 \times (10 - 5.50) = 4500$. At a price of $\$5.50$ per unit, M would realize a margin of $\$5.50 - \$1 = \$4.50$ a unit. Hence, $\Pi = \$4.5 \times 4500 = \$20{,}250$.

Observe that $\Pi > \Pi_M + \Pi_R$. Furthermore, the downstream price is lower in scenario #2 than scenario #1. Consumers are better off *and* the firms, collectively, are better off. Given that consumers and the two firms have interests that are antagonistic to each other, this is surprising. Before continuing with our discussion, we should check if what has just been observed is limited to the example selected.

Example 6 *Let M have a constant marginal cost of production of c. Denote by $D(p)$ the demand in the downstream market when the unit price set by R is p. If M chooses a wholesale price w, then R will choose p to solve*

$$\max_{p \geq 0}(p - w)D(p).$$

Let $p^*(w)$ denote the optimal choice of p. The notation is chosen to make explicit the dependence of R's optimal price on w.

Because whatever R sells must be bought from M, M's profit will be $(w - c)D(p^*(w))$ and M will choose w to maximize this expression. Let $\bar{w}$ be M's optimal choice of w. Hence, the joint profit of the two firms will be

$$\Pi_1 = (w - c)D(p^*(\bar{w})) + (p^*(\bar{w}) - w)D(p^*(\bar{w})) = (p^*(\bar{w}) - c)D(p^*(\bar{w})).$$

Now, let Π_2 be the joint profit that would be obtained if M and R coordinate prices. In this case the joint firm will choose the downstream price p to solve

$$\Pi_2 = \max_{p \geq 0}(p - c)D(p). \tag{2.3}$$

Notice that $p^*(\bar{w})$ is a feasible solution to the optimization problem above. Hence, $\Pi_1 \leq \Pi_2$. ☐

Figure 2.2 gives a graphical illustration of double marginalization. Monetary amounts are displayed on the vertical, and quantities on the horizontal. There are three curves displayed. The first is the marginal revenue curve $(MR(q))$, which is downward sloping. The second is the marginal cost curve of M. This is a horizontal line through c because we have assumed constant marginal cost of c. The third is the marginal cost curve of R. This is a horizontal line through the wholesale price w because M sells to R at w a unit. We know that $w > c$ because M would set a price above its marginal cost to turn a profit.

Given w, R will choose the quantity q^R to maximize its profit. This is the quantity where marginal revenue is equal to the retailer's marginal cost. The retailer's profit will be determined by the area of the triangle marked: R's profit. M's profit is determined by the area of the rectangle marked: M's profit. Joint profit is the sum of these two areas.

Now suppose M and R merge. The merged enterprise will choose the quantity q^I, where marginal revenue equals its marginal cost c. The profit of the merged enterprise will be the area of the triangle below the marginal revenue line and above the

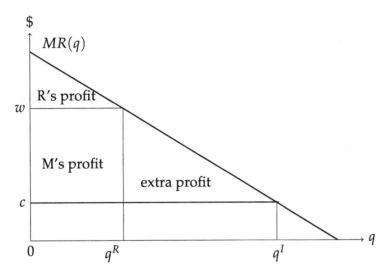

Figure 2.2 Double marginalization

horizontal line through c. The area of the triangle labeled "extra profit" represents the increase in joint profit that would be enjoyed by M and R merging.

Why is the joint profit of M and R ($\Pi_M + \Pi_R$) when pricing independently lower than when they coordinate pricing (Π)? Because each ignores the effect of its action on the other in the chain. This results in lower profits and a higher retail price than if they coordinated their pricing actions. This is the problem of **double marginalization**. How might M and R recover those "lost" profits?

1. Integration
   M and R merge into a single firm; also called vertical integration.
2. Resale price maintenance
   M controls the price that R charges. In the double marginalization case, M would like to place a ceiling on the price set by R.
3. M introduces a competitor to R in the downstream market
   It is easy to see that if R competes with another retailer selling the same product, that would place a ceiling on the price that R sets.
4. M changes the way it prices to R
   The goal is to induce R to select a lower price by rewarding R with a share of the money previously left on the table. One way to do this is to deploy a two-part tariff. M offers to sell to R each unit at marginal cost (i.e. c per unit) in return for a fixed fee F. In retailing, F is often called a franchise fee. See the example below for details.

Example 7 *We continue with Example 6. Suppose M chooses a franchise fee of F in return for selling as many units of Soma as R wishes for a price of c per unit. If R chooses a downstream price of p per unit, R's profit will be $(p - c)D(p) - F$. Thus, R* *will choose p to maximize this. Notice that this is precisely the optimization problem in (2.3) modulo the term involving F. As F does not depend on p, the optimal choice of p here is the same as the optimal choice of p in (2.3). Hence, R achieves a total profit of $\Pi_2 - F$. In other words, R has been incentivized to choose the downstream price that maximizes the joint profit of the firms. The franchise fee F simply determines how Π_2 is to be shared between M and R. In particular, there is a choice of F that would give each of M and R more profit than they would enjoy when pricing independently of each other.* □

What does this analysis suggest about the three-tier distribution system in some states? Alcohol prices are higher than they otherwise would be. In fact, the system of tied houses could be interpreted as one solution to the double marginalization problem via vertical integration. However, as the UK experience with tied houses shows, while prices might be lower, the variety of beers on offer might be diminished.

2.4.1   Keystone Pricing

Often, retailers follow a simple pricing rule, called **keystone pricing**: double the wholesale price. If M sets a wholesale price of w, R sets a downstream price of $2w$. The rule ignores the elasticity of demand in the downstream market. Therefore, it cannot be profit maximizing for R. Are retailers who follow such a rule simpletons?

Suppose that R follows a simple doubling rule to set the downstream price and M knows this and can't alter R's behavior. If M sets a wholesale price of w per unit, R will charge a price of $2w$ per unit downstream. At this downstream price, R will enjoy a demand of $1000 \times (10 - 2w)$. Since R must buy every unit it sells from M, it means that R will order $1000 \times (10-2w)$ units from M. Therefore, if M sets a wholesale price w, it will see a demand of $1000 \times (10 - 2w)$. Again, we can use the relative markup formula to determine M's profit-maximizing wholesale price. Since the demand curve that M now faces is $1000 \times (10 - 2w)$, the elasticity of demand will be $\frac{2w}{10-2w}$. By the markup formula, the profit-maximizing value of w must satisfy

$$\frac{w-1}{w} = \frac{10-2w}{2w} \Rightarrow w - 1 = \frac{10-2w}{2} \Rightarrow w = 3.$$

This means the price that R will charge is $6.

R's margin on each unit is $6-\$3 = \$3$ and the demand it sees is $1000 \times (10-6) = 4000$. Hence, R's profit is $\$3 \times 4000 = \$12{,}000$. Now, M's margin is $\$3 - \$1 = \$2$ and so its profit will be $\$2 \times 4000 = \$8000$. In total, the two firms make $\$12{,}000 + \$8000 = \$20{,}000$. This is $\$250$ less than in scenario #2 but higher than in scenario #1. Notice that R is better off than in scenario #1! Does this mean idiocy pays? In scenario #1, R was forced to respond to M's price. However, under keystone pricing, when R commits to a rule like doubling the markup, M is forced to react to R. In effect, R has given M the power to determine the downstream price but dictated what share of the profits it (R) will keep.

2.5   Calculating Consumer Surplus

In Example 1 a table of incremental reservation prices was used to compute the consumer surplus enjoyed by a single buyer at various prices. This is tedious, and even more so with more than one buyer. However, given a demand curve (either for an individual or an aggregation of them), determining the consumer surplus at any price can be calculated via integration. First, we describe how consumer surplus can be calculated using the inverse demand curve. Subsequently, we show that it can be determined from the demand curve.

2.5.1   Inverse Demand Curve

Suppose our seller, facing an inverse demand curve of $p(q)$, has chosen to sell q^* units. The total amount paid by buyers will be $p(q^*) \times q^*$. The total reservation price of all buyers who purchased will be $\int_0^{q^*} p(x)dx$ (i.e. the area under the inverse demand curve). To see why, divide the interval $[0, q^*]$ into tiny intervals of width Δ. Let q be the endpoints of one of these intervals. If we increase the quantity sold to $q + \Delta$, we pick up Δ extra buyers. The RPs of each of these buyers are approximately $p(q + \Delta)$. The *increase* in total RP of these buyers is $p(q + \Delta)\Delta$. Hence, the total RP from the acquisition of q units is approximately

$$p(0 + \Delta)\Delta + p(\Delta + \Delta)\Delta + p(2\Delta + \Delta)\Delta + \cdots + p(q^*)\Delta. \qquad (2.4)$$

It will be useful to see this more concretely in Figure 2.3. The inverse demand curve is the downward-sloping curve. Quantities are marked off on the horizontal. Consider what happens when we increase the quantity from seven to nine units. We pick up two additional units of demand. This is the length of the base of the shaded rectangle between 7 and 9 on the horizontal axis. The RPs of these additional "two" buyers

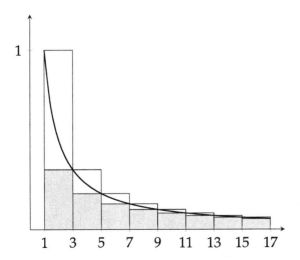

Figure 2.3 Consumer surplus

is approximately $p(9)$, which is the height of the shaded rectangle between 7 and 9. Hence, the increase in total surplus is the area of the relevant rectangle. If we sum up the areas of the shaded rectangles, we get an estimate of the total surplus from acquiring 17 units. Hence, the area under the inverse demand curve, which is what the shaded area approximates, is the total surplus. If we let $\Delta \to 0$ in expression (2.4), we obtain a Riemann sum which converges to the integral of $p(q)$. Therefore, the total RP from the acquisition of q units is

$$\int_0^{q^*} p(x)dx. \tag{2.5}$$

Hence, total consumer surplus at q^* units is

$$\Sigma(q^*) = \int_0^{q^*} p(x)dx - p(q^*)q^*. \tag{2.6}$$

2.5.2   Demand Curve

If we wish to derive total consumer surplus as a function of the demand curve, it is helpful to think of $D(p)$ as the number of buyers with an RP that exceeds p. Let p^* be the price chosen by the monopolist. The number of buyers with an RP in the interval $[p^*, p^* + \Delta]$ is roughly $D(p^*) - D(p^* + \Delta)$. Each of these buyers enjoys a surplus of at most Δ at price p^*. Therefore, the total consumer surplus for buyers with an RP in $[p^*, p^* + \Delta]$ is approximately $[D(p^*) - D(p^* + \Delta)]\Delta$.

Similarly, the total consumer surplus for buyers with an RP in $[p^*, p^* + 2\Delta]$ will be approximately $[D(p^* + \Delta) - D(p^* + 2\Delta)]2\Delta$.

Now, look at $[p^* + 2\Delta, p^* + 3\Delta]$, $[p^* + 3\Delta, p^* + 4\Delta]$, all the way up to the choke price $\bar{p}$. Total consumer surplus $S(p^*)$ will be, roughly,

$$[D(p^*) - D(p^* + \Delta)]\Delta + [D(p^* + \Delta) - D(p^* + 2\Delta)]2\Delta + \cdots .$$

Rearranging and simplifying yields

$$D(p^*)\Delta + D(p^* + \Delta)\Delta + D(p^* + 2\Delta)\Delta + \cdots . \tag{2.7}$$

If we let $\Delta \to 0$ in (2.7), this gives us an integral. Thus, total consumer surplus will be

$$\int_{p^*}^{\bar{p}} D(x)dx,$$

where $\bar{p}$ is the choke price.

2.6   Regulating a Monopolist

It is estimated that at least 0.05% of the world's population is susceptible to anaphylaxis. This is an allergic reaction that in minutes produces an itchy rash, throat or tongue swelling, shortness of breath, vomiting, lightheadedness, low blood pressure, and, if untreated, death. The primary treatment is an injection of epinephrine into a muscle.[9] The World Health Organization lists it as among the most important medications needed in a basic health system. The wholesale price is between $0.10 and $0.95 a vial, so it would seem that access to epinephrine should not be a problem. The challenge is delivering epinephrine to the body when needed. It would appear that a syringe is the obvious solution, but it is risky. The user must measure the dose precisely and avoid injecting themselves in a vein (which can be fatal), all while the heart races and the hands shake. The current solution of choice is an autoinjector based on a design developed for the US military by Sheldon Kaplan of Survival Technology, Inc. for treating exposure to nerve agents.

The autoinjector for delivering epinephrine is called an EpiPen and the underlying technology is under patent. In 2007 Mylan acquired the right to market the EpiPen. As late as 2016, Mylan had the US monopoly for the product. Generic and non-generic alternatives were expected to enter the market in 2015, but regulatory hurdles and production problems prevented this. The US list price of a single EpiPen in 2016 was about $300, six times larger than the list price at the time Mylan acquired the rights.[10] Note that users typically buy the EpiPens in packs of two or more. The actual price paid by a user depends on the kind of insurance coverage they have. Users with low-deductible plans, for example, might pay as little as $73 per pack of two. The difference is absorbed by the insurance company, which eventually works its way back into higher premiums.[11]

On July 11, 2016, an on-line campaign began with the goal of shaming Mylan into lowering its prices. A petition called "Stop the EpiPen Price Gouging" was filed at Petition2Congress.com. Some 80,000 signatures later, it caught the attention of US legislators. Former presidential candidate Bernie Sanders "tweeted"

There's no reason an EpiPen, which costs Mylan just a few dollars to make, should cost families more than $600.

There is, it's called the profit motive. Senator Charles Grassley, head of the Senate Judiciary Committee, demanded an explanation from Mylan for the price increases. In short, there is a view, held by many, that Mylan's prices are "too high" and that it would be a "good thing" if they were to lower their prices on the EpiPen. Would it? Stepping back from the specific case of Mylan, we might ask more generally, would it be a good idea to regulate the price charged by a monopolist by placing a ceiling on it? Equivalently, regulating the quantity produced?

Lowering the price charged by the monopolist (equivalently, increasing output) benefits consumers. However, a monopolist is a person too. Forcing them to lower their price (increase output) makes them worse off. How should we balance the two? It depends on how we choose to measure the benefits to each and weigh one against

---

[9] Epinephrine (also known as adrenaline) is a hormone, first isolated in 1901.

[10] *New York Times*, August 25, 2016.

[11] List prices and price paid are considerably lower outside the USA. In Europe there are at least eight generic versions approved for use.

the other. Here we will measure the benefits to consumers by consumer surplus, and to the monopolist by their profit. In each case what we measure is denominated on a common monetary scale so we can sum them. In other words, the monopolist's money is as good as and no worse than the consumer's. The sum is called **total surplus**. If $\Pi(q)$ is the monopoly profit at output q and $\Sigma(q)$ is the total consumer surplus at q, then total surplus is

$$\Sigma(q) + \Pi(q).$$

The goal is to determine the value of q that maximizes total surplus. We have framed the problem in terms of a choice of quantity rather than price. We could conduct the analysis in terms of price, but this is inconvenient.

As we increase q (lower price) above (below) the profit-maximizing quantity (price), $\Sigma(q)$ increases and $\Pi(q)$ declines. It is not obvious which of these changes is larger, and neither prose nor poetry are sufficient to settle the matter.

Suppose our hypothetical monopolist has a cost function $C(q)$ that satisfies decreasing returns to scale. Then $\Pi(q) = p(q)q - C(q)$. Using equation (2.6), we see that total surplus is

$$\left[\int_0^q p(x)dx - p(q)q \right] + [p(q)q - C(q)] = \int_0^q p(x)dx - C(q).$$

Our problem is to solve

$$\max_{q \geq 0} \left[\int_0^q p(x)dx - C(q) \right]. \tag{2.8}$$

Differentiating the expression for total surplus in (2.8) with respect to q and setting to zero yields

$$p(q) - \frac{dC}{dq} = 0.$$

Note that the second derivative is $\frac{dp(q)}{dq} - \frac{d^2C}{dq^2}$, which is negative for all q. This is because $p(q)$ is decreasing in q and the second derivative of C is positive.

In words, total surplus is maximized by forcing the monopolist to choose a quantity that forces price to marginal cost. Equivalently, requiring the monopolist to price at marginal cost will maximize total surplus. This reveals that consumer surplus grows faster than monopoly profit falls as quantity (price) increases (decreases). Why is this?

As the monopolist lowers their price from p^*, say, to $p^* - \epsilon$, the consumers who were prepared to purchase at p^* are better off. Each enjoys ϵ more surplus. Their increase in surplus exactly matches the profit reduction the monopolist suffers from this reduction. But lowering the price allows more consumers to purchase the good! There are buyers who were not prepared to purchase when the price was p^* but will purchase at $p^* - \epsilon$. It is these additional buyers who tip the balance in favor of lowering the price. Note that we are making the assumption that the monopolist will continue to produce even when the price is set as marginal cost.

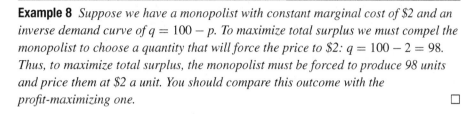

Example 8 *Suppose we have a monopolist with constant marginal cost of $2 and an inverse demand curve of $q = 100 - p$. To maximize total surplus we must compel the monopolist to choose a quantity that will force the price to $2: $q = 100 - 2 = 98$. Thus, to maximize total surplus, the monopolist must be forced to produce 98 units and price them at $2 a unit. You should compare this outcome with the profit-maximizing one.*   ☐

Example 9 *Suppose a monopolist with a total cost of $1.5q^2$ to produce q units faces an inverse demand curve of $q = 100 - p$. To maximize total surplus we must compel the monopolist to choose a quantity that will force the price to marginal cost (i.e. $3q$). Thus, $q = 100 - 3q \Rightarrow q = 25$. Thus, to maximize total surplus, the monopolist must be forced to produce 25 units and price them at $75 a unit. You should compare this outcome with the profit-maximizing one.*   ☐

Should the government step in to regulate the price of Mylan? The analysis by itself cannot answer this question, because it has focused only on the immediate trade-off between consumer surplus and monopoly profit. It ignores at least two things:

1. What is the incentive for the monopolist to keep working as its price is reduced? While the analysis reveals that reducing price (or increasing quantity) will increase total surplus, it does not follow that we can push price all the way down to marginal cost. The monopolist must be left with sufficient profit to give it the incentive to continue operating.
2. What is the source of monopoly power? In the case of pharmaceuticals and medical devices, it is a government-granted monopoly (i.e. patent). It is granted to encourage the company to invest in invention and development. Regulating the price and quantity at the back end will reduce the incentives to make these investments.

Nevertheless, the analysis is still useful because it highlights the trade-offs involved with regulating price or quantity.

2.7   Credibility

The department store sale was invented by John Wanamaker to increase traffic into his store after Christmas (and avoid laying off workers). Wanamaker bought from wholesalers in bulk and resold at small margins for a limited time only, in January. It was a smashing success, rapidly emulated by others. By 1992 the *New York Times* reported that

Merchants now treat their shoppers to a rich diet of one-day sales, pre- and post-holiday sales, seasonal sales, clearance sales, sacrificing their profit margins in the process.

While the quote notes a drop in margin, it says nothing about the effect on volume. Could the increase in volume compensate for the smaller margins? To analyze the trade-off, consider a monopoly seller of widgets. There is no other seller of widgets and the unit cost of production is zero. For simplicity, suppose we are at the beginning of the year (i.e. January 1). At the end of the year, no matter when they are bought, these widgets become obsolete.

There are equal-sized buyer segments, called high and low types, for the product, each of whom will buy at most one widget. The RP of each high-type buyer for a full year's use of a widget is $800, and the RP of each low-type buyer for a full year's use is $250.

If the monopolist chooses to sell widgets in January only, the profit-maximizing price is $800 and the average profit per person is $400.[12] At this price, a low-type buyer (one with an RP of $250 for a year's use) does not buy. Thus, the monopolist sells to half the market only.

Now July arrives. Half the buyers are bereft of a widget. Since the cost of production of a widget is zero, any price that a widget can fetch goes straight to the bottom line. Why not attempt to sell a widget to the low-type buyers? If a buyer chooses to buy a widget in July instead of January, her RP is reduced by half, since she obtains only half a year's use. Thus, by dropping the price in July to $125, our seller can sell one widget to each low-type buyer. Therefore, at year's end, the seller collects an average profit per person of $\frac{800+125}{2} = \$462.50$.

At the end of the year, the widgets held by the two buyers become obsolete. In January of the next year, the widgets are again priced at $800. Now what happens?

If high-type buyers believe the monopolist will discount in July, some who bought in January may switch to buying in July. To illustrate, consider a high-type buyer with an RP (for the year) of $800. Such a buyer now has three choices compared to the two from the year before. She can buy now, buy in July, or refuse to purchase at all. Which will she do? It will depend on the surplus she enjoys from each option.

If she decides not to buy, her surplus will be zero. If she buys in January, her consumer surplus will be zero. If she decides to postpone her purchase to July, her RP becomes $400 (i.e. she gives up $400 in value). So, postponing the purchase is not costless. Her surplus will depend on what price she anticipates the seller will set in July. Suppose she expects a price of $125. Then her surplus will be $400 − $125 = \$275$, more than 0. If she believes the monopolist will sell for $125 in July, she will switch from buying in January to buying in July. In making this switch, the supplier loses $800 − $125 = \$675$.

What happens in July? If every high-type buyer has decided to postpone their purchase, the seller will price at $400 in July.[13] This price is higher than the one anticipated by a high-type buyer. But look at things from the point of view of the seller. In the previous year, the seller earned a profit per person of $462.50. Now the seller's profit per person is $200. This is a more than 50% drop in profit for a seller that faces no competition!

---

[12] You should be able to work this out.
[13] If only some high-type buyers choose to postpone, the analysis become complicated. We take up this possibility in Section 2.7.2.

The lesson here is that every seller competes against themselves. In our story of the widgets, the seller is competing against his future self, born of the buyer's anticipation of a price cut. In our example, the seller's profits are eroded because there is an expectation of future price cuts. The behavior is not uncommon, as Kinglake himself observed in the *Kapilcarsi*. Many firms regularly drop their prices at the end of the quarter to meet sales and revenue targets. Buyers learn to anticipate this and purchase accordingly. Not only does this play havoc with profits, it also complicates production planning since the seller must now plan for demand that is "bursty" rather than smooth. In other cases sellers compete with their past selves as well. For example, secondhand goods and previous generations of an operating system.

In each case, what determines the intensity of competition between the selves of the seller is the relative cost of postponing the purchase for buyer and seller. If the buyer has a lower cost of postponing the purchase (delay, making do with an inferior model) than the seller (inventory, staff salaries), the buyer has the bargaining power.

Return now to our monopoly seller of widgets. It's year three and suppose our seller has learnt their lesson. The seller announces a January price of $800 and a promise never to have a sale later in the year. What will happen? It depends on how many of the high-type buyers believe the seller's promise. What if a large portion are skeptical and decide to postpone? The seller will make few sales in January. Come July, the seller must choose between forgoing substantial revenues to keep a promise or making some money but breaking their word. If the second, they confirm the low opinion that the skeptics had. It's a difficult choice.

How might a seller deal with this? Credibility on either supply or price. The first is restricting supply. Ferrari, for example, does this by committing to produce a limited number of cars each year, safe in the knowledge that no buyer can reproduce a Ferrari in their home office. In the second case this means announcing a price and sticking to it. Apple has a reputation for this. It works hard to ensure that the price for an Apple product is the same no matter what channel it is purchased through. Furthermore, it will remove or restrict the supply of older versions of a product before the introduction of a new version.

2.7.1   J. C. Penney

The first J. C. Penney store opened in 1902. At its peak, the company operated 2000 stores throughout the USA. It now has about half that many, a consequence of changing consumer tastes and competition. Sales played a big part in the company's cash flows. By 2011, 72% of J. C. Penney's revenue came from products sold at a discount of 50% or more. Less than 1% of company revenues came from items sold at full price. J. C. Penney had become like Kinglake's merchant, who begins by asking for a perfectly hopeless price. Rajiv Lal of the Harvard Business School described the situation this way:

Here's how it works. You start off pricing something at $100, but you end up selling it at, say, $50. All the actual sales take place at 50 bucks.

The problems that high–low pricing cause are tremendous. Customers come into the store, they look at the new merchandise, and they look at the prices. They like the merchandise, but don't like the price, and so they don't buy. As a result, this new merchandise sits on the shelves. The first markdown takes place after six weeks, and only then does the merchandise begin to move. So for six weeks, not much happens.

In 2011, J. C. Penney appointed a new CEO, Ron Johnson, credited with making Apple's stores the success they are today. Upon taking command, he announced five changes. The company's stock increased 24%.

1. A move to everyday low prices
   Previous years' sales data would be used to mark down current-year prices on all of their merchandise by at least 40%. For example, a Liz Claiborne purse regularly priced at $49.99 could have an "everyday" price of $25.
2. Fewer sales
   A red tag shows the everyday price. A white tag will display a "month-long value" that means the item is on sale for that entire month. Blue tags will be used on items that did not sell well. These items will go on sale on the first and third Friday of every month (payday).
3. Whole-number pricing
   Jeans previously priced at $19.99 would now be priced at $19 or $20 instead.
4. New logo and advertising
5. Store-within-a-store areas for brands like Sephora and Martha Stewart
   Each store to be divided into about 100 small boutiques with a central service center called a "town square." This would be coupled with a reduction in private label brands.

The first three items were designed to regain credibility on price. The last two, to update the store's offerings and appeal to customers. However, by the fourth quarter of 2012, same store sales fell by 31.7%. After 12 months the company posted a net loss of $985 million. Many critics saw this as inevitable. A *Time* magazine article from April 2013 reflecting the popular view had this to say:

Johnson thought it made sense to cut to the chase by listing realistic prices from the get-go and foregoing nonstop sales. It does make logical sense, after all. But shoppers aren't purely logical creatures. They're often drawn to stores not by the promise of fair pricing, but by the lure of hunting for deals via coupons and price markdowns.

The writer believes that J. C. Penney customers were stupider than Johnson gave them credit for. We suggest an alternative explanation. Given the company's history of discounting, it is sensible for a customer to be skeptical about Johnson's commitment to forgo sales. The easiest way to test J. C. Penney's credibility is to postpone a purchase. If it is not costly to do so, it is in their interest to do so. On J. C. Penney's side, the only way they can convey credibility is to "not blink."

The cost to a J. C. Penney customer of postponement is low, unless J. C. Penney was offering items that were both attractive and unavailable elsewhere. Johnson was clearly aware of this, hence the "store-within-a-store" idea he promoted to build up product lines that would differentiate J. C. Penney from its competitors. However, these were still in the process of being rolled out.

With the sharp drop in sales, Johnson authorized a return to limited sales and promotions like free haircuts for children. The word "clearance" reappeared in advertisements. J. C. Penney blinked and confirmed its customers' initial skepticism. Johnson lasted all of 17 months in the job. William Ackman, the hedge fund Croesus who had championed Johnson as the man to save J. C. Penney, described Johnson's tenure as "something close to a disaster." [14]

2.7.2   Two-Period Monopoly

Earlier, we glossed over the possibility that some, not all, high-type buyers would choose to postpone their purchase. The fewer high-type buyers that choose to postpone, the lower the mid-year price can be. However, the lower the mid-year price, the greater the incentive for a high-type buyer to postpone purchasing. But the more of them that choose to postpone, the higher the mid-year price becomes. To sort out these competing forces we will need a more detailed model than the one presented so far. It is described below:

1. There will be two periods, denoted $t = 1, 2$.
2. A monopoly seller has a good that can be sold in period 1 and period 2.
3. The good is durable, meaning it lasts two periods.
4. The marginal cost of production is zero.
5. Seller and buyers have the same discount rate $\delta < 1$. Each dollar obtained in period 2 is worth only δ period-1 dollars. Discounting captures the idea that waiting is costly (impatience). The lower δ is, the more "impatient" everyone is; the value of a future dollar is dropping.
6. The inverse demand curve is $1 - q$. A buyer that does not buy in period 1, will be present in period 2.

The benchmark is the profit the monopolist can make if she *only* sells in period 1. Her problem is to choose a quantity q to maximize $q(1 - q)$. It is straightforward to verify that the profit-maximizing quantity is $q = \frac{1}{2}$ and the profit-maximizing price is $\frac{1}{2}$, yielding a profit of $\frac{1}{4}$.

Now suppose the monopolist will sell in both periods. Counterintuitively, we will work backwards. This is because decisions made in period 1 affect demands in period 2. To avoid this difficulty we start the analysis in period 2, taking the period-1 price or quantity as given.

Suppose q_1 units were sold in period 1. How many units should be sold in period 2? Given that q_1 units were already sold in period 1, the customer base in period 2 will be smaller and this is reflected in the new (period-2) inverse demand curve: $1 - q_1 - q_2$.

---

[14] For a fuller account, see http://fortune.com/2014/03/20/how-to-fail-in-business-while-really-really-trying/.

Holding q_1 fixed, in period 2 the monopolist will solve

$$\max_{q_2 \geq 0} q_2(1 - q_1 - q_2).$$

The profit-maximizing period-2 quantity is $q_2 = \frac{1-q_1}{2}$. Notice that as period-1 sales volume q_1 increases, the period-2 sales quantity diminishes. Put differently, the more that buy in period 1, the fewer that remain to buy in period 2.

The inverse demand in period 1 must account for the fact that not all buyers will choose to purchase in period 1. A customer will buy in period 1 if and only if their surplus from buying in period 1 exceeds that from buying in period 2. If RP is the reservation price of a period-1 customer, the following two conditions must hold:

1. $RP \geq p_1$ (i.e. a customer will not pay more than it is worth to them).
2. $RP - p_1 \geq \delta(RP - p_2)$ [i.e. the surplus from buying in period-1 (measured in period-1 dollars) should be at least as large as the surplus in period 2 (measured in period-1 dollars)].

Therefore, $RP \geq \frac{p_1 - \delta p_2}{1-\delta}$. Hence, only buyers with a reservation price of at least $\frac{p_1 - \delta p_2}{1-\delta}$ will purchase in period 1. Using the period-1 inverse demand curve, we can determine the number of such buyers:

$$\frac{p_1 - \delta p_2}{1 - \delta} = 1 - q_1.$$

Therefore:

$$p_1 = (1 - q_1)(1 - \delta) + \delta p_2 = (1 - q_1)(1 - \delta) + \delta(1 - q_1 - q_2) = 1 - q_1 - \delta q_2.$$

The *total* profit of the monopolist measured in period-1 dollars is

$$\Pi = q_1 p_1 + \delta q_2 p_2.$$

Recall that the inverse demand in period 1 is $p_1 = 1 - q_1 - \delta q_2$ and in period 2 it is $p_2 = 1 - q_1 - q_2$. Hence

$$\Pi = q_1(1 - q_1 - \delta q_2) + \delta q_2(1 - q_1 - q_2).$$

However, q_2 is a function of q_1: $q_2 = \frac{1-q_1}{2}$. Substituting this into the expression for profit yields

$$q_1\left(1 - q_1 - \delta\frac{1 - q_1}{2}\right) + \delta\frac{1 - q_1}{2}\left(1 - q_1 - \frac{1 - q_1}{2}\right).$$

Therefore, in period 1, the monopolist chooses q_1 to solve the following:

$$\max_{q_1} q_1\left(1 - q_1 - \delta\frac{1 - q_1}{2}\right) + \delta\frac{1 - q_1}{2}\left(1 - q_1 - \frac{1 - q_1}{2}\right).$$

A straightforward calculation shows that the optimal choice of q_1 is $q_1 = 2\frac{(1-\delta)}{(4-3\delta)}$. Note that the second-order condition is satisfied. It follows that $q_2 = 0.5\frac{(2-\delta)}{(4-3\delta)}$.

Profit is

$$0.25\frac{(2-\delta)^2}{(4-3\delta)} = 0.25\left[1 - \frac{\delta}{4} + \frac{\delta^2}{4(4-3\delta)}\right],$$

which is *smaller* than the profit of selling in period 1 only (0.25). Hence, having the sale lowers the monopolist's profit.

2.8 Production Function

No firm is "born" with a cost function. Rather, its costs are the results of its choices about the mix of inputs (raw material, human capital, automation) that it acquires to deliver the goods and services promised. Characterizing a firm in terms of its cost function is a convenience that allowed us to ignore these input choices. However, we sometimes care very much about these input choices.

Consider a firm that purchases a variety of inputs in order to produce its output. A seller of one of the inputs will be interested to know how a change in the price of another input will affect the firm's demand for their input. If that input is your labor and the other input is automation, this question will cause sleepless nights. To answer questions of this kind we model a firm as being endowed with a function that relates the inputs to the quantity of the output produced. It is called a **production function** and it specifies the *maximum* amount of an output that can be produced from a given combination of inputs. The qualifier maximum is present so we can ignore cases where a firm does not exploit its productive capabilities to their fullest extent. One can think of the production function as a description of the firm's chosen technology for producing and delivering the goods and services it promises. Subsequently we show how to get from a description of the firm's production technology to its cost function.

Custom and tradition suppose that a production process has two inputs, called labor and capital, that are combined to produce an output that is subsequently sold. The inclusion of labor grows out of a desire to understand how a firm's input choices affect the wages of workers. Capital is a catchall to describe inputs other than labor, like money, raw material, or automation. There is nothing that requires us to be limited to just two inputs, but for economy of exposition we assume two.

If L units of labor (which could be measured in hours or number of workers, depending on context) and K units of raw material (land, oil, rubber, etc.) are combined, they generate q units of output, where $q = f(K, L)$. Here, f is the firm's production function. Examples of production functions, along with their names, are listed below.

1. Linear (perfect substitutes): $q = \alpha L + \beta K$.
2. Fixed proportions (perfect complements): $q = \min(\alpha L, \beta K)$.
3. Cobb–Douglas: $f(K, L) = AK^\alpha L^\beta$, where $\alpha, \beta \geq 0$.
4. CES (constant elasticity): $q = [K^\rho + L^\rho]^{1/\rho}$.

The **marginal product of labor** is $\frac{\partial f}{\partial L} \geq 0$ while the **marginal product of raw material** is $\frac{\partial f}{\partial K} \geq 0$. These have the obvious interpretation of the incremental output from an infinitesimal change in labor and raw material, respectively. If the firm wishes to produce q units of output, there could be many different combinations of labor and raw material that will work. There can be many choices of L and K such that $q = f(K,L)$. The set of all $K, L \geq 0$ such that $f(K,L) = q$ is called an **isoquant** at threshold q.

Example 10 *Consider the production function $f(K,L) = K^{0.5}L^{0.5}$. Its isoquant at threshold q is the set of all (K,L) combinations such that*

$$f(K,L) = q \implies K^{0.5}L^{0.5} = q.$$

If we were to graph this with K on the horizontal axis and L on the vertical, we would rewrite the last expression as follows:

$$L = \frac{q^2}{K}.$$

A sketch of this curve for various values of q is displayed in Figure 2.4.   □

A firm's costs are determined by the money spent to acquire the inputs for its production process. To formalize this, suppose each unit of labor costs w (for wage), irrespective of how much labor is required. Let r be the unit price of the raw material; again, it does not change with the amount of raw material purchased. The assumption is restrictive and in Section 2.9 one implication of relaxing it is explored.

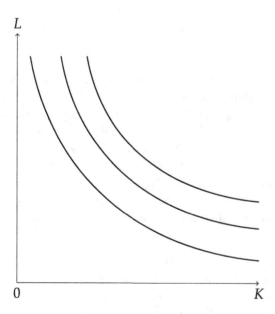

Figure 2.4 Isoquant at various thresholds

The minimum total cost incurred to produce q units of output using labor and raw material is denoted $C(q)$.

If K units of raw material and L units of labor are purchased, the firm will spend $rK + wL$ in total. If the firm wishes to produce q units of output, it must choose K and L so that $f(K,L) = q$. There might be many choices of K and L that will deliver q units of output. All these choices will lie on the level-q isoquant of the production function. $C(q)$ is the least-cost way to generate q units of output and is derived from the following optimization problem:

$$C(q) = \min_{L,K} rK + wL$$

$$\text{s.t. } f(K,L) = q$$

$$K,L \geq 0.$$

Equivalently, it is the point on the level-q isoquant with lowest cost.

Example 11 *Suppose the firm's production function is $q = L^{1/2}K^{1/2}$, $w = 4$, and $r = 1$. Then the optimization problem to be solved to determine the firm's cost function is*

$$C(q) = \min 1K + 4L$$

$$\text{s.t. } L^{1/2}K^{1/2} = q$$

$$K,L \geq 0.$$

One way to solve this is via substitution. Let's use the equality constraint to write L in terms of K $\left(i.e.\ L = \frac{q^2}{K}\right)$. Substituting this into the function we are trying to minimize gives us

$$C(q) = \min K + 4\frac{q^2}{K}$$

$$\text{s.t. } K \geq 0.$$

Ignoring the non-negativity constraint for the moment, setting the first derivative of the function to be optimized to zero yields

$$\frac{-4q^2}{K^2} + 1 = 0 \implies K = 2q.$$

As the second derivative $\frac{8q^2}{K^3}$ is non-negative, we know this is the minimum. Notice also that $K = 2q$ satisfies the omitted non-negativity constraint.

Hence, to produce q units of the output at minimum cost, we must acquire $2q$ units of raw material and $\frac{q}{2}$ units of labor: For this choice:

$$C(q) = 2rq + w\left(\frac{q}{2}\right) = \left(2r + \frac{w}{2}\right)q.$$

Substituting in the given values for r and w, we see that $C(q) = 4q$. Notice that this cost function satisfies constant returns to scale.

One can also use the method of Lagrange multipliers. First, ignore the non-negativity constraints and write down the Lagrangian:

$$\mathcal{L} = 1K + 4L + \lambda(q - L^{1/2}K^{1/2}).$$

The relevant first-order conditions are

1. $\frac{\partial \mathcal{L}}{\partial L} = 4 - \lambda(\frac{1}{2})L^{-1/2}K^{1/2} = 0.$
2. $\frac{\partial \mathcal{L}}{\partial K} = 1 - \lambda(\frac{1}{2})L^{1/2}K^{-1/2} = 0.$
3. $\frac{\partial \mathcal{L}}{\partial \lambda} = q - L^{1/2}K^{1/2} = 0.$

Rearranging the first two conditions yields

$$4 = \lambda\left(\frac{1}{2}\right)L^{-1/2}K^{1/2},$$

$$1 = \lambda\left(\frac{1}{2}\right)L^{1/2}K^{-1/2}.$$

Dividing the first by the second gives $4 = \frac{K}{L} \Rightarrow 4L = K$. Hence:

$$q = L^{1/2}(4L)^{1/2} = 2L \Rightarrow L = \frac{q}{2}, \quad K = 2q.$$

These satisfy the omitted non-negativity constraints. Furthermore, the appropriate second-order conditions can be checked to verify that this solution is indeed optimal.

A geometrical view of the optimization problem can be useful and is found in Figure 2.5. Suppose the minimum total cost to produce q units is C^*. The straight line represents all (K, L) combinations that cost exactly C^*. The isoquant at threshold q is displayed. Where the two are tangent to each other is the cost-minimizing combination of (K, L) denoted (K^*, L^*). □

This formulation of how the firm's cost function is obtained allows us to analyze how the mix of inputs varies as their unit price changes. The **marginal rate of technical substitution** (MRTS) shows the rate at which inputs can be substituted with each other while maintaining the output level constant. For example, the MRTS of raw material with respect to labor is the incremental amount of raw material needed to replace one unit of labor so as to keep the output level constant. Formally, it is

$$\frac{\frac{\partial f}{\partial L}}{\frac{\partial f}{\partial K}}.$$

Geometrically, it is the slope of the isoquant.

Example 12 *Suppose $f(K, L) = 4K + 2L$. Then*

$$\frac{\partial f}{\partial K} = 4$$

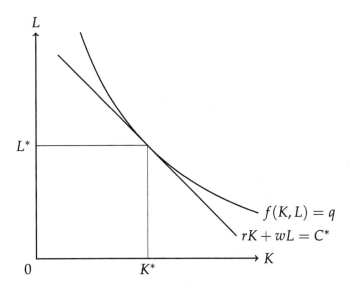

Figure 2.5 Cost minimization

and

$$\frac{\partial f}{\partial L} = 2.$$

Hence, the MRTS of raw material with respect to labor is $\frac{2}{4} = \frac{1}{2}$. In words, for each one unit decrease in labor we must increase raw material by 1/2 a unit to maintain the same level of output. □

More generally, we can have many inputs, say n. If x_i is the quantity of input i for $i = 1, 2, \ldots, n$, then the output generated is given by $f(x_1, x_2, \ldots, x_n)$. If each unit of input i costs c_i per unit, the minimum cost expended to produce q units of output is given by the following:

$$\min \sum_{i=1}^{n} c_i x_i$$

$$\text{s.t. } f(x_1, x_2, \ldots, x_n) = q$$

$$x_1, x_2, \ldots, x_n \geq 0.$$

2.8.1 Automation

The factory of the future will have only two employees, a man and a dog. The man will be there to feed the dog. The dog will be there to keep the man from touching the equipment.

Warren Bennis

Ned Ludd entered history when, in a fit of rage, he took a hammer to a knitting machine. News of his vandalism spread, making his name a byword for the sabotage of knitting machines. Eventually, the Nottingham weavers, who were being displaced by the new weaving machines, banded together under the Luddite banner to put pressure on employers by breaking the machines. The Luddites were not "anti-progress," but a labor movement that, in Eric Hobsbawm's words, "engaged in collective bargaining by riot."

The concern with automation displacing labor did not vanish with the Luddites. Now that it threatens "nescafe society" as well, it commands more attention. In this section we take up the question of whether automation makes workers better or worse off. Our analysis will not be completed until Section 6.7.

Suppose the output of a firm is generated by combining labor with other ingredients, one being automation. As the price of automation falls, what will happen to the amount of labor that the firm buys? Will suppliers of labor be better or worse off? The answer depends on how labor interacts with automation. We examine two polar cases.

In the first case, automation is a substitute for labor. That is, automation can perform the same tasks that labor is contracted to execute. For example, a greeter in a "big box" store can be replaced by a robot equipped with a cheerful disposition. An example of a production function with this substitute property is $f(L, K) = L + K$, where L is the number of units of labor acquired and K denotes the number of units of automation deployed. Observe that if one reduces labor by one unit and increases automation by one unit, total output remains unchanged.

Let us determine the firm's minimum total cost to produce q units of output. Let w be the price per unit of labor and r the price per unit of automation. Then the firm must solve the following optimization problem:

$$\min rK + wL$$

$$\text{s.t. } K + L = q$$

$$K, L \geq 0.$$

The solution to this optimization problem is derived below.

Example 13 *We use substitution. Using the constraint $K + L = q$, we write K in terms of L (i.e. $K = q - L$). Then, the optimization problem becomes*

$$\min r(q - L) + wL$$

$$\text{s.t. } q - L \geq 0$$

$$L \geq 0.$$

This simplifies to

$$\min rq + (w - r)L$$

$$\text{s.t. } 0 \leq L \leq q.$$

The optimal solution will depend on the sign of $(w - r)$. If negative, we should make L as large as possible (i.e. $L = q$). If positive, we should make L as small as possible (i.e. $L = 0$). When $w - r = 0$, any choice of L between 0 and q is optimal. Let us set $L = q$ in this case. Then we can summarize the optimal solution as follows:

1. If $w \leq r$, $L = q$ and $K = 0$.
2. If $w > r$, $L = 0$ and $K = q$.   □

In words, if the price per unit of automation exceeds the price per unit of labor, the firm chooses to produce using labor only. If the price per unit of automation is lower than that of labor, the firm relies exclusively on automation. If automation is sufficiently inexpensive relative to labor, the anticipated "nightmare" outcome obtains. It happens because labor and automation are perfectly interchangeable. That is baked into the production function $K + L$. If we reduce automation by one unit, we can recover the original output level by replacing it with exactly one unit of labor and conversely.

Is the nightmare outcome inevitable? No. It depends, as will be seen shortly, on the production function. By way of contrast, consider the production function $f(K, L) = \min\{K, L\}$. In this production function labor and automation complement each other. To increase output, one must increase both labor *and* automation. An example of this can be found in the Lowes chain of hardware stores. They have introduced a robot (called a LoweBot) to help customers navigate the store to find products and assist employees with scanning inventory. In one sense it displaces labor, but what Lowes has found is that it frees workers to spend more time with customers who need advice regarding home repair and improvement projects. Thus, automation complements labor by boosting its effectiveness.[15]

In this example, the firm's cost minimization problem is

$$\min rK + wL$$

$$\text{s.t. } \min\{K, L\} = q$$

$$K, L \geq 0.$$

The solution is described below.

Example 14 *The reader should verify that neither the method of Lagrange nor the method of substitution will work. The key observation is that the optimization problem can be rewritten as*

$$\min rK + wL$$

$$\text{s.t. } K \geq q$$

$$L \geq q$$

$$K, L \geq 0.$$

---

[15] The phenomenon is not new. The Excel spreadsheet is an earlier example.

It is easy to see that we achieve a minimum by selecting K and L to be as small as possible. In this case, $K = L = q$. Notice that this choice does not depend on the relative magnitudes of r and w.   □

In this case, whether labor is cheaper or more expensive than automation, the amount of labor selected to minimize cost remains the same. This is because labor and automation complement each other. To increase output (i.e. q), we must increase both K and L.

To conclude, whether automation displaces labor or not depends on whether they complement or substitute each other. Thus, it is possible that in some industries automation will displace labor and in others it may actually increase the demand for labor.[16]

If automation and labor are substitutes for each other, then a drop in the price of automation will result in a drop in the demand for labor. Does it follow that workers are worse off? As will be discovered in Section 6.7, not necessarily.

2.9   Monopsony

After playing in the St. Louis Cardinals baseball team for 11 years, Curt Flood was traded away to the Phillies. Flood, who had won seven consecutive Gold Glove awards, balked. In doing so, he stood to lose roughly $700,000 in 2016 dollars. Under the terms of what was known as the reserve clause, Flood had only two choices; exit baseball or move to Philadelphia.

The clause had been a part of baseball since 1879. Unless dismissed by his team, a player was forbidden to offer his services for competitive bidding to other teams. In fact, players entered Major League Baseball through a draft that allowed only one team to bid for any one player. Thus, at all times during their career, a player faced only one potential employer, a classic case of monopsony, from the Greek meaning "alone to buy."

In a letter to Bowie Kuhn, the Baseball Commissioner, Flood demanded to be declared a free agent:

After twelve years in the major leagues, I do not feel I am a piece of property to be bought and sold irrespective of my wishes. I believe that any system which produces that result violates my basic rights as a citizen and is inconsistent with the laws of the United States and of the several States.

He expressed the same sentiments more forcefully elsewhere:

In the history of man there's no other profession except slavery where one man is tied to one owner for the rest of his life. In slavery they can ship you from one plantation to the other. In

---

[16] It would be more accurate to think of a job as a portfolio of tasks. Some of these tasks will be automated away, while others would be complemented by automation. Rather than thinking of the job going away, it is better to think of the nature of the job changing with the introduction of automation.

baseball they do the same thing. They ship you from one franchise to the other depending on the whims of 24 millionaires . . . I don't want anyone to own me.

While not the first player to request "free agency," he was the first to fight back by filing suit:

I doubt even one of the 24 men controlling the game would touch me with a 10-foot pole. You can't buck the Establishment.

When Flood's case went to trial, no active member of the league, including his teammates, was present in court. Flood's roommate with the Cardinals had this to say:

Was I behind Curt? Absolutely. But I was about 10 steps back just in case there was some fallout.

Only Jackie Robinson and Hank Greenberg, both retired, showed up in support. Flood lost the case, but, on appeal, it went all the way to the US Supreme Court. This brought hate mail and death threats. In 1972 the court ruled 5–3 in favor of Major League Baseball. By then Flood was out of baseball, drunk, in debt, and in a Barcelona psychiatric hospital. Four years later, the reserve clause was abandoned. Average annual salaries for baseball players rose from about $50,000 in 1975 to nearly $1.4 million in 1997. Such was the power of monopsony.

Monopsony is the mirror image of monopoly. While a monopolist faces buyers, a monopsonist faces suppliers. The suppliers behave in a manner similar to a rational buyer. We can think of each supplier as being characterized by a reservation price. In this case it is the *minimum* dollar amount that the supplier will accept to give up a unit of supply. If the supplier can supply more than one unit, then they will be characterized by a sequence of incremental RPs that *increase*. We can represent the way in which the quantity supplied by an individual or group varies with its unit price (holding the price of other things fixed) by a **supply curve** or **supply function**. An example of a supply function is $S(w) = 100 + 2w$, where w is the price paid per unit of supply. The choice of the letter "w" follows from the tradition of thinking of the good being supplied as labor and the price paid for labor is called a wage.

Suppose our monopsonist converts each unit of supply into one unit of output that it subsequently sells. If q is the units of output produced, denote by $R(q)$ the total revenue earned by the monopsonist. The monopsonist's problem is to determine the price per unit of supply to pay so as to maximize its profit, as well as the quantity of output to produce.

If the monopsonist offers a price per unit input of w, she will receive $S(w)$ units of supply. If she chooses to produce q units of output, her revenue will be $R(q)$. Hence, her total profit will be $R(q) - wS(w)$. What links q and w? The fact that one unit of supply produces one unit of output [i.e. $q = S(w)$]. Hence, the monopsonist's problem is to choose q and w to solve

$$\max_{q,w} R(q) - wS(w)$$

$$\text{s.t. } q = S(w)$$

$$q, w \geq 0.$$

We can use the equality constraint to eliminate the q variable and rewrite her problem as follows:

$$\max_{w} R(S(w)) - wS(w)$$

$$\text{s.t. } w \geq 0.$$

Example 15 *The Weyland-Yutani Corp. is monopsony on the input side and monopoly on the output side. On the input side it faces a supply curve for input of $S(w) = w$. It takes one unit of supply and converts it into one unit of output. On the output side it faces an inverse demand curve of $p(q) = 100 - 2q$. We will determine the output level q and input price w that Weyland-Yutani should set to maximize profit.*

The monopsonist's problem is to choose q and w to solve:

$$\max_{q,w} qp(q) - wS(w)$$

$$\text{s.t. } q = S(w)$$

$$q, w \geq 0.$$

Substituting in the relevant expressions:

$$\max_{q,w} q(100 - 2q) - w^2$$

$$\text{s.t. } q = w$$

$$q, w \geq 0.$$

We can use the equality constraint to eliminate q:

$$\max w(100 - 2w) - w^2$$

$$\text{s.t. } w \geq 0.$$

The optimal value of w is $\frac{100}{6}$. So, $\frac{100}{6}$ units of output will be supplied.   □

Just as we could measure the well being of buyers using consumer surplus, there is an analogous notion for suppliers, called supplier or producer surplus. If the monopsonist faces a supply curve of $S(w)$, and offers a wage of $w^* - \Delta$ per unit of input, $S(w^* - \Delta)$ units of supply show up. Now raise the wage per unit of output to w^*.

This increases supply by $S(w^*) - S(w^* - \Delta)$. The "additional" suppliers who step forward must all have opportunity costs between $w^* - \Delta$ and w^*. Hence, each of these $S(w^*) - S(w^* - \Delta)$ workers enjoys a surplus of about $w^* - (w^* - \Delta) = \Delta$. Thus, the total net benefit enjoyed by these suppliers is $[S(w^*) - S(w^* - \Delta)]\Delta$. Hence, by analogy with the calculation of consumer surplus, producer surplus will be $\int_0^{w^*} S(x)dx$.

As in the monopoly case, we can ask what choice of w would maximize the sum of monopsony profit and producer surplus. Under the assumption that the monopsonist *must* buy all supply offered at the stipulated price, we can formulate this problem as the following optimization problem:

$$\max_w R(S(w)) - wS(w) + \int_0^w S(x)dx$$

$$\text{s.t. } w \geq 0.$$

Example 16 *Recall Example 15. The value of w that maximizes monopsony profit and producer surplus solves*

$$\max_w w(100 - 2w) - w^2 + \int_0^w x\,dx$$

$$\text{s.t. } w \geq 0.$$

This simplifies to

$$\max_w w(100 - 2w) - w^2 + \frac{w^2}{2}$$

$$\text{s.t. } w \geq 0.$$

The optimal value of $w = \frac{100}{5}$. *Notice that this is higher than the monopsonist would choose when maximizing profit.*   □

Examples 15 and 16 are interesting if we interpret the input being purchased by the monopsonist as labor. They say that raising the wage above the profit-maximizing level would increase total surplus. Furthermore, the amount of labor supplied and purchased would rise! This is happening because we have forced the monopsonist to buy *all* labor supplied at the regulated price. What if we relaxed this? If we force the monopsonist to pay more for labor, would it not respond by buying less labor?

2.9.1 Minimum Wage

The Code of Hammurabi contains 282 distinct regulations. While a number end with "shall be put to death," most deal with the terms of trade, which result in less condign punishments. Some specify a minimum wage for various specialities. For example:

If a man hire a sailor, he shall pay him six gur of corn per year.
If any one hire a field laborer, he shall pay him eight gur of corn per year.

A gur was a unit of volume corresponding to about 80 gallons.

The first minimum-wage legislation that we would recognize was enacted in New Zealand in 1894. Australia and the UK followed soon after. The USA instituted a minimum wage under Franklin Delano Roosevelt in 1938. Since then, the US minimum wage has been raised 22 times by 12 different presidents. Every increase faces huge debates about both the justice and the effect of such an increase. In this section we examine the effect of a minimum wage on the behavior of a monopsonist employer.

A minimum wage clearly makes the employer worse off, but does it make the workers better off? It depends on how the employer responds to the imposition of a minimum wage. If it reduces its workforce, then the workers let go are clearly worse off. The workers who remain are better off. If an employer increases hiring, then the workers are clearly better off. What about the employer? By increasing the number of workers, an employer can increase output. This may compensate for the increased labor costs. To see which of these forces will dominate, we need a model.

Suppose that OmniCorp, a producer of Soma, is the only employer in the city of Detroit. The company faces an inverse demand curve for Soma of $p(q) = 100 - q$. Its production technology converts one unit of labor into one unit of Soma.

No one will work for OmniCorp for free. If OmniCorp offers a wage of w per unit of labor, other things held fixed, it can expect w units of labor to be supplied in Detroit. Notice that the higher the wage, the larger the number of units of labor available.[17] Let us first work out the profit-maximizing choice of q and w.

If OmniCorp wishes to produce q units of output it must purchase q units of labor. To attract q units of labor, the wage needs to be set at q. Therefore, total cost is $C(q) = q^2$. Hence, profit will be

$$\Pi(q) = R(q) - C(q) = 100q - 2q^2.$$

A straightforward calculation reveals that the profit-maximizing quantity is $q^* = 25$ and the profit-maximizing wage is $w^* = 25$.

Now, suppose a minimum wage law is passed in Detroit and it is set *slightly* above the wage identified above. To be specific, the minimum wage is equal to $25 + \Delta$. While OmniCorp is obliged to pay the new wage, it is not obliged to hire all labor prepared to work for that wage. What effect will this have on OmniCorp's output level, as well as the number of workers it hires?

OmniCorp has at least two choices. OmniCorp does not increase output and therefore does not increase the amount of labor it acquires. In this case, its profit will be

$$25 \times (100 - 25) - 25 \times (25 + \Delta) = [25 \times 75 - 25 \times 25] - 25\Delta.$$

---

[17] Think of this as the higher the wage (other things held fixed), the more people are willing to work for OmniCorp.

Therefore, its profit declines by 25Δ compared to the unregulated case. If OmniCorp wanted to put the boot in, they could choose to acquire less than 25 units of labor (i.e. hire fewer workers than in the unregulated case). Should they choose an output level $q \le 25$, they need only acquire $q \le 25$ units of labor. Given that they will pay $25 + \Delta$ per unit of labor, the profit earned will be

$$q(100 - q) - q(25 + \Delta).$$

For $q \le 25$, this profit function is increasing in q, so OmniCorp is better off choosing $q = 25$ after the imposition of the minimum wage.

A second choice would be to exploit the fact that at the minimum wage of $25 + \Delta$, they can increase output to $25 + \Delta$. In this case, OmniCorp's profit will be

$$(25 + \Delta)(100 - 25 - \Delta) - 25 \times (25 + \Delta) = [25 \times 75 - 25 \times 25] - 2\Delta^2.$$

For Δ sufficiently small, this is better than the first option. Hence, OmniCorp would actually *increase* the amount of labor hired with the passage of the minimum-wage regulation.[18] Notice that the increased output will be coupled with lower prices for Soma, so consumers will also benefit from the wage increase!

Let us step back from the algebra to see why OmniCorp might respond by increasing output. Assuming Δ is small, an increase of labor costs from 25×25 to $(25 + \Delta)(25 + \Delta)$ will not be very large. So, the labor costs don't change very much. However, the increase in output will result in an increase in revenue. How do we know this? Prior to the imposition of the minimum wage, OmniCorp must have set the price at a point where elasticity exceeded 1. Therefore, by dropping the price slightly (i.e. increasing output slightly) they will increase revenue. Recall that the revenue-maximizing price occurs where elasticity is exactly 1.

2.10 Increasing Returns to Scale

What happens if the firm enjoys increasing returns to scale? It is still the case that the profit-maximizing output occurs at a point where marginal revenue equals marginal cost. However, there can be more than one such point. A picture will be useful. Consider Figure 2.6. Quantity is displayed on the horizontal axis, and monetary values on the vertical.

Marginal cost decreases until it hits the horizontal axis and then becomes zero. There are two points where marginal revenue equals marginal cost. The first is at q_1 and the second at q_2. For quantities smaller than q_1, marginal cost exceeds marginal revenue. Therefore, if the firm chooses to produce q_1 units, its total profit will be negative. This clearly cannot be profit maximizing. If the firm increases production beyond q_1, marginal cost falls below marginal revenue. Thus, each unit beyond q_1

---

[18] This analysis shows that if a small increase in the minimum wage benefits workers, it does not follow that a large increase will benefit them more.

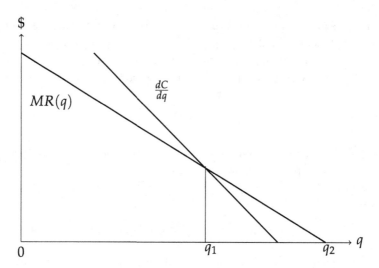

Figure 2.6 Increasing returns (a)

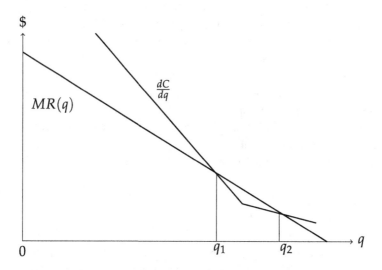

Figure 2.7 Increasing returns (b)

generates a profit for the firm. Hence, profit is maximized at q_2, the point at which revenue is maximized because $MR(q_2) = 0$. This does not mean that profit will be positive though, because the profit earned on each unit after q_1 may not cover the losses incurred up to q_1 units.

Figure 2.7 provides another illustration. Again we see that there are two quantities (q_1, q_2) where marginal revenue equals marginal cost. Again, q_2 is the profit-maximizing output level. This suggests the following rule: among the quantities where marginal revenue equals marginal cost, choose the one with largest revenue. In this sense, firms that enjoy increasing returns to scale are revenue focused.

2.11   Multi-product Monopoly

Many sellers sell more than one good or service. When these multiple products interact with each, the price of each product must be set in coordination with the others. For simplicity, consider a monopolist selling two goods called 1 and 2.

The two goods can interact with each other in two ways. The first is that their production requires a common, scarce resource. For example, the firm may have a capacity constraint that limits the total output of the two products.

The second is that the demands for the two goods interact with each other. This can happen in two ways. First as substitutes, for example Mayo and Miracle-Whip, or consuming today vs. consuming tomorrow. In other words, if the price of one good rises, the demand of the other good increases, holding its price fixed. This can be formalized in the following way. Let p_i be the price per unit of good i and suppose the demand for good 1 is a function of the price of good 1 *and* good 2 [i.e. $D_1(p_1, p_2)$]. Similarly, $D_2(p_1, p_2)$ is the demand for good 2 as a function of the price of good 1 and good 2. Goods 1 and 2 are **substitutes** for each other if

$$\frac{\partial D_1}{\partial p_1} \leq 0 \, , \frac{\partial D_1}{\partial p_2} \geq 0$$

and

$$\frac{\partial D_2}{\partial p_1} \geq 0 \, , \frac{\partial D_2}{\partial p_2} \leq 0.$$

Example 17 *Here is an example of substitutes:*

$$D_1(p_1, p_2) = 3 - p_1 + 2p_2,$$

$$D_2(p_1, p_2) = 5 + 0.75p_1 - 3p_2. \qquad \square$$

The two goods are **complements** if

$$\frac{\partial D_1}{\partial p_1} \leq 0 \, , \frac{\partial D_1}{\partial p_2} \leq 0$$

and

$$\frac{\partial D_2}{\partial p_1} \leq 0 \, , \frac{\partial D_2}{\partial p_2} \leq 0.$$

In words, if the price of one good increases, the demand of the other good falls, holding its price fixed. The classic examples are copper and zinc. Both are needed to make brass. If the price of copper increases, this makes brass more expensive to produce. The brass producer will reduce zinc output. However, this results in a reduction in the consumption of zinc as well.

Example 18 *Here is an example of complements:*

$$D_1(p_1, p_2) = 3 - p_1 - 2p_2,$$
$$D_2(p_1, p_2) = 5 - 0.75p_1 - 3p_2. \qquad \Box$$

3   Price Discrimination

Macbeth murdered sleep and the railway did the same for distance. The poet Heinrich Heine mourned distance's demise:

I feel as if the mountains and forests of all countries were advancing on Paris. Even now, I can smell the German linden trees; the North Sea's breakers are rolling against my door.

The railways made travel accessible to the working classes, crowded into third or fourth-class carriages that were little more than roofless boxcars with wooden benches. The novelist Alphonse Daudet described the atmosphere:

I'll never forget my trip to Paris in a third class carriage in the midst of drunken sailors singing, big, fat peasants sleeping with their mouths open like those of dead fish, little old ladies with their baskets, children, fleas, wet nurses, the whole paraphernalia of the carriage of the poor with its odor of pipe smoke, brandy, garlic sausage and wet straw.

Conditions for plebeians were spartan. In England, for example, lower-class riders were initially classified as freight goods. Parliamentary action was required to force the railways to cover third and fourth-class carriages to protect riders from hot coals and soot from the locomotive.[1] This suggests that railway owners were just the sort of people to be first against the wall come the revolution. Not so, as the Belgian railway engineer and economist Jules Dupuit (1804–1866) explained:

It is not because of the several thousand francs which they would have to spend to cover the third class wagons or to upholster the benches that a particular railway has uncovered carriages and wooden benches; it would happily sacrifice this for the sake of its popularity. Its goal is to stop the traveler who can pay for the second class trip from going third class. It hurts the poor not because it wants them to personally suffer, but to scare the rich.... Thus, it is for the same reason that companies, after being cruel to travelers in third class and miserly for those in second, become prodigious for those in first class. After having refused the poor some necessary comforts, they give the rich what is superfluous.

Dupuit observed that the railways were trying to charge different buyers different prices for what was essentially the same service. Why? Buyers differ in the value they assign to the same product or service. This difference in valuation allows one to earn a greater profit by matching the price to a buyer's RP. This is called price discrimination. To see how the arithmetic plays out, consider a monopolist facing the demand function

---

[1] The Gladstone Act of 1844.

$9 - p$, where p is the unit price. So, there is one customer with an RP of 8, another with an RP of 7, and so on. When the monopolist was restricted to charging a single price, we worked out that she should charge $5 a unit, yielding a profit of $16. Suppose the monopolist could get away with charging a different price to each buyer. Say $7 to the buyer with an RP of $8, $6 to the buyer with an RP of $7, and so on till the buyer with an RP of $2.[2] The profit would be $6 + 5 + 4 + 3 + 1 = 19$.

Price discrimination is vulnerable on two fronts. The first is competition from another firm. If the incumbent responds by lowering its prices, then a price war might ensue where eventually every flyer pays the same price.

The second is arbitrage possibilities between the buyers, of which there are two kinds. The first is associated with **transferability of the commodity**. If the transaction costs of the resale of the commodity from one buyer to another are low, price discrimination will collapse. If I offer you and not your neighbor a discount, you could turn around and sell the goods to your neighbor at a lower price than I can. If transaction costs are high (medical services, travel) this sort of arbitrage is unlikely. An example of something that falls between the extremes of no transaction costs and high transaction costs is student discounts. One needs only a student ID card to make use of them. I could transfer this discount to someone who is not a student by selling them a fake ID.

The second type is associated with the **transferability of demand** between different packages or bundles offered to the customer. There is no transfer of goods in this case. Consider airlines offering first and second-class seats. The trick is to get the passenger to whom first class is targeted to buy the first-class seat and not second class. To do this, the airlines must ensure that the perceived value difference in the two service classes is at least as large as the difference in airfare.

Price discrimination comes in three varieties. **First-degree price discrimination**, the ideal,[3] is where the firm identifies the RP of every buyer and prices accordingly. This is unlikely to exist, because of arbitrage and the absence of perfect information about buyers' tastes.

Second-degree price discrimination identifies, imperfectly, the RPs of the buyers through a form of self-selection. Buyers choose among different packages of goods offered by the seller, and in doing so they reveal something about their RP's. The trick is to match the package with the RP. We'll discuss a specific example of this later.

Third-degree price discrimination involves the use of a customer signal (age, time of day, occupation, usage, income, race) to price discriminate. The important difference between second and third-degree price discrimination is that third-degree price discrimination uses a direct signal about demand, whereas second-degree price discrimination selects indirectly between buyers through their choice of different packages.

---

[2] Why don't we consider the others?
[3] For the firm, not the customer.

Every form of price discrimination presents an arbitrage opportunity. Therefore, no prescription for price discrimination is complete without a discussion of how the resulting arbitrage possibilities will be handled.

3.1 An Example of the Third Degree

In Section 2.6, the tale of opposition to Mylan's pricing of the EpiPen was told. Mylan's immediate response to the furor was to reduce the out-of-pocket costs of users. The discounts were not uniform, but tied to the kind of insurance plan a user had. So, families on insurance plans with high deductibles, 70% of the total customer base, received a coupon worth up to $300. The uninsured (5% of the total) got free EpiPens provided their income was below 400% of the US Federal poverty level. Those covered by Medicare, Medicaid, and Tricare saw no difference, because such coupons were considered an illegal financial inducement. However, about 90% of such users had coverage for the EpiPen. Keep in mind that Mylan (as other pharmaceutical companies) has always employed such co-pay schemes as a way to price discriminate. In the case of Mylan, they simply increased the size of the discounts they offered to users.

Example 19 *To see how this plays out numerically, suppose a monopolist produces Soma which is used as an input by two industries producing two different goods (say Amos and Mosa). Because of intense competition in their markets, these two firms charge prices that are close to marginal cost.*

Assume that both industries convert one unit of Soma into one unit of output. The demand for Amos has a constant elasticity of demand of 1.5, and for Mosa the elasticity of demand is 2. Finally, assume that the monopolist's constant marginal cost of production is $1.

Consider the Amos-producing industry first. Since input equals output, its demand for Soma will have an elasticity of 1.5. Hence, by the markup formula, the price p that the monopolist will charge to firms in this industry will satisfy

$$(p - 1)/p = 1/1.5 = 2/3$$
$$\Rightarrow p = 3.$$

Similarly, the price charged to the Mosa-producing industry will be $2 a unit (less than to the Amos-producing industry). Notice that the monopolist is charging different prices for the same good depending on the market; an example of third-degree price discrimination. Discrimination is based on an observable, the elasticity of demand associated with the markets that each industry is serving.

How does the monopolist prevent the Mosa-producing industry from selling Soma to the Amos-producing industry? One way (and you should think of others) is by vertically integrating with one of the firms in the Mosa market. The monopolist buys one of the Mosa-producing firms and sells Mosa at $2 a unit. To all other firms, it sells Soma at $3 a unit. Now, no other Mosa-producing firm can compete with the monopolist's subsidiary if it is buying Soma at $3 a unit. So, the Mosa competition is squeezed out. The Amos-producing firm continues to buy Soma at $3 a unit.   □

3.2   Examples of Second-Degree Price Discrimination

In second-degree price discrimination, the seller offers a menu of choices to the buyer and the buyer chooses from the menu. The two most popular instances of this menu idea in practice are **versioning** and **bundling**.

3.2.1   Versioning

The problem with offering the same product to all buyers is that not all of them value all of the features of the product in the same way. Therefore, it is useful to add or subtract features from the product to generate multiple versions of the same basic product. Different versions of the same product can be customized to different buyer segments. Tesla, for example, sells (as of 2016) two different versions of their Model S and X electric cars. One has a 60 kw-h battery which allows the car to travel 200 miles per charge. The other is a 75 kw-h version, allowing the car to go 230 miles per charge. The 75 kw-h version is $9000 more expensive than the 60 kw-h version. However, both versions have the same 75 kw-h battery. The company adds a line of code to reduce the storage capacity of the battery.

In deciding how many versions of a product to make and what to price them at, the firm needs to worry about the costs of producing and distributing the versions chosen and the consequent cannibalization of sales. The latter occurs when a product intended for one segment attracts buyers from another segment. This is the second form of arbitrage mentioned earlier (arbitrage of consumption). A simple numerical example illustrates the trade-offs involved.

Example 20 *Suppose you are the monopoly seller of two types of electric vehicles, that vary in how far they can travel per charge. Call them "SHORT" and "LONG." For simplicity, assume that the unit cost of each type is zero. As pointed out earlier, LONG and SHORT cost the same to make.*

There are two customer segments, A and B, of equal size (suppose one of each). The RPs of each segment for each type of vehicle are shown in Table 3.1.

Table 3.1 RPs

	LONG	SHORT
A's RP	$100K	$40K
B's RP	$49K	$30K

As the seller, you cannot tell whether a buyer belongs to segment A or B. In other words, there is no observable signal (like gender, age, etc.) that indicates the segment a buyer belongs to. This excludes the possibility of third-degree price discrimination.

You have three options to consider. First, price and sell the LONG version only. Second, price and sell the SHORT version only. Third, offer both versions simultaneously. To determine which option is best, we calculate the profit consequence of each.

If you were to sell the LONG version only, there are only two prices worth considering. Slightly under $49K and slightly under $100K. At a price below $49K, both segments will purchase because the surplus offered is positive. At a price between $49K and $100K, only segment A will purchase. However, any price well below $100K leaves money on the table. Finally, at a price that exceeds $100K, no one will buy. Hence the two prices: slightly under $49K and slightly under $100K. To avoid having to write and read the phrase "slightly under" repeatedly, we simply drop it. In other words, if buying confers zero surplus and not buying confers zero surplus, assume that the buyer will break the tie in favor of buying.

Table 3.2 records the demand and revenue consequences from charging each of the two possible prices. Recall that since costs are zero, profit is the same as revenue.

Table 3.2 Revenue from LONG

Price	Demand	Revenue
$49K	2	$98K
$100K	1	$100K

Therefore, if you sell the LONG version only, it should be priced at $100K.

Now let us repeat the same analysis for the SHORT version (see Table 3.3).

Table 3.3 Revenue from SHORT

Price	Demand	Revenue
$30K	2	$60K
$40K	1	$40K

In this case, a price of $30K for the SHORT version would maximize revenue.

Of the two options considered so far, the best is to sell the LONG version only and price it at $100K. In this case one shuts out the B segment completely. To make more money, one must sell to both segments but get the A segment to pay more. How?

The idea is to offer both vehicles, and charge a higher price for the LONG version. Clearly, the LONG version should be directed to the A segment while the SHORT version is directed to the B segment. To squeeze the A segment, the LONG version should be priced higher than the SHORT one. However, if the LONG version is priced too high, the A segment will switch down to buying the SHORT version (this is arbitrage associated with the transfer of consumption). To illustrate, suppose the LONG version is priced at $100K and the SHORT version is priced at $30K. When *faced with these two versions, a buyer in the B segment will choose the SHORT version. A buyer from the A segment will also choose the SHORT version. Why? Consider the surplus that such a buyer obtains from each version. The surplus on the LONG version will be $100K − $100K = $0. The surplus from the SHORT version will be $40K − $30K = $10K (i.e. the surplus on the SHORT version is larger). If you find this odd, keep in mind that the rational buyer model assumes that buyers make trade-offs. In this case, if a short-range vehicle is priced low enough, it looks better.*

To recap. If one sells only one type of vehicle, it should be the LONG version at $100K. If one now introduces the SHORT version as well for a price of $30K, it will appeal to the B segment as well as cannibalize sales from the LONG version. Thus, to keep the A segment paying for a LONG version, we have to (in this example) lower the price of the LONG version just enough that it will look more attractive than the SHORT version. The A segment will buy the LONG version as long as the LONG version delivers at least as much surplus to them as the SHORT version. The surplus of a buyer from the A segment on the SHORT version is currently $40K − $30K = $10K. So, if we price the LONG version at $90K (or just a hair beneath), the A segment will purchase the LONG vehicle. The result is a revenue of $90K + $30K = $120K. This is $20K more than selling the LONG version only. □

Example 20 shows that introducing a variant of a product produces two effects. On the positive side, the variant allows one to cater to a segment not previously being served. On the negative side, the variant competes with the original product. This competition manifests itself in the cannibalization of sales from the original version, which may require lowering the price of the original version. In the example above, the positive effect outweighed the negative effect. The next example illustrates that this is not always the case.

Example 21 *As Example 20, except that the RPs of the segments are changed as in Table 3.4.*

Table 3.4 Modified RPs

	LONG	SHORT
A's RP	$100K	$65K
B's RP	$49K	$30K

As before, if one sells only the LONG version, its revenue-maximizing price is $100K, yielding a total revenue of $100K. If one sells only the SHORT version, its revenue-maximizing price is $65K, yielding a total revenue of $65. Can one do better by selling both versions?

If both versions are sold, then the SHORT version must be priced at $30K. A buyer from the A segment receives a surplus of $35K from the purchase of the SHORT version. Hence, to ensure that the A buyer will buy the LONG version, it must be priced at $65K. However, total revenue will be $95K only (buyer in segment A buys LONG at $65 and buyer in segment B buys SHORT at $30K). This is less than the revenue obtained from selling the LONG version only. □

The reason versioning does not increase profit in Example 21 is that the A segment perceives less of a difference between the two versions. This can be seen in the difference in RPs. In Example 20, the difference in RPs for the A segment between LONG and SHORT is $60K. In Example 21 that difference is $35K. In other words, the added benefits of a LONG version over a SHORT version have diminished, making them more alike in the buyer's mind.

Is offering two versions always better than a single version? It seems like it can't be worse. The underlying profit-maximization problem has more control variables, giving the seller greater flexibility. However, selling two versions also imposes more restraints, preventing arbitrage of consumption. The end result is that it could go either way, depending on the numbers.

While it may appear unseemly for Tesla to intentionally damage their product to increase revenue, an inspection of Example 20 shows that in such an instance, versioning *increases* consumer surplus.

3.2.2 Bundling

A bundle is a collection of distinct products or services that are sold together as a package. A suite of software programs sold together, season tickets to the theater, round-trip air tickets, and *prix fixe* menus are examples. The meaning of "distinct" requires clarification. A BLT (bacon–lettuce–tomato) sandwich, for example, consists, amongst other things, of bread, bacon, lettuce, and tomatoes. As these are distinct products, a BLT is a bundle. It would seem, then, that pretty much everything under the sun constitutes a bundle. This is not helpful. Instead, what constitutes a bundle should be evaluated from the perspective of the buyer. For the buyer at a sandwich shop, the BLT is not a bundle because there is no expectation that the shop will offer the ingredients of the BLT for sale individually. In contrast, for the buyer at home contemplating a meal, the BLT is a bundle because they can go to the supermarket to buy its individual components.

There are two kinds of bundling.

1. **Pure bundling**

   The seller does not make the items in a bundle available for sale individually, even though they could. For example, until 2010 the Windows operating system could not be purchased without Internet Explorer. Thus, one buys both or neither.

2. **Mixed bundling**

   In any McDonald's one can choose to buy the value meal (hamburger, soft drink, and fries) or each component or pair of components separately.

   Sellers bundle for reasons other than price discrimination, but these will not concern us here. In this section we will show how bundling can be used to price discriminate.

Example 22 *Our numerical example consists of four buyers (A, B, C, and D) and two products. One is a subscription to CNN and the other to ESPN. Each buyer is interested in at most one subscription for each channel. Since most of the costs of putting on the channel are fixed, we will assume that the goal is to maximize revenue.*
   The RP of each buyer for each channel is shown in Table 3.5.

Table 3.5 Subscription prices

	CNN	ESPN
A's RP	$80	$40
B's RP	$40	$80
C's RP	$90	$10
D's RP	$10	$90

There are three ways in which subscriptions can be sold:

1. *Price and sell each channel as an individual item.*
2. *Price and sell the channels in a bundle of two only (pure bundling). The option of subscribing to a single channel is unavailable.*
3. *Price and sell a bundle as well as the channels individually (mixed bundling).*

Which will generate the most revenue?
   If we price and sell CNN by itself, the revenue generated at each price point is shown in Table 3.6.

Table 3.6 Price, demand, and revenue for CNN

Price	Demand	Revenue
$10	4	$40
$40	3	$120
$80	2	$160
$90	1	$90

So, the revenue-maximizing price for CNN is $80. A similar analysis applies to the pricing of ESPN, yielding the same price. This generates a total revenue of $320.
   Now suppose we bundle the channels together. There are three possibilities for how buyers may value the bundle. The first is that there are synergies (i.e. the whole

is greater than the sum of its parts). In this case, it is obvious that bundling will be beneficial. If one delivers more value, one can capture more of it with higher prices. The second is that bundling destroys value. For example, no buyer can view more than one channel because of time constraints. Therefore, the RP of buyer A for the bundle will be $80. If one can watch only one channel, one would watch the channel that is of most value. If bundling destroys value, then clearly selling a bundle makes no sense. The third possibility is that the RP of a bundle will simply be the sum of the component RPs. So, A's and B's RP for the bundle is $120, while C's and D's RP for the bundle is $100. Pricing the bundle at $100 yields a revenue of $400, while setting the bundle price at $120 yields a revenue of $240. Thus, in the pure bundling case, pricing at $100 maximizes revenue. Notice that more revenue is generated in this case than in the first.

With mixed bundling, buyers have the option to buy a bundle or just one of the channels. Here is a combination that generates more revenue than the pure bundling case. Price the bundle at $120 and each individual subscription at $90. Faced with these prices, A and B maximize their surplus by purchasing the bundle, while C and D do so when they purchase one channel subscription each (C buys CNN, D buys ESPN). Total revenue is $420.   □

Pure bundling generates higher revenues than selling individually in Example 22 because it increases demand. When the channels are sold individually, a total of four subscriptions are sold. However, under pure bundling, eight subscriptions are sold. To see why this happened, compare the spread or variance in RPs for a single product vs. the variance in RPs for the bundle. The variance for the bundle is lower. The reduction in variance helps the seller. With a single price, the seller loses in two ways. First, there are buyers who do not buy and second, there are buyers who pay much less than their RPs. The magnitude of these losses increases with the variance of the RPs.

Now consider the mixed bundling option in Example 22. The average price per unit paid by A and B is $60. The average price per unit paid by C and D is $90. So, the same product is sold to different buyers at different prices. Naturally, there must be an arbitrage possibility here. A can buy the bundle and then resell the components for $85 each to C and D. In practice such arbitrage opportunities are forestalled by making resale illegal or designing the product so as to make resale difficult. For example, season ticket holders are given a ticket that cannot be split up into individual tickets or are required to present a valid ID when using the ticket.

3.3   Two-Part Tariff

At the northern end of the island of Sumatra is the territory of Aceh. While a part of Indonesia, it enjoys a degree of autonomy denied other provinces, the result of a prolonged fight for independence. The territory has a bloody history of resisting control going back to the arrival of the Portuguese, 600 years earlier. It required an act of God, the 2004 tsunami, for Aceh to achieve a measure of independence from Indonesia.

As of 2009 there were two overland routes for the shipment of goods into Aceh from North Sumatra, the Indonesian province adjacent to it. One runs from Medan to Banda Aceh, the capital of Aceh. It takes about a day to traverse, and along the way is a weigh station at Gabang. A truck weighing more than 5% above the maximum limit must be both ticketed and shed the excess weight. To compound the punishment, the driver is required to face a magistrate and pay a fine. As drivers receive a flat payment for all expenses incurred on the road, they are prepared to pay a bribe to avoid the fine. Unsurprisingly, weigh station officials at Gabang are delighted to accept.

Interestingly, truckers are given a choice for how they wish to pay the bribe.[4] A trucker who arrives at the weigh station from Medan must pay a fixed fee of approximately Rp. 170,000 (US$18.50) and about Rp. 11,000 (US$1.20) per ton overweight for each ton over 10 tons overweight. However, before departing Medan, a trucker can buy a coupon from a criminal organization for about Rp. 150,000 (US$16.30). The coupon allows the trucker to pay a flat fee of Rp. 50,000 (US$5.50) to the weigh station officials, regardless of how overweight they are. A trucker more than 16 tons overweight will prefer the second option to the first.

Each of the options has two parts. The first is a fixed payment (low in the first and high in the second), independent of the weight of the cargo. The second is a per-unit fee tied to the excess weight (high in the first and low in the second). Such a pricing scheme is called a two-part tariff.

To understand why such a pricing scheme might be useful, it is helpful to consider the case of a single buyer who enjoys diminishing marginal benefits from consumption. Consider a Soma-producing monopolist with constant marginal costs of production of $1. There is only one customer, say Mariko, and her *incremental* RP for various amounts of Soma is shown in Table 3.7.

Table 3.7 Incremental RPs

Quantity	First unit	Second unit	Third unit	Fourth unit
Mariko's RP	7	5	3	1

Assume that the RP for the fifth and higher units is zero. Notice that her RP for the fourth unit is less than her RP for the third unit, and so on, consistent with diminishing marginal benefits.

Table 3.8 shows how many units Mariko will buy at various prices.

---

[4] Barron, P. and B. A. Olken (2009). The simple economics of extortion: Evidence from trucking in Aceh. *Journal of Political Economy*, 117(3), 417–452.

Table 3.8 Price and demand

Price per unit	1	2	3	4	5	6	7
Mariko's demand	4	3	3	2	2	1	1
Profit	0	3	6	6	8	5	6

It is easy to see that the profit-maximizing unit price is $5, yielding a profit of $8. Can one do better than a profit of $8? Yes, because selling each unit at the same price leaves money on the table. At the $5 a unit price, Mariko buys two units. Her surplus on this purchase is $7 + 5 - 2 \times 5 = 2$. So, $2 is left on the table. Here is one way to get (most of) the surplus. Charge $7 for the first unit, $5 for the second unit, $3 for the third unit, and so on. This may not seem like bundling, but that is cosmetic. One could just as well have set a price of $7 for one unit, $12 for a pack of two units, $15 for a pack of three, and so on.

Announcing a price for each unit or a price for each possible bundle is impractical, and for that reason one is interested in simpler pricing schemes that approximate what the ideal price looks like. Here is an illustration of one. Charge a fixed fee of $1.99 and sell every unit for $5. The fixed fee of $1.99 will not affect the quantity bought. It will determine if the buyer chooses to accept the offer. Suppose she does. Then she can buy as many units as she likes for $5. At this price she would maximize her surplus by acquiring two units. This will leave her with a surplus of $2. Since the fixed fee of $1.99 is less than that, by accepting this offer her surplus will exceed zero. Thus, given a choice between buying and not, she will buy. Profit will now be $1.99 + 8 = 9.99$. Such a pricing scheme is called a **two-part tariff**. It is composed of a fixed fee F and a per-unit price p. If you purchase q units, the total payment will be $F + pq$. We have seen such a scheme before in Section 2.4.

A two-part tariff is an example of bundling. The buyer is offered one unit for $F+p$, a bundle of two units for $F+2p$, and so on. The two-part tariff recognizes that Mariko does not value all units the same. To extract as much surplus from her as possible, we should sell her the first unit for $7, the second unit for $5, and so on. The two-part tariff attempts to do just this. Here is why. If the fixed cost is F and the per-unit price is p, consumer A will spend $F + p \times Q$ to purchase Q units. The *average* price per unit she pays will be

$$\frac{F}{Q} + p.$$

Notice that this quantity declines as Q, the amount she purchases, increases. Thus the average price per unit decreases with the volume of purchase.

Can one do better than the two-part tariff just identified? Yes. Here is a two-part tariff that does better: $F = 12$ and $p = 1$. The surplus for various purchase quantities under this tariff is shown in Table 3.9.

Table 3.9 Quantity and surplus

Quantity	1	2	3	4
Mariko's surplus	< 0	< 0	0	0

Breaking ties in favor of the larger quantity, we see that Mariko will buy four units, yielding a profit of $12.

Such tariffs are ubiquitous. Sometimes the fixed fee F is associated with an entry fee or cover charge. Some night clubs charge a fee to enter and then more depending on the number of drinks ordered. Water and electricity bills are sometimes of this form. In other cases, possibly more interesting, the fixed fee is associated with a durable good like a razor or e-book reader. The per-unit price p is associated with a consumable like a blade or an e-book. The durable and the consumable are linked in that the durable is needed to access the consumable. Thus, a blade is worthless without the razor and one needs a reader to access an e-book. The obvious question is how to set F and p.

3.3.1   Optimal Two-Part Tariff

How does one determine the profit-maximizing two-part tariff for a monopolist? When selling to a single buyer (or multiple buyers with identical preferences), it is calculated using the following procedure.

1. First set the per-unit rate p, at marginal cost.
2. For this value of p, determine how many units the consumer will purchase to maximize her surplus. Set F equal to this surplus.

As the per-unit rate of the tariff is set to the seller's unit cost, profits are made with the fixed fee. Lowering p stimulates demand, so increasing the buyer's surplus. The seller captures this increase in surplus by raising F.

To prove the assertion just made about the optimal two-part tariff, suppose a single buyer is characterized by the inverse demand curve $p(q)$.[5] The seller has constant marginal costs of c per unit.

If the seller charges p^* per unit, the buyer will purchase q^* units where $p(q^*) = p^*$. Hence, the buyer will enjoy a consumer surplus of

$$\int_0^{q^*} p(x)dx - p^*q^*.$$

Thus, assuming the outside option of the buyer yields zero surplus, the largest the seller can set F to be is that surplus:

$$F = \int_0^{q^*} p(x)dx - p^*q^*.$$

---

[5] This argument would apply to multiple buyers with identical inverse demand curves.

Setting F to exceed this will cause the buyer to exit. Setting F to be lower than this leaves money on the table. Therefore, the seller's profit is

$$\int_0^{q^*} p(x)dx - p^*q^* + (p^* - c)q^* = \int_0^{q^*} p(x)dx - cq^*.$$

This expression should be familiar to you from Section 2.6.

The seller wants to choose p^* to maximize profit. However, p^* does not appear in the profit expression, q^* does, but recall that it depends on p^*. So, we can choose q^* to maximize profit and then use the optimal choice of q^* to back out the optimal choice of p^*. Differentiating the seller's profit function with respect to q^* and setting it to zero (check the second-order condition) yields

$$p(q^*) - c = 0, \quad \Rightarrow p(q^*) = c.$$

In words, choose q^* so that inverse demand equals marginal cost (i.e. $p^* = c$).

Example 23 *Suppose we have a buyer with an inverse demand curve of $p = 9 - q$ (equivalent to $q = 9 - p$). Suppose that the seller has constant marginal costs of $1 a unit. Set the unit price to $1. At this price, demand will be 8. The fixed fee F will be*

$$F = \int_0^8 (9 - x)dx - 8 \times 1 = \left[9x - \frac{x^2}{2}\right]_0^8 - 8 = 32. \qquad \square$$

If we apply this logic to razors and blades, we should set a high price for the razor and sell the blade at cost. In other words, make the money off the razor not the blade. According to a 1929 issue of *Time* magazine, this gets it backwards:

As everyone knows, safety razor manufacturers derive the bulk of their profit, not from razors, but from the replaceable blades.

Glucometer manufacturers sell millions of blood-sugar-monitoring devices (the durable) to diabetics below cost and receive their profits from hundreds of testing strips (the consumable) used annually by each diabetic. Printer companies sell their printers (the durable) below cost and recover their profits on the ink cartridges (the consumable). Is our two-part tariff analysis out of touch with reality?

3.3.2 Razors and Blades

The strategy of a low-priced durable (possibly below cost) and a high-priced consumable is called a razors and blades pricing model. It is credited to King Camp

Gillette, the inventor of the disposable razor. Other than the name, nothing in the previous sentence is correct. Even the name beggars belief.[6]

Before 1904, razor blades were not disposable. Blades were expensive to produce because of the amount of steel needed to prevent them from buckling under the pressure of a man's stubble. The Montgomery Ward catalog of 1895 devotes one and a half pages out of 624 to razors and blades.[7] The price for a razor ranged from $0.60 to $3.50, while the price for a (non-disposable) blade was as much as half that of the razor. The catalog also offered stropping machines and strops, devices needed to sharpen a blade. Sharpening a blade required time and skill, so it was not uncommon for men to have their blades sent out for sharpening.

One of the more popular razor brands of the time was the Star Razor. The father of US Supreme Court Justice Oliver Wendell Holmes, who was a popular travel writer, endorsed the product with these words:

> It is pure good-will to my race which leads me to commend the STAR RAZOR to all who travel by land or by sea, as well as to all who stay at home.

In 1903 Gillette announced, in *System* magazine, his disposable blade with these words:

> ... so that the blades require but a small amount of material and can be ground very quickly and easily, and hence I am able to produce and sell my blades so cheaply that the user may buy them in quantities and throw them away when dull without making the expense as incurred as great as that of keeping the prior blades sharp, and, moreover, will always have the cutting edge of his razor-blade in the same perfect condition a that [of] the new blade.

Gillette had hit upon the idea of a disposable blade, but to make it a reality had to lower the cost by making them thinner, so consuming less steel. A thin blade, however, was fragile. Enter William Nickerson, an MIT-educated engineer who solved the problem. The razor to hold the blade would be designed to prevent the blade from buckling. The two of them patented the idea in 1901.

The initial offer was a razor plus a pack of 20 blades for $5. Gillette claimed this was 2 years' supply and new blades could be purchased for 5 cents a unit. However, used blades could be returned for sharpening at 2.5 cents a blade.[8] By way of comparison, the average weekly industrial wage was $15 and a low-end man's suit ran for $12. Gillette emphatically did not embrace a low-priced razor, high-priced blade strategy. In fact, within a year he had modified the offer to one razor and a 12-pack for $5 with subsequent packs offered at $1 a piece, effectively increasing the price of the

---

[6] Gillette was also a writer, anticipating the modern fashion of industry titans giving advice to one and all. He advocated that all industry be controlled by a single publicly owned corporation, and that everyone in the USA should live in a giant city called Metropolis powered by Niagara Falls.

[7] Montgomery Ward was the Amazon.com of its time.

[8] The Montgomery Ward catalog offered these services for as much as 50 cents a blade.

blades. He sold 51 razors and 48 blades in his first year. In the second he "went viral," selling 91,000 razors and 100,000 blades![9]

It was estimated that a Gillette razor would last 6 years. This means, at the initial offer, for $7 one could purchase 6 years' worth of shaves.[10] At these numbers, Gillette had at least three other ways to price his razor-blade system.

1. $7 for a razor and a lifetime's worth of free blades.
2. A free razor but each blade would be priced at about 12 cents.
3. $7 for a bundle consisting of one razor and 60 blades.

Why prefer one of these over the other?

The low-priced razor, high-priced blade strategy frequently credited to Gillette was not adopted until *after* 1920, when it faced competition. Joseph Spang, CEO of the company in 1951, described the goal this way:

> Every effort was made to get the Gillette razor in the hands of as many men as possible. The idea of making a profit on the razor became unimportant. That period might be termed the "give-away" years.

Razors were given away with Wrigley's gum, pocket knives, and canned meat.[11]

3.3.3 Kindle and E-books

Amazon's Kindle e-book reader was introduced in November 2007 at a price of $399. It was not the first e-book reader. The idea for such a device had already been proposed in the 1930s.[12] Devices that we would recognize as dedicated readers were already being offered by companies like Sony before the Kindle.

Amazon also offered e-versions of new bestseller hardbacks at $9.99. Publishers charged Amazon the same wholesale price for the e-book version as for the new hardbacks. The wholesale price was typically 50% of the list price. Therefore, hardbacks listing for a retail price of $25.99 would have cost Amazon $13 to buy from the publisher. If a customer purchased the e-version for $9.99, Amazon would lose $5.[13] Again, Amazon was not following the low-priced razor, high-priced blade strategy.

The unit cost of the first-generation Kindle was roughly $250. This meant the margin on the first-generation Kindle was roughly $150. At a $5 loss per e-book, the profit on the Kindle would be consumed after 30 books. This seems likely, as the initial set of buyers of the Kindle would be heavy readers. Why would Amazon operate at a

---

[9] The US entry into WWI made Gillette. In 1914 he offered the US army 4.8 million razors at cost. Returning doughboys, having used his razors, became enamored of them. By war's end in 1918, he had sold over 1 million razors and 120 million blades.

[10] $5 for the razor and initial pack. Then, two more packs for $1 each.

[11] Picker, R. C. (2010). The razors-and-blades myth(s). *University of Chicago Law Review*, 78, 225–255.

[12] The *Hitchhiker's Guide to the Galaxy*, which contains all the knowledge in the galaxy, fits into a device the size of a paperback book, with updates received over the "Sub-Etha."

[13] This comes from the $3.01 loss on the e-book plus the $2 loss on the physical version that is cannibalized by the e-book.

loss? Let's dismiss one explanation: Amazon wants to save on shipping by encouraging readers to switch to the e-book. Amazon generally ships items for free if the bill is over $25. Assume a customer buys two physical books for $30 and qualifies for free shipping. If they choose expedited shipping, this will cost $3 plus $0.99 per book. So, the customer pays $4.98 in shipping for two books. Amazon's shipping cost for two books was about $3 at the time. If the customer opts for free shipping, Amazon makes a net profit of $1 ($4 profit on the two books minus $3 shipping cost). If the customer opts for expedited shipping, Amazon makes a profit of $5.98 (the $4 profit on the two books plus the $1.98 on shipping).

3.3.4   Reconciliation?

The intuition that monopoly profits are made with the cover charge rather than the per-unit fee is at variance with the generally accepted view that one should do the opposite. We have summarized two examples where the seller departed from the generally accepted view. However, there are also examples of firms following the low-priced durable, high-priced consumable strategy (recall the glucometers). How do we reconcile this?

Recall the logic of the two-part tariff; the monopoly seller should first determine the buyer's lifetime value of shaving, say V. Since the incremental value of a blade diminishes only upon death, V is uncertain. Assuming a long life, V will be some impossibly large number. If death were at the doorstep, V would be vanishingly small. Thus, uncertainty on the part of the buyer about the number of blades he will consume reduces his incentive to pay a large sum (the cover charge) upfront. The uncertainty can have many sources. A buyer may fear being locked into one kind of razor until death. He may decide at some later date that he looks better in a beard. Further, what is to prevent the seller from subsequently raising the price of blades or going out of business? Or an innovation in shaving technology that would make the present razor obsolete. In short, the two-part tariff with a large fixed-cost component imposes huge risks on the buyer when they are uncertain about consumption, so making them reluctant to accept such an offer. One can overcome this reluctance by lowering the fixed-cost component (F) and compensating for this by raising the per-unit price (p). This shifts the risk associated with the uncertainty in the volume of consumption onto the seller. In the case of razors and blades, the seller bears the cost of the razor, gambling that the buyer will spend enough on blades to recoup that cost and more. In other contexts, the seller may limit risk for both himself and the buyer by placing time limits. For example, F could be an annual or monthly fee that entitles the buyer to unlimited consumption during the relevant period for a per-unit fee. In fact, a seller could offer a menu of two-part tariffs. One with a large F but low p and another with a low F and large p. Health clubs are an example. Annual membership (large F) in return for unlimited use of the facilities for a year ($p = 0$). Or no membership fee ($F = 0$) but a daily use fee (high p). The first offering would be attractive to users confident that they will use the facilities with high frequency, and the second to those uncertain about how often they will use the facilities.

This last observation highlights an important assumption in our analysis of the optimal two-part tariff. It assumed that all buyers had the same demand curve (i.e. they were entirely homogeneous in their tastes). We now examine the consequence of dropping this assumption. For this case imagine a monopoly supplier of single-serve coffee machines (Keurig, Nespresso) and the pods. Consumers receive utility from the pods but not the machine. However, no one can use the pods without the machine. The unit production cost of a machine is $5 and the unit production cost of a pod is $1.

There are two types of customers (assume one of each), heavy and light. Heavy users are prepared to pay more for each incremental pod than light users. The incremental reservation prices of the heavy users are shown in Table 3.10.

Table 3.10 Incremental RPs of heavy users

Unit	1	2	3	4	5	6	7	8	9
RP	$9	$8	$7	$6	$5	$4	$3	$2	$1

The incremental reservation prices of the light users are displayed in Table 3.11.

Table 3.11 Incremental RPs of light users

Unit	1	2	3	4	5	6	7
RP	$7	$6	$5	$4	$3	$2	$1

If the monopolist were selling only to the light user, what price would it charge for the machine and pod to maximize profit? This would just be the optimal two-part tariff. Sell the pod at cost (i.e. $1 a unit). At this price the light user maximizes his surplus when he buys seven units (he purchases to the point where the incremental RP is $1). At seven units the surplus of the light user is 21. So the optimal two-part tariff is to charge $21 for the machine and $1 a unit for the pods. Profit is $21 − $5 = $16.

If the monopolist were selling only to the heavy user, a similar analysis would suggest that the machine should be priced at $36 and each pod at $1. Profit is $36 − $5 = $31.

To summarize, when selling to light users, the seller would set $F = 21$ and $p = 1$. When selling to heavy users, $F = 36$ and $p = 1$. Such a scheme works provided that the seller is in a position to distinguish between heavy and light users. What happens if the seller is limited to imposing the same two-part tariff on all buyers?

At a machine price of $21 and pods at $1 a unit, both types of users would have an interest in buying the machine and pods. However, this leaves money on the table with respect to the heavy users. In contrast, a machine price of $36 and pods at $1 would make the products unattractive for the light users. Is there a combination of machine and pod prices that would be attractive to both heavy and light users as well as generate more profit than selling to one kind of buyer alone? A good starting point is the first pricing schedule: machine at $21 and pods at $1 a unit. At these prices both buyers make purchases, yielding a total profit of $42 − $10 = $32. Now there is money left on the table with the heavy users. We can capture that in one of two ways. Raise the price of the machine or the price of the pods. In the first case, we would shut out the light users, which is unprofitable. Let us consider the second case.

Increase the pod price to $2 a unit. At this price, the light users buy six pods and the heavy users buy eight. The surplus of the light users will be $15. The surplus of the heavy users will be higher. If we wish to serve both markets, the surplus of the light users will be the upper limit we can charge for the machine. So, set the machine price to $15 and each pod to $2. Total profit is $30 − 10 + 6(2 − 1) + 8(2 − 1) = $34. This is larger than before. Now suppose a pod price of $3 a unit. Light users will buy five pods, heavy users will buy seven. The surplus of the light users will be $10. So, set the machine price to $10. At these prices, profit will be $34. Profit is unchanged. In fact, it is easy to see that by raising the pod price further we can only lower profits.

Thus, with customers of various kinds, to maximize profits we may have to increase the price of the consumable and drop the price of the durable. As consumers become heterogeneous in their incremental RPs, we may be forced to take our profits from the pods.

Now, suppose a drop in the production cost of the pods. In this case, one would drop the per-unit price of the pods and increase the price of the machine. Selling each pod for less gives the buyers more surplus, raking it back with a higher machine price.

Example 24 *In this example we determine the optimal two-part tariff when there are heterogeneous consumers. The information about consumer preferences is given in terms of demand curves rather than a table of incremental RPs.*

Suppose two segments: heavy and light users. There is one heavy user and their inverse demand curve is $q_H = 9 − p$. There are two light users and each has the following inverse demand curve: $q_L = 6 − p$. What distinguishes a heavy user from a light one is that at any unit price p, the heavy user always demands more than the light user. The monopoly seller has a constant marginal cost of $1 a unit.

To acquire a feel for the problem, consider two cases first.

1. *Set unit price to $1*
   The demand of the heavy user will be 9 − 1 = 8. The surplus of the heavy user will be

$$\int_0^8 (9 − x)dx − 8 \times 1 = 32.$$

   The demand of each light user will be 6 − 1 = 5 and their surplus will be

$$\int_0^5 (6 − x)dx − 5 \times 1 = \frac{25}{2}.$$

If we set $F = 32$, only the heavy user will buy, yielding a profit of $32. If we set $F = 12.5$, everyone buys, yielding a profit of $12.5 \times 3 = $37.5.

2. *Set unit price to $2*
   The demand of the heavy user will be 7 and his surplus will be

$$\int_0^7 (9 - x)dx - 7 \times 2 = \frac{49}{2}.$$

The demand of each light user will be 4 and their surplus will be

$$\int_0^4 (6 - x)dx - 4 \times 2 = 8.$$

If we set $F = \frac{49}{2}$, only the heavy user buys, yielding a profit of $24.5 + 7 = \$31.5$. If we set $F = 8$, all three buy, yielding a profit of $\$3 \times 8 + 2 \times 4 + 7 = 39$. Notice that profit is higher than in the previous case.

How do we find the profit-maximizing two-part tariff when selling to two segments? We need to break the analysis down into two possibilities:

1. *Do we want to sell to both segments?*
2. *Do we want to sell to just one of the segments and if so, which one?*

Focus first on finding the (F, p) combination that maximizes profit subject to selling to all buyers. Denote by $q_L(p)$ the quantity bought by a light user at price p. Let $q_H(p)$ be the quantity bought by a heavy user at price p.
   Denote the surplus of a light user at unit price p by $S_L(p)$. Similarly, let $S_H(p)$ denote the surplus enjoyed by a heavy user at unit price p. Assuming both segments purchase, the total profit will be

$$3F + (9 - p)(p - 1) + 2(6 - p)(p - 1).$$

To sell to all buyers, F cannot exceed the surplus of any of the buyers. So, the profit-maximization problem faced by the seller is

$$\max_{F,p} 3F + (p - 1)q_H(p) + 2 \times (p - 1)q_L(p)$$

$$\text{s.t. } F \leq S_L(p)$$

$$F \leq S_H(p).$$

Given that heavy users demand more than light users at each price, it follows that $S_H(p) \geq S_L(p)$. Hence, to maximize profit we should set F equal to the surplus of light users. Higher than that, and the light users will walk away. Less than that, and money is being left on the table. Under this choice of F, total profit will be

$$3 \times S_L(p) + (p - 1)q_H(p) + 2 \times (p - 1)q_L(p).$$

We need to choose p to maximize this expression. Now

$$S_L(p) = \int_0^{6-p} (6 - x)dx - p(6 - p) = (6 - p)\left[3 - \frac{p}{2}\right].$$

Therefore, profit is

$$3 \times (6-p)\left[3-\frac{p}{2}\right] + 2(p-1)(6-p) + (p-1)(9-p) = 33 + 6p - \frac{3}{2}p^2.$$

Differentiating, setting to zero, and verifying the second-order condition we find the profit-maximizing choice of p is p = 2. Notice that $S_L(2) = 8$. Hence, the optimal two-part tariff when we sell to all segments is $F = 8$ and $p = 2$. Total profit is $39.

If we decide to sell to exactly one segment, which one? If it is just the heavy user, we set $p = 1$ and $F = 32$. This combination will not attract light users but clearly generates less profit than the case above.

What about selling to just the light users? This is not a possibility. It is straightforward to verify that any two-part tariff attractive to a light user will also attract heavy users. Thus, one winds up selling to both segments anyway. □

How does the presence of a competitor affect the analysis? First, assume a competitor develops a low-cost substitute for the pods that sell for less than $1 each. The competitor does not sell a machine, but their pods are compatible with your machine. As the incumbent you should increase the price of the machine. In fact, if the numbers work out right, you might be better off having the competitor come in to provide the pods at a lower price than you can. This encourages buyers to buy more pods, so increasing their surplus. This increase can be captured by raising the price of the machine.

What if the competitor has a machine compatible with your pods, but no pods of their own? In this case, you would drop the price of your machine but raise the price of the pods. What if the competitor has their own machine–pod system?

4 Competition

In 1890, Alexandre Delcommune left Kinshasa upon two steamers towards the Katanga region of what was then known as the Congo Free State. Free in name only, the state was the personal property of Leopold II, King of the Belgians, an Atilla in modern dress. Delcommune's mission was to find gold and explore the feasibility of settling the region. Among his company, briefly, was Joseph Conrad who had hoped for command of one of the two steamers. A falling out with Delcommune's brother put paid to this ambition, but Conrad was permitted to accompany the expedition part way. That experience made its way into *The Heart of Darkness*.

Now a province of the Democratic Republic of the Congo, Katanga is rich beyond the wildest dreams of avarice in copper, cobalt, and diamonds. Mining involves roughly 2 million people, divided into three-man teams, digging 60 feet below the surface to scratch out about 220 pounds of copper ore a day. After taxes this generates about $4. By comparison, a loaf of bread is $1.50. The situation is summarized in the April 24, 2008 issue of the *Washington Post*:

As world mineral prices soar, the former soldier makes less than $5 on a good day of toiling 20 yards underground, at the literal end of a chain of predatory middlemen, gold-wearing labor bosses and shadowy mineral traders stretching from here to China and India and places he only imagines.

Effectively, the miners make zero margin. How can that be? The next section introduces a model of price competition due to Joseph Bertrand (1822–1900) to explain this. Miners are like competing firms who set a price for their labor.

4.1 Bertrand Model

Suppose two firms sell identical widgets to a market of 100 buyers. Each buyer has an RP for a widget of $2 and will buy no more than one widget. Therefore, not one of them will spend more than $2 for a widget.

Each widget costs $0.50 to make. Production is instantaneous and defect-free, so neither firm need worry about inventory, returns, and the other complications of real life. Production capacity is unlimited for both firms.

Both firms and buyers live exactly one day. The firms must simultaneously and independently set prices at which they will sell their widgets at the start of the day.[1] Prices, once set, are communicated instantly to all 100 buyers and cannot be adjusted. The buyers purchase from the seller that gives them the largest surplus. In case the surplus offered by each firm is the same, the buyers divide equally between the two firms.

What price do you expect each firm to post? What price would you, as firm 1, post? To simplify, suppose firms 1 and 2 are limited to charging one of two prices: $2 a unit and $1.50 a unit. Table 4.1 (called a **payoff table**) summarizes the profit consequences of various price choices. The rows correspond to the price/strategy choices of firm 1 (you), while the columns represent the price/strategy choices of firm 2 (opponent). The left-hand entry of each cell is the profit to firm 1, while the right-hand entry is the profit to firm 2.

Table 4.1 Payoff table #1

Firm 1/Firm 2	Price = $2	Price = $1.50
Price = $2	$75, $75	$0, $100
Price = $1.50	$100, $0	$50, $50

If you select the low price ($1.50) because you are risk-averse, let us make the choice even starker. Suppose that each firm incurs a fixed cost of $55 of doing business, independent of the number of widgets sold. Table 4.2 displays the payoffs for this case. Would you still choose the low price ($1.50)?

Table 4.2 Payoff table #2

Firm 1/Firm 2	Price = $2	Price = $1.50
Price = $2	$20, $20	−$55, $45
Price = $1.50	$45, −$55	−$5, −$5

Suppose I offered to tell you what price your rival will pick *before* you had to choose your price? Would you accept my offer? Would knowing what your opponent will do in advance make a difference? Focus on Table 4.2.

If I told you (firm 1) that firm 2 intends to choose the high price $2, what would you do? Matching firm 2 on price yields a $20 profit. Undercutting (to $1.50) yields a $45 profit. Since more money is better than less, undercutting is the best option. Thus, in this case, you (as firm 1) would choose the low price.

Suppose now I told you that firm 2 was going to choose the low price. If you respond with the high price, you lose $55. If you select the low price, you lose $5, which is less. In this case you would choose the low price.

---

[1] In particular, collusion is ruled out.

Notice that, no matter which price firm 2 picks, you (firm 1) are always better off choosing the low price. The same argument applies with equal force to firm 2. So, both firms would select the low price, losing $5.

If both firms had picked the high price, they would each generate a profit of $20, making each better off. Recognizing this, why doesn't each choose the high price? Why didn't you?

The same conclusion holds for Table 4.1 as well (the one without fixed costs). Again, logic impels both firms to choose the low price.

Does the conclusion change if the firms are permitted to choose any price? No. The argument is more elaborate and involves an idea that we use repeatedly. In this argument assume that fixed costs are zero.[2]

If one allows the firms to choose any price, no firm will choose a price that exceeds $2. No buyer values a widget at more than $2. It is also obvious that no firm will choose a price below variable cost of $0.50.

Is it sensible to predict, say, that firm 1 will price at $1.57 and firm 2 will price at $1.63? To check, place yourself in the shoes of each firm in turn. As firm 1, you get the entire market, making a profit of $107. As firm 2, however, you make nothing. What's more, as firm 2, if you predicted that these would be the prices, it is silly for you to choose the $1.63 price. After all, if you, as firm 2, predicted that firm 1 would post a $1.57 price, then you should have priced just below that. So, firm 1 pricing at $1.57 and firm 2 pricing at $1.63 is implausible.

How about firm 1 at $1.89 and firm 2 at $1.76? Again, not sustainable. At this pair of prices, firm 1 would rather undercut firm 2.

The two examples illustrate that the firms offering unequal prices is implausible. The firm with the higher price would be better off dropping their price.

How about the firms matching their price? For example, $1.70 each. At this pair of prices firm 1 makes $60. However, if firm 1 drops its price by a penny to $1.69 and firm 2 does not, firm 1 can sell to the entire market and increase profits above $60 by an amount equal to $69. So, even equal prices is implausible, because at least one firm could improve its own profit by dropping prices.

Where does that leave us? Each firm pricing at cost (i.e. $0.50). No firm can improve its profit by unilaterally undercutting the other. No firm can improve its profitability by unilaterally raising its price. Therefore, pricing at cost is the only plausible outcome.[3]

4.1.1   Game Theory Digression

Underlying the reasoning employed above is an idea from game theory known as the Nash equilibrium. Here we will review some basic ideas from game theory that will prove useful in the remainder of this chapter.

---

[2] Assuming otherwise makes no difference, since such costs are sunk.

[3] One may think that the price of a penny above $0.50 is also correct. Yes, if we are limited to pricing in increments of a penny. Let's assume that it is possible to charge any fraction, however small, of a penny.

The word "game" in game theory applies to any situation where the actions of each player affect the payoffs to others. Defining a game completely is not always easy, and failing to do so can lead to confusion. What does defining a game involve?

1. Identify who the **players** in the game are and their **objectives**.
2. Identify the **strategies** that each player has at their disposal. For example, can they choose prices as well as capacities? Can they threaten other players? Is it possible to collude with other players in the game?
3. What are the **outcomes** and their associated **consequences** from players choosing each of their strategies. It is important to distinguish outcomes that are the result of strategy choices and those produced by factors beyond the players' control.
4. Who knows what and when? It is not always the case that all players know the same things. Some may be better informed than others, and information can be revealed as the game progresses.

Some games involve a single simultaneous move by all players, such as rock–paper–scissors. These are called **simultaneous-move** games. Others involve a sequence of moves over time and are called **sequential** games. The two kinds of games are represented in different ways. The representation of simultaneous-move games is described first. Assume that players play for money and all prefer more money to less.

Simultaneous-move games are represented by

1. A list of players.
2. For each player, a list of their strategies.
3. For each strategy, one for each player, a list of (monetary) payoffs that each player receives.

These lists are assumed to be known by all players.

In a game with just two players, these lists can be combined into a table, as illustrated in Example 25 below.

Example 25 Two firms, two locations. *Two competing fast food chains, M and W, have each decided to open one restaurant in a small town. The town has two shopping centers, denoted by L and S, constituting the two natural places for such restaurants. It is estimated that the expected daily number of buyers is 1200 at L and 800 at S. It is assumed that if they locate at the different centers, they would each get the local traffic and that if they locate at the same center, they will split the number of local customers equally, while the customers from the other center will be lost.*

We can summarize the payoff data as in Table 4.3. It describes two choices, or strategies in the language of game theory, for each of the two players, M and W. The table entry corresponding to every pair of strategies is a pair of numbers, describing the corresponding pair of payoffs that result from the selected pair of strategies. So, for example, the top-left entry is (600, 600) because these are the expected number of customers they each receive if they both choose location L. But the top right entry, corresponding to M choosing L and W choosing S, has the payoffs (1200, 800). The left-hand entry in each cell is the payoff to M and the right-hand entry the payoff to W. □

Notice that when M chooses strategy L, he forces the game to be played in the top row (with the final choice being determined by the choice made by W) and when he chooses strategy S, the game is restricted to the bottom row. For this reason, we often refer to player M in this game as the row player. Similarly, every strategy choice of W restricts the game to a certain column and thus, we refer to W as the column player. When the row player chooses a row and the column player chooses a column, the outcome of the game is the pair of payoffs corresponding to the selected entry. In general, the entries in the payoff table do not have to be symmetric and the number of strategies each player has may be greater than two.

Table 4.3 Payoff table

M/W	L	S
L	600, 600	1200, 800
S	800, 1200	400, 400

When players make moves in rounds with dependencies between the rounds, the stages of the game are represented by **vertices,** and the vertices are linked by arrows, called **directed edges** that specify the order in which stages occur. A path from one vertex to another represents a sequence of moves and counter-moves by the players. This congregation of vertices and edges is called a **game tree**.

In a two-player game, the vertices come in three colors, black, white, and red, say. A white vertex represents a stage in the game at which player 1 must make a move. The edges directed out of the vertex represent the strategy choices that player 1 has at that stage of the game. A black vertex represents a stage in the game at which player 2 must make a move. A red vertex represents a point in the game where "chance" makes a move (i.e. a dice throw). We will not consider games with "chance" moves in this book.

Example 26 *A benevolent plutocrat proposes the following three-stage game between Joanna and Oscar, who are not allowed to collude.*
Stage 1: The plutocrat offers Joanna $1 million. If Joanna accepts, the game ends. If Joanna rejects the offer, the game goes to stage 2.
Stage 2: The plutocrat offers Oscar $2 million. If Oscar accepts, the game ends. If Oscar rejects, the game moves to stage 3.
Stage 3: The plutocrat offers Joanna $3 million. If Joanna accepts, the game ends. If Joanna rejects, the game ends.
The extensive form representation of the game is displayed in Figure 4.1.

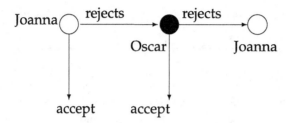

Figure 4.1 Centipede game

The white circles represent stages where Joanna moves and the black circle where Oscar moves. The arrows that emanate from each circle represent the moves that each player can make at that stage of the game.   ☐

A strategy in a sequential game is a complete plan that specifies what move will be made in every contingency. In the game tree, a strategy reduces to a set of instructions on which directed edge is chosen at *every* white (black) vertex.

Playing the Game

The natural question is, what strategy should one choose? It is easier to consider a related question first. What, if any, strategies should one *not* play?

Consider the Bertrand model (BM) introduced earlier. A portion of the payoff table is reproduced as Table 4.4.

Table 4.4 BM payoff table

Firm 1/Firm 2	Price = $2	Price = $1.50
Price = $2	$75, $?	$0, $?
Price = $1.50	$100, $?	$50, $?

Consider firm 1. No matter what firm 2 does, firm 1 is always better off choosing a price of $1.50. If firm 2 chooses a $2 price, firm 1 makes $100 as opposed to $75. If firm 2 chooses a $1.50 price, firm 1 is better off choosing a $1.50 price than a $2 price. The $2 price is an example of a **strictly dominated strategy**. A strategy is strictly dominated if there is some other strategy in the game that does strictly better than this strategy *no matter what* the opponent does. The dominance principle says that one should never choose a dominated strategy. The dominance principle does not require any information about the payoffs that one's opponents will receive.

Example 27 *This example illustrates the dominance principle in a more elaborate context. The strategies of the column (she) player are labeled with lowercase letters,* *while those of the row (he) player with uppercase letters. Only the payoffs to the row player are shown.*

Row/Column	a	b	c
A	4	5	−3
B	−100	−200	0
C	5	7	0

Row player's strategy A does not strictly dominate his strategy B. Strategy A does better than strategy B only if the column player chooses a or b. If the column player chooses c, then the row player is better off choosing his strategy B. Now, row player's strategy C strictly dominates his strategy A. No matter what strategy column chooses, row is always better off choosing C over A. What about C over B? C does not strictly dominate B. It is true that if column chooses a or b, row is better off choosing C over B. However, and this is crucial, when column chooses c, strategy B delivers the same payoff as C to row. Strict dominance requires that one strategy beats the other every time. It is not enough for C to beat B sometimes and tie other times. This distinction may seem like hair splitting, but cannot be ignored. □

To give a formal definition of strict dominance, let a_{ij} be the payoff to the row player from playing row i and from the column player choosing column j. Strategy row p **strictly dominates** i if $a_{pj} > a_{ij}$ for all column strategies j.

To deal with the situation where one strategy beats another sometimes and ties with it other times, we have the notion of **weak dominance**. Formally, strategy row p **weakly dominates** strategy i if $a_{pj} \geq a_{ij}$ for all column strategies j, with strict inequality for at least one j. In Example 27 row's strategy C weakly dominates B.

The idea that no one should play a strictly dominated strategy is a compelling one. It should apply with equal force to weakly dominated strategies. For the moment suppose yes, with a caveat to be revealed later.

Sequential Elimination

By eliminating strictly dominated strategies in the BM, we can determine what firm 1 should play. This by itself does not determine the outcome of the game. To do that we need to know the payoffs to firm 2 (Table 4.5).

By symmetry, the $2 price strategy is strictly dominated for firm 2 as well. Given this, we expect that each player will choose the $1.50 price strategy. Notice the use of the word "we" in the previous sentence. As the outside observer of the game, we can tell what the outcome will be. What about the players themselves? Put yourselves in the shoes of player 1. If all you know are your payoffs, then you can deduce only that you should choose the low price. You cannot predict what your rival will do without

Table 4.5 BM payoff table

Firm 1/Firm 2	Price = $2	Price = $1.50
Price = $2	$75, $75	$0, $100
Price = $1.50	$100, $0	$50, $50

knowing their intentions. This is where the rationality assumption bites. Knowing both your rival's payoffs and that they are rational allows you to deduce that they will pick the low price.

In the BM each player has only two strategies, so the presence of strictly dominated strategies for each of them is enough to determine the outcome. What about in more elaborate games?

Example 28 *Consider the payoff table below*

Row/Column	B	N
H	1, 1	0, 0
M	2, 0	0, 0
L	3, −1	0, 0

Place yourself in row's shoes. Strategies H and M are weakly dominated by strategy L. Thus, as the row player you will choose strategy L. Can you predict what your opponent will do? Not unless you know their payoffs. Suppose you do. Notice that the column player has no strictly (or even weakly) dominated strategies. So, you cannot with certainty predict what they will do. But suppose now that the column player knows your payoffs and knows that you are rational as well.

Column can deduce that you, player row, will play L. So column, in choosing a strategy, will ignore your strategies H and M. Thus, as far as column is concerned, the game reduces to (after eliminating rows H and M)

Row/Column	B	N
L	3, −1	0, 0

However, you know that column knows your payoffs and that you are rational, so that you can deduce that column will be looking at the reduced game above. At this point, player column's strategy B is strictly dominated by strategy N. You can thus predict that the outcome is (L,N). □

Two things drive the game to a single possible outcome. The first is that both players know the entire game and they know that they know this and so on. This is called **common knowledge of the game**. The second is that both players know that each is rational and they know that they know this and so on. This is called **common knowledge of rationality**. In this book we assume both kinds of common knowledge hold.

Example 29 *Consider a more elaborate example*

Row/Column	B	N
H	3, 6	7, 1
M	5, 1	8, 2
L	6, 0	6, 2

In this game column does not have a strictly dominated strategy. Row, however, does; row H is strictly dominated by row M. So, row will eliminate row H. Now, assume that column knows that row will do this. Thus, column can conclude that row H will never be played. Delete row H from the table.

Row/Column	B	N
M	5, 1	8, 2
L	6, 0	6, 2

In the 2-by-2 table that remains, column B is strictly dominated by column N. So, column will eliminate column B.

Row/Column	N
M	8, 2
L	6, 2

Row knows this and will eliminate row L. Thus the outcome will be (row M, column N). □

Does the outcome of the game depend on the order in which dominated strategies are eliminated? Yes, when the strategies eliminated are weakly dominated. The order of elimination does not matter when only strictly dominated strategies are eliminated.

Backward Induction

The analog of eliminating strictly dominated strategies in extensive form games is called **backward induction**. To illustrate the idea, recall the centipede game of Example 26.[4]

If you are Joanna, what should you do? It is common to frame the analysis in terms of how long each is prepared to stay in before they lose their nerve and bolt with the money. They reason *forward* from the first round of play. The reasoning goes something like this. I could take the $1 million now or pass; at worst I don't get $1 million, which was found money anyway. Now the pot goes to $2 million. What is the chance that Oscar will pass? If he does, then I could get $3 million, and so on.

Assuming Joanna and Oscar are rational, the correct thing to do is to reason backwards. In the last round of the game (if it is ever reached) we can tell precisely what will happen. Joanna has a choice between $3 million or nothing. Assuming that Joanna is rational, she'll take the money. So, on the last round we know she'll take the money and we know that she knows and she knows that we know, and so on. So, in the next to last round what should we do? If we pass, we know that Joanna takes the money and we get nothing. So, in the next to last round we should take the money. In the round before that Joanna knows that if she passes, Oscar will take the money in round 2. So, what will she do? Take the money in round 1.

Equilibrium

Many games cannot be solved by the sequential elimination of dominated strategies. Rock–paper–scissors is an example. In these cases we resort to an equilibrium principle due to John Nash (1928–2015). To motivate its definition, consider the BM. If both firms chose the $2 strategy, they would be better off! Knowing this, why don't they agree on a $2 price? They could agree to fix the price at $2, but what incentive is there for either to keep the agreement. If firm 1 believes that firm 2 will charge a $2 price, its best course of action is to renege and lower its price to $1.50. The ($2, $2) agreement is not an **equilibrium**. A pair of strategies, say x for player 1 and y for player 2, is an equilibrium if player 1 cannot do strictly better by playing something other than x if player 2 plays y, and vice-versa. An equilibrium is a pair of strategies that form a *self-enforcing agreement*. If I believe that you will play y, my best course of action is to play x; and if you believe that I will play x, your best course of action is to play y.[5] The price pair ($2, $2) is not an equilibrium, because at least one firm can do better by unilaterally deviating. The price pair ($1.50, $1.50) is an equilibrium. Neither firm is made better off by unilaterally switching to another strategy.[6]

This version of the BM is an instance of the Prisoner's Dilemma. The dilemma lies in the fact that the outcome of the game that is *individually* rational ($1.50, $1.50) is not *collectively rational* (where both firms choose the $2 price).

---

[4] So called because the game tree looks like a centipede, see Figure 4.1.

[5] It is self-enforcing in the limited sense that a single player cannot do better by deviating.

[6] If a game is dominance solvable, the outcome will be an equilibrium.

To recap, a collection of prices, one for each firm, form a **Nash equilibrium** if no single firm can generate more profits for itself by unilaterally raising or lowering its price from the equilibrium level.[7] In what follows we use the Nash equilibrium of the competitive situation as a prediction of what the outcome will be. For brevity we will omit the honorific "Nash" when referring to an equilibrium.

Determining equilibrium prices is sometimes difficult, but this need not concern us, because we are usually interested in a simpler (and more interesting) question:

Is it an equilibrium for each firm to price at its marginal cost?

Here is a three-step recipe for deciding this issue.

1. First, assume that each firm is pricing at its marginal cost.
2. Under this profile of prices, determine how the market divides between the firms (i.e. who buys what from whom at the prices identified in step 1).
3. Now check if there is a firm that could increase its profits by it (alone) raising its price above its marginal cost. If there is one, then all firms pricing at their respective marginal cost is not an equilibrium. Otherwise it is.

Notice that we don't have to consider the possibility of a firm dropping its price below cost.

In what follows, this will be the approach taken. When possible, we will determine equilibrium prices.

Mixed Strategies

Not every game has a Nash equilibrium as we have defined it (however, many of the games we will discuss in this book will have a Nash equilibrium as defined). As an example, consider the game of rock–paper–scissors. Its payoff matrix is shown in Table 4.6.

Table 4.6 Rock–paper–scissors

Row/Column	Scissors	Paper	Rock
Scissors	0, 0	1, −1	−1, 1
Paper	−1, 1	0, 0	1, −1
Rock	1, −1	−1, 1	0, 0

The reader can verify that the game does not have a Nash equilibrium in the sense defined above.

To guarantee the existence of an equilibrium in *all* games,[8] we must allow the players to randomize.[9] Thus, a player's strategies are described by a probability vector.

---

[7] The equilibrium idea doesn't require that firms choose the same price or that their profits be equal. There can be equilibria where firms choose different prices and have different profits. Further, there can be multiple equilibria for the same situation.

[8] At least those with a finite number of strategies.

[9] This is not without controversy, but a full discussion is beyond the scope of this book.

In rock–paper–scissors, row's strategies would be the set of vectors (p_1, p_2, p_3) such that

1. $p_1 + p_2 + p_3 = 1$,
2. $p_1, p_2, p_3 \geq 0$,

where p_i is the probability that row chooses row i.

The original set of strategies (in this case scissors, paper, and stone) are called **pure strategies**, while the strategies obtained by randomizing are called **mixed**. The payoff from a randomized strategy is just the expectation of the payoffs of the various pure strategies.

Randomized strategies pose a problem in how they should be interpreted, but as they will not play a role in this book, we ignore this issue.

4.1.2   Objections to the Bertrand Model

If one takes the BM seriously, why would anyone choose to participate in a business that is anticipated to yield zero profit? To answer this, modify the BM. Suppose each player must first decide to play the game (before knowing what the other player has decided). Once these decisions are made, they become public. Then, each player that decided to play, chooses a price. Table 4.7 summarizes the profit consequences of the four possible scenarios. The payoffs in the upper left-hand corner come from the fact that if both firms decide to play, they would choose prices that are in equilibrium (i.e. $0.5 each). Hence, they make zero profit. The payoffs in the lower left-hand corner come from the fact that if firm 1 decides not to play and firm 2 does, firm 2 becomes a monopolist and will charge $2. As the reader can verify, the only equilibrium is for both firms to choose to play. The point is that both firms are attracted to the possibility of supplying a market with a total value of $2 \times 100 = \$200$.

Table 4.7 Play vs. don't play

Firm 1/Firm 2	Play	Don't play
Play	$0, $0	$150, $0
Don't play	$0, $150	$0, $0

There are five features of the BM that force prices to be at marginal cost.

1. The BM assumes just one chance to set prices.
2. Costs are the same.
3. No capacity constraints.
4. The products sold are undifferentiated.
5. Buyers and sellers have full information. That is, buyers are aware of each seller's offering and the price charged. Sellers are aware of each other's costs, offerings, and prices.

These features, in concert, eliminate any incentive to price above marginal cost. In this sense the list is useful because it describes the characteristics of an industry in which one should expect margins to be razor thin. Here is the same list reinterpreted.

1. Are sellers focused on short-term gains? This can happen because compensation is tied, for example to quarterly targets. Or the business may be one where only a few deals are signed each year. The consequences of losing a couple of large orders in a row may result in layoffs. The jet engine industry is an example.
2. Do sellers have similar cost structures?
3. Is there excess capacity?
4. How much differentiation is there between sellers in the market?
5. How much transparency is there?

If the answers to these questions are yes, yes, yes, none, and a great deal, respectively, then the industry resembles the BM and we should expect slender margins. This is the world of the Congolese miners. Anyone who can dig can mine. As there are few alternative sources of income, the supply of miners, mainly ex-soldiers, is huge. Second, the costs of mining are essentially the same for all miners; sweat! Third, they are all selling the same thing, raw ore. Fourth, the miners are focused on short-term gains; today's meal, which will fuel tomorrow's digging.

Not every industry resembles the world that the Congolese miners inhabit. Airlines, for example, change their prices hour by hour. Firms add and subtract capacity regularly. In the following pages we will investigate the consequences of relaxing each of the assumptions about the BM, some in more detail than others.

4.1.3   More than Once

Does the outcome of the BM change if there is more than one round of play? Perhaps, because the game is no longer a simultaneous one but a sequential one. Suppose the BM was to be played for exactly 10 rounds. For simplicity, focus on the version of the BM where the sellers are limited to just two possible prices; recall Table 4.1.

We will use backward induction to determine the outcome. At the last round, round #10, each firm will choose the low price of $1.50 as the other price is strictly dominated. On round #9, you and your rival know that on round #10 each of you will choose the $1.50 price. Hence, there is nothing one can do in round #9 to influence what happens in round #10. Therefore, one can treat round #9 in isolation to round #10, and again one should price at $1.50. Repeating this analysis, we see that the outcome is each firm choosing the low price in *every* round. Clearly, what drives this conclusion is a terminal round. What happens otherwise?

Suppose the two firms will interact with each other for an indefinite number of rounds. We can formalize this idea by flipping a coin at the end of each round to see if they will play another round. If the coin comes up tails, they stop, otherwise they play a further round. By increasing the chance of a heads, we increase the chance of a prolonged interaction. Now, how one firm prices in the current round could influence a rival's behavior in a future round. Why? Because there is a possible "future."

Notice "could" rather than "will." You and your rival could end up charging low prices in every round (perpetual price war) or high prices in every round, or something in between.

In repeated play of the BM, a strategy is no longer what price you pick in each round but rather a rule that uses the history of the game played so far to determine the price in each round. Here are three examples of such rules:

1. Choose the low price in each round. This rule ignores the entire history of what has transpired.
2. Choose a high price in the first round. In subsequent rounds, choose a high price if the rival chose a high price in the previous round. If the rival chose a low price in the previous round, then choose the low price in every round thereafter. This rule is called **grim trigger**.
3. Choose a high price in the first round. In subsequent rounds, choose the price that the rival chose in the previous round. This rule is known as **tit-for-tat** (TFT).

If you believed your rival was guided by the first rule, the best you could do against them is to choose the low price in each period. Notice that if you could convince your rival that you would play by the first rule, the best they could do is to respond with the low price in each period. So, in the repeated version of the BM, both sellers playing by the first rule is an equilibrium.

What if your rival plays by the second rule? If you pick the high price in each period, you enjoy an income stream of $75 in each period. If you undercut your rival in the first period, you earn $100 in that period. But, in all subsequent periods, because your rival will choose the low price, you will also choose the low price. In this case your profit will be $50. Hence, the extra $25 gained in the first period is paid for by an income stream of $50 in all subsequent periods. If you give any reasonable weight to future income, an income stream of $75 in every period is better than one that yields $100 in the first period followed by $50 in all subsequent periods. If you give no weight to future income, then you are essentially playing once.

If you adopt a rule that will choose a low price at some other time (does not matter when), then from that time on the best you can do is garner a profit of $50 in all following periods. If the game goes on long enough, average per-period profits will be close to $50. However, if you play by the rule that chooses the high price in each round, average per-period profits will be $75. So, against the second rule, your best option is to choose the high price in each round. Thus, both firms adopting the second rule is an equilibrium of the repeated version of the BM.

The third rule, TFT, combines sticks and carrots. If you follow it and your rival undercuts you, it dictates that you respond in kind; the stick. If they subsequently raise their price, then you follow; the carrot. You reward a move to higher prices by your rival by doing the same, and punish them when they don't by cutting the price. The reader may verify that the rival's best response to a TFT on your part is to choose the high price in each round.

One way in which the TFT can be implemented is with a price-matching guarantee. Suppose firm 1 sells its output for $2 a unit, along with the following guarantee: should the buyer get the same product elsewhere for a lower price, they will refund the buyer the difference in price. Assuming the guarantee to be credible, what effect, if any, does it have? Since the guarantee is public knowledge, firm 2 is aware of it. What price should firm 2 charge? If it charges $2, it gets $75. If it decides to undercut firm 1 by charging $2.50, it gets only $50. This is because the guarantee has the effect of automatically reducing firm 1's price the moment firm 2 lowers its price.

The guarantee is actually a threat: "if you don't keep prices high, I will instantaneously punish you by dropping prices." Instantaneous retaliation is crucial. Otherwise, firm 2 might make a quick killing before firm 1 realizes that firm 2 has lowered prices. The guarantee is such that firm 2's price drop cannot be kept concealed from firm 1 because it encourages customers to police firm 2. The entire scheme depends on firm 1's ability to follow through on the guarantee. If there is any doubt about this, the guarantee may have no effect. Thus it is not sufficient to offer such a guarantee. One must make it credible.

So far we have two possibilities. One where the seller's average is $50 per period and the other where they average $75 per period. It turns out that for any number between 50 and 75, there is an equilibrium that gives each player that much per period (on average), suggesting anything can happen.

Just because anything can happen doesn't mean it will. It seems more plausible to believe that firms will be thinking and doing things that lead them to the equilibria with high per-period payoffs. In particular, the firms will use the repeated interactions to signal each other and effectively collude on higher prices. Nevertheless, there are obstacles.

First, the signaling hypothesis relies on the ability of firms to monitor each other's prices. This may be difficult to do. Price cuts can be disguised using rebates, changes in payment terms as well as warranties, changing product serial numbers or adding features. Indirect observations of prices like changes in demand and profit are also imperfect. For example, the fact that the volume of business one does with a client is steady is not a sign that one's rival has not cut price. Imagine that the client's business is growing but they are sending a larger share of it to one's rival. Where there is evidence of signaling succeeding, it has usually been the case that sellers offer a standardized product or service and prices are easily monitored. Airlines are an example. In 1992, the US Justice Department filed suit against the then eight largest American airlines because they were using the common computerized reservation system to fix air fares. Using the common reservation system an airline could, for example, signal that starting on January 1 it would increase its unrestricted economy fare by $75 between Washington DC and Boston. In some cases, airline A, for example, would signal its intention to reduce a fare on a profitable route for airline B. Airline B would respond by signaling its intention to reduce a fare on a route that was lucrative for airline A (e.g. tit-for-tat). Subsequently, both fare reductions would be abandoned. United Airlines and USAir agreed to end the practice of using the reservation system to "feel" out rivals about price increases. The other six eventually settled in 2000.

Second, the period between price changes may be quite large, on the order of months or years. This could be because purchases are infrequent (think aircraft) or buyers sign long-term contracts. Thus, profits made on the tenth round are not the same as profits made on the second round (i.e. discounting matters). If the discount factor is high enough, then in the eyes of the firms, round 5, say, and higher, don't matter and we are back to charging low prices every round.

Collusion and Signaling

Can collusion allow the firms to avoid price competition? Agreements to fix prices or quantities (tacitly or otherwise) are usually illegal in most countries.[10] However, even if firms were to flout such laws, price-fixing agreements do not eliminate competition. Rather, they shift competition from the marketplace to haggling in hotel rooms. Colluding firms must bargain over how to split the profits amongst themselves. In the longer term they must coordinate capacity expansions and whether to include new entrants into the cartel. This often results in a falling out amongst thieves.

Predation

In 2003, the European Commission fined the French internet provider Wanadoo about 10 million euros for deterring competition by pricing below cost. Pricing below cost in order to drive out a competitor or discourage entrants is called predatory pricing. It is outlawed in a number of countries, but definitions and standards of proof vary.

The logic behind the strategy appears straightforward. If one prices below a rival's marginal cost for a sustained period, this should drive one's rival out and leave one a monopolist in the market. During the period in which one is a monopolist, one recoups sufficient profits to cover the costs of ejecting the rival. First, even if one succeeds in driving out one's rival, what happens to their capacity? As long as it remains in the market, it poses a competitive threat. Second, when the rival departs, presumably one raises prices. When that happens, what is there to prevent a new entrant?

Predatory pricing is also risky. This can be seen most clearly in a stylized setting called an **all-pay auction**. Imagine you and a rival are to bid on an envelope containing $50. Bidding takes place in rounds and continues as long as the second highest bidder is willing to top the current high bid. The highest bidder wins but, *each* bidder must pay the highest bid they have made so far. Hence the term "all pay." For bidders and firms, the money in the envelope represents the dollar value of the market they are competing for and their bid in each round represents their daily costs of business. These costs must be paid whether or not the market is "won."

How should you bid? Suppose you have $10 and your rival has $5 and this is common knowledge. Then it is clear that your rival will walk, leaving you with the envelope for a nominal bid. Therefore, when budgets are common knowledge, the bidder with the deeper pockets wins.[11] If budgets are not common knowledge, one would like to convince the other bidder that your budget is larger. The only credible

---

[10] Firms rarely fix prices. Instead, they fix shares or volumes. These agreements divide up the market either geographically or customer by customer.

[11] There are details that arise when budgets differ by very small amounts relative to the bid increments that we ignore.

way to do so is to put your money where your mouth is and bid aggressively. If they suspect you are bluffing, they will bid as well. Before you know it, you've reached your budget or bids exceed $50. How can this be? Consider two bidders, Leena and Meena. Suppose Leena has the current high bid of $49, and Meena the second highest bid of $48. Suppose it is Meena's turn to bid or drop out. If she drops out, by the rules she will be down $48. In contrast, she could top the current high bid, say with a bid of $50. If Leena drops out, then Meena is only out zero. So, it makes sense for Meena to top the current high bid. Now switch to Leena. She faces a high bid of $50. If she drops out now, she is down $49. If she tops the high bid with a bid of $51 and wins, she is only out a dollar. Which is better? Clearly, bidding above $50. One wins the envelope, but pays exactly what it is worth; a Pyrrhic victory.[12]

4.1.4   Capacities

Here we examine the impact of capacity on prices. Return again to the version of the BM with two possible prices but suppose that each seller has the capacity to supply only 20 widgets each. In this case, total industry capacity is 40 widgets while the number of potential buyers is still 100. Since demand exceeds capacity, intuition suggests that prices should be high. This is correct. The possible outcomes are summarized in Table 4.8. We assume that when a firm cannot serve all the demand it faces, the excess demand goes to the rival. The reader should verify that each firm pricing at $2 is an equilibrium.

Table 4.8 Each has 20 units

Firm 1/Firm 2	Price = $2	Price = $1.50
Price = $2	$30, $30	$30, $20
Price = $1.50	$20, $30	$20, $20

Now let us see what happens when capacity is increased. Suppose each firm has 60 units of capacity. Now industry capacity is 120, which exceeds the total number of buyers. Would the equilibrium price fall? To answer this, consider Table 4.9.

Table 4.9 Each has 60 units

Firm 1/Firm 2	Price = $2	Price = $1.50
Price = $2	$75, $75	$60, $60
Price = $1.5	$60, $60	$50, $50

You should verify that each firm pricing at $1.50 is *not* an equilibrium. In fact, the equilibrium is each firm pricing at $2. How can that be? First, firms were limited to one of two prices: $2 and $1.50. Hence, dropping the price by 50 cents a unit in order

---

[12] In fact, the US Supreme Court has declared predatory pricing to be "inherently uncertain," and noted its "general implausibility."

to increase the number of buyers to be served by 10 is not worth it. While cutting the price will bring the entire market to one's door, one does not have the capacity to serve this additional demand. In the case of firm 1, for example, cutting the price brings in an additional 40 customers. However, it can serve only 10 of them. The 10 additional customers bring in $10 in additional profit. But this does not offset the revenue loss of $25 from the lower prices to the initial 50 customers. Thus, cutting the price is a bad idea for firm 1. The same logic applies to firm 2.

If the firms were free to choose *any* price, the equilibrium price would indeed fall.[13] However, and this is the important part, the equilibrium price will not fall to cost. Why is this? Suppose both firms were to price at cost (i.e. $1 a widget). At these prices, the market divides evenly between the two sellers (i.e. each sells 50 units). Consider firm 1. If it raises its price, how many buyers can it lose? Since their rival has only 60 units of capacity, there will still be 40 units of demand unserved. Firm 1 will find it more profitable to charge $2 and sell to these 40. Hence, each firm pricing at marginal cost is *not* an equilibrium.

Therefore, what determines price is not just the balance between capacity and demand, but how that capacity is allocated between the firms.

4.1.5   Differentiation

There are two kinds of differentiation, vertical and horizontal. Vertical differentiation means that your product/service is superior to your competitor's product/service in the eyes of *all* buyers. In other words, every buyer assigns a higher RP to your offering than the competitor's. This superiority allows one to extract a premium in price. In horizontal differentiation one segment of buyers rates your offering as superior to the competition and is prepared to pay a premium over the competitor's offering. Another segment rates your rival's offering as superior to yours and will pay a premium over your price for their offering. For example, your widgets are colored blue while the rival's product is painted red. Some customers value the blue color more than the red color, and vice-versa. This manifests itself in a higher RP for the blue widget than for the red widget. This differentiation allows, in some cases, firms to sell at prices above cost.

The model we analyze is a variation of the BM.[14] Firm 1 decides to paint its widgets blue (blue firm), while firm 2 paints its widgets red (red firm). Manufacturing costs for both firms are $1 a unit. Each firm has unlimited capacity. Of the 100 buyers, 50 prefer blue widgets to red widgets (blue lovers). These 50 value blue widgets at $5 and red widgets at $3 (blue lovers). The other 50 prefer red widgets to blue ones (red lovers). These 50 value red widgets at $5 and blue ones at $3 (red lovers). This

---

[13] We can see this by establishing that both firms pricing at $3 is *not* an equilibrium. If both firms price at $3, profits for each are $100. Suppose firm 1, say, drops its price to $2.99. This will attract more buyers. In particular, firm 1 will be able to sell 60 units rather than 50. Its profit will now be
$(2.99 − 1) \times 60 = 119.40$, more than $100.

[14] Though simple to describe, we are limited in what can be done with it. A more sophisticated model, the Bertrand–Hotelling model, is discussed later in this chapter.

is summarized in Table 4.10. Further, assume that firms are free to charge any price they like. Because someone prefers, say, blue to red widgets does not mean that they will only buy blue widgets. If red widgets are priced low enough they may switch to buying red widgets. To illustrate this, suppose the price of blue widgets is $3.50 while the price of red widgets is $1.00. Consider a blue lover. If they buy blue, their surplus is $5−$3.50 = $1.50. If they buy red instead, their surplus will be $3−$1 = $2. Since the surplus on a red widget is higher, this blue lover buys a red widget, even though they prefer blue widgets. In other words, the red widget is an imperfect substitute for the blue widget, and vice-versa.[15]

Table 4.10 Distribution of RPs

Buyer type	RP for blue	RP for red	Number
Blue lover	$5	$3	50
Red lover	$3	$5	50

Let's check that each firm pricing at cost is *not* an equilibrium. Suppose both firms charge $1 for their widgets. Now ask: could any one firm do better by raising its price? If it could, then pricing at cost is not an equilibrium.

Consider the blue firm, for example. At a $1 price, it makes zero profit. If it raises its price by 1 penny, does it lose all its customers to the competition? No. The surplus for a blue lover from a blue widget at the new price is 5 − 1.01. The surplus from a red widget would be 3 − 1. Notice that 5 − 1.01 > 3 − 1, so the blue lovers continue to buy from the blue firm. At this new price the blue firm makes a penny profit from each sale. So, it is better off. Therefore, pricing at marginal cost is not an equilibrium.

Let's check that each firm charging a high price (of $5) is an equilibrium. As always, it suffices to determine if any one firm has an incentive to undercut. Consider the blue firm. When blue and red both charge $5, the blue firm makes (5 − 1) × 50 = 200. Could the blue firm make more by dropping its price? The only reason to drop the price is to get new customers. These new customers have to be red lovers. To induce them to buy a blue widget, the blue firm has to drop its price to something slightly below $3 [i.e. 3 − ϵ (why?)]. But this means that its profits will be 100 × (3 − ϵ − 1) < 200, less than before. So the blue firm has no unilateral incentive to cut the price. Similarly, the red firm has no unilateral incentive to cut the price.

Differentiation, as this example shows, blunts price competition. Why? Because differentiation imposes switching costs (of the psychological kind in this case) on buyers. A blue lover gives up $2 in value in order to consume a red widget. Because it is costly for the blue lovers to switch to red widgets, the blue firm can afford to raise prices above marginal cost.

---

[15] In the event that prices lead to the same surplus for a buyer, we assume she will buy the color she prefers.

Differentiation naturally divides customers into segments. From the point of view of the blue firm, the market consists of a **strong market** (those customers who prefer blue) and a **weak market** (those who prefer red). When blue thinks about cutting the price, it must balance the profit gain from the weak market against the revenue loss from the strong market. If the strong market is sizable enough relative to the rest of the market, the incentive to cut prices is reduced. To see why, consider the modification summarized in Table 4.11. The products of the two firms are still differentiated. Can a price of $5 each be sustained? No. Suppose both firms post prices of $5 each. This cannot be an equilibrium. Consider the firm selling red widgets. At the $5 price it makes $5 - 1 = 4$ in profit. If it drops its price to $2, for example, it captures the whole market and makes $(2 - 1) \times 100 = 100$ (i.e. more profit). Even though the red firm is differentiated from its rival, it is along a dimension, color, that hardly anyone cares about.

Table 4.11 Modified distribution of RPs

Buyer type	RP for blue	RP for red	Number
Blue lover	$5	$3	99
Red lover	$3	$5	1

The lesson of the last example is that one should differentiate in a way that leads to a sizable strong market. The less obvious lesson is that one should differentiate in a way that leaves a sizable (relative to the market) strong market for one's rival. If they have no strong market, they have nothing to lose by cutting the price. Dropping their price makes their product more attractive to your strong market. More generally, to determine a rival's incentive to cut price, one should compare the size of their strong market with the incremental volume they will attract from a price cut.

Return to the case summarized in Table 4.10. Suppose you as the red firm could offer two prices. A high price to red lovers and a lower price, for the same red widgets, to blue lovers.[16] For example, red lovers pay $5 for red widgets but blue lovers pay $2.50. Would you want to engage in this kind of price discrimination?

Let us see what happens if you did. At a $2.50 price for red widgets offered to blue lovers, they would receive a surplus of $0.50. This is more than the surplus they receive on the blue widgets priced at $5. Therefore, in order for the blue firm to keep its buyers, it must drop its price. In the market consisting of just blue lovers, what would the price of a red widget and the price of a blue widget be in equilibrium? The red firm would price its red widgets to blue lovers at cost (i.e. $1) and the blue firm would price its blue widgets at $3. All blue lovers would buy blue widgets. So, the red firm gains no additional revenue but ends up lowering the price that the blue firm charges. However, the market is more than just blue lovers. The blue firm faces the

---

[16] And suppose also that you could prevent resale of red widgets bought at the lower price to red lovers.

following choice. Price its widgets at $3 and sell only to blue lovers or drop its price slightly below $3. Why contemplate a further price drop? If red lovers are paying $5 for red widgets, they would switch to blue widgets priced below $3 because it gives them more surplus. It is easy to see that dropping price below $3 is more profitable for blue. This in turn forces red to drop the price of its red widgets to red lovers to keep them. The net effect is that *both* firms end up lowering prices on their strong markets without necessarily gaining share from the other!

This kind of price discrimination destroys the benefits of differentiation. By going after your rival's customers, you force them to lower the price on their product. This makes their product more attractive to your strong market. To keep your strong market, you are forced to lower the price to the strong market. And so prices spiral downward. The example above is an extreme one to make the point. In this example, lower prices lead to lower profits. This is not always so because there are two effects of this kind of price discrimination. One is positive and the one that most sellers identify right away. It allows you to sell to a segment that you were not previously selling to and this brings additional profit. The other is negative and often overlooked. Doing this encourages your competitor to lower their prices and so forces you to lower prices to your strong segment. This reduces profits. In the example above, the negative effect outweighs the positive one. But it can go the other way as well.

Loyalty Programs

Loyalty programs are one way in which firms can induce differentiation when none was initially present. To see how, we consider a twist on the BM.[17] Firm 1 produces blue widgets while firm 2 produces red widgets. Marginal costs for each are a constant $1 a unit.

On the demand side, buyers behave a little differently than they do in the BM. When the prices quoted for widgets by each firm are **unequal**, all 100 buyers buy from the lowest-priced seller. When quoted prices are equal, 50 of these buyers always buy from firm 1. Call them **blue bloods**. The other 50 always buy from firm 2; call them **red bloods**. Each firm knows which customers are blue bloods and which are red bloods. All buyers are willing to pay up to $3 for a widget of any color. Each seller has sufficient capacity to serve the entire market and they have one chance to set the price.

Suppose you are firm 1. If you could choose any price between 0 and $3 per widget, what price would you charge? Equilibrium analysis dictates that the price will be $1 per widget. This should be clear because if you charge any price greater than cost, the other firm can undercut you and gain 100% of the market.

Now suppose you and you alone issue a coupon good for $1 off the price of a blue widget but **only** to blue bloods. What price would you charge? The obvious response is: how can the coupon make a difference? It adds no value to the buyers, so how can the firms do more than price at cost? Nevertheless, it does. To see why let's see

---

[17] Klemperer, P. (1987). Markets with consumer switching costs. *Quarterly Journal of Economics*, 102(2), 375–394.

whether pricing at cost is an equilibrium. Pricing at cost would mean that firm 2 (the red one) posts a price of $1. Firm 1 (the blue one), if it is to price at cost, must price at $2. Anything less generates negative profits, given the coupons in circulation. So, firm 1 (blue) is at $2 and firm 2 (red) is at $1. At these prices they split the market. The blue bloods buy from firm 1. Why? With the coupon, the effective price of a blue widget is $1. The red bloods buy from firm 2.

Could this combination of prices (firm 1 at $2 and firm 2 at $1) be an equilibrium? *No.* Firm 2 could do better by unilaterally raising its price. In fact, raising its price from $1 to $2. Will firm 2 lose its customers from a unilateral price increase? *No.* The red bloods can buy their favorite widget from firm 2 for $2. Their alternative is to buy blue widgets from firm 1 for $2, since red bloods do not have a coupon for blue widgets. Since prices from their viewpoint are equal, they buy the color they prefer (i.e. they stay with firm 2). Hence, firm 2 has raised its price and kept its buyers, therefore its profits must go up.

Could firm 1 pricing at $2 and firm 2 at $2 be an equilibrium? Again, no. Firm 1 has an incentive to raise the price. Suppose firm 1 prices at $3 while firm 2 is at $2. To see that firm 1's profits must increase, it is enough to check that it does not lose any customers. Observe that blue bloods will pay $2 for blue widgets because they have the coupon. If they go to firm 2 instead, they must pay $2 for red widgets. Since prices from their viewpoint are equal, they buy the color they prefer (i.e. they stay with firm 1).

Could firm 1 pricing at $3 and firm 2 pricing at $2 be an equilibrium? Again, no. In fact, as the reader can verify, there is no pure strategy equilibrium. It does not matter what the mixed-strategy equilibrium is.[18] What matters is that pricing at cost is no longer an equilibrium. This is remarkable because in the absence of the coupon, equilibrium profits were zero. In other words, there is now an upward incentive price whereas before there was none. The availability of this coupon, that has no effect on either costs or how customers value the product, introduces an incentive to raise prices. Why? When firm 1 issues a coupon to blue bloods only, it is effectively announcing two prices; one for blue bloods and one for red bloods. Furthermore, the price to red bloods is *higher* than the price to blue bloods. Firm 2, recognizing this, knows that it can raise its price without losing customers. Since firm 2 is going to raise prices, this gives you, firm 1, room to raise your own price above $2 and turn a profit.

Does it matter if firm 2 also issues coupons to its customers only? No, equilibrium profits will still be positive. In fact, they will be higher because the coupons mutually reinforce the incentive to raise prices. For example, each firm will make $100 in profit if both firms charge $4 with a $1 off coupon.

What if you, firm 1, issue coupons to everyone? In this case, equilibrium profits will be zero. Why? If every buyer has the coupon, they don't care where they buy from. This intensifies price competition.

---

[18] One can show that expected profits are positive for each firm.

The coupon story illustrates that loyalty programs act like a "no poaching of customers" agreement. The drawback is that the initial cost of signing customers up may wipe out the subsequent benefits from higher prices. Competition switches from price to the rewards in the program.

Airline frequent flyer miles are an example of the coupon logic in reality. They solve the problem of who should get which coupon by allowing customers to self-select. What prevents someone signing up with every program? The rewards are designed in such a way that spreading your purchases between different airlines delays the date at which you receive a reward, thus reducing its value. The program is not a traditional quantity discount because it links the reward to the *cumulative* volume of purchases. This is what encourages buyers to concentrate their purchases.

4.1.6 Competing with Complements

Suppose competing sellers have offerings that complement each other. It will be useful to have a concrete example in mind. Assume two firms, A and B. Each makes a graphics card and a monitor. Label the graphics card and monitor made by A as AG and AM, respectively. Label the graphics card and monitor made by firm B as BG and BM, respectively. For simplicity, the marginal costs of all products are zero.[19]

Buyers are interested in purchasing a **system** rather than individual components. That is, they want to purchase a graphics card and a monitor. The buyers are divided into three equally sized groups, labeled AA, BB, and AB. They differ in the value they place on different graphics card and monitor combinations. These valuations are summarized in Table 4.12.

Table 4.12 Table of RPs

Buyer segment	AG, AM	BG, BM	AG, BM	AM, BG	Number
AA	$10	$5	$5	$5	100
BB	$5	$10	$5	$5	100
AB	$5	$5	$10	$0	100

The AAs prefer a system that is made up entirely of A components and the BBs prefer one that is made up of B components only. The ABs have a preference for a system that combines a particular component from each firm. In particular, they have value for combining a graphics card from A and a monitor from B but not a graphics card from B and a monitor from A. If the ABs did not exist, the systems would be imperfect substitutes for each other. It is the ABs that see value in combining a component from one seller with a component from another seller.

Given the price of a system, buyers will buy the system that generates the largest surplus. For example, if the price of an A system is $8 while that of a B system is $2,

[19] Mattutes, C. and P. Regibeau (1988). Mix and match: Product compatibility without network externality. *RAND Journal of Economics*, 19(2), 221–234.

the AAs will buy the B system because their surplus is $2 for the A system but $3 for the B system.

There are two scenarios to consider. In scenario 1, the graphics card of A is incompatible with the monitor of B and the graphics card of B is incompatible with the monitor of A. In scenario 1, firms set prices on systems and sell only whole systems.

In scenario 2, each firm's products are compatible with the other firm's products. In this scenario firms set prices on individual components and sell individual components.

As one of the sellers, is there a reason to prefer one scenario to the other? Making the components incompatible increases differentiation and presumably supports higher prices.

Observe first that the largest revenue that any firm can achieve is when it is a monopolist. In this case it is revenue maximizing to price a system at $5 and sell to all three segments. This yields a revenue of $5 \times 300 = \$1500$. Is there an equilibrium in scenario 1 that supports this outcome or even comes close? No. For example, suppose each firm were to price their (incompatible) systems at $10. Firm A will sell its system to the AAs only and firm B will sell its system to the BBs only. Each will generate a revenue of $1000. Let us see if firm A has an incentive to unilaterally cut the price. From firm A's point of view its strong market consists of the 100 AAs. Its weak market is the 100 BBs and the 100 ABs. For a price cut to be worthwhile, firm A must cut sufficiently to attract buyers from its weak market. If firm A drops the price of its system to $5, it will attract the ABs but not the BBs.[20] Such a drop does not increase profit, since it results in a $5 loss in revenue from each AA buyer and a $5 increase on each AB buyer. Since these segments are of equal size, the loss is exactly balanced by the gain. If firm A drops the price of its system below $5, say $4.99, then this will attract the BBs as well. This price will capture all three segments, yielding a revenue of 4.99×300, which exceeds $1000. Furthermore, it will give firm A profit close to the monopoly profit. But firm A at $4.99 and firm B at $10 cannot be an equilibrium. This is because firm B will have an incentive to undercut A. High prices in scenario 1 are hard to sustain because of the ABs. Their number makes the size of the weak market dwarf the size of each seller's strong market, putting downward price pressure on each seller.

Consider scenario 2 now. In this case each firm pricing each of its components at $5 is an equilibrium. At these prices firm A sells two components to the AAs and one to the ABs. Firm B sells two components to the BBs and one to the ABs. Revenues for each firm are $5 \times 300 = \$1500$, equal to the monopoly profits. To check that it is an equilibrium, examine firm A's choices (a similar analysis will hold for firm B).

Suppose A raises the prices of any one of its components. Then it will lose the AAs because the price of A's system will exceed their RPs. Suppose A drops the price of any one of its components. The only reason to drop is to attract the BBs and get the ABs

---

[20] The surplus for the BB segment is zero for B's system as well as A's system. In this case the BBs choose the B system.

to switch to buying two components. This can only work if A drops the price enough to hand them at least $5 of surplus. But any surplus given to attract the BBs means a corresponding revenue loss on the AAs. Any surplus given to the ABs means zero revenue on them. The last possibility is to raise the price of one component and drop the other. Whether this increases profits depends on whether this changes the surplus enjoyed by the BBs and the ABs. From the reasoning above, this will not happen.

Scenario 2, then, benefits both firms. Why is this? The first reason is that by switching to compatible systems they have reduced the intensity of price competition. This can be seen from the fact that the gains from cutting the price of a component in terms of volume are not sufficient to compensate for the drop in price. A second reason is that compatibility increases value in the sense that ABs are catered to, and this may permit higher profits for both firms.

Now let us put flesh on this example. Suppose we have two sellers, each offering cellular phones and applications that run on them. For the moment we are making the unrealistic assumption that the seller produces both the phone and the applications.[21] Buyers have no interest in a phone by itself or the applications by themselves. They do, however, care about a package of the two. Should each seller design their applications to operate on their rival's phone?

The analysis above highlights the justification for doing so. There is also an argument for making their systems incompatible. If the goal of one of the sellers is to drive out the other, then making the systems incompatible will do that. It forces buyers to make a choice. If the seller can get enough buyers to commit to their system (by pricing aggressively), it kills interest in the competing system. Thus, the choice facing the seller is whether they are better off sharing the market, or incurring the cost of securing the market for themselves.

Now, let us consider what happens when applications are produced not by the phone producer but by third parties. There is now, unsurprisingly, a conflict of interest between application providers and phone manufacturers. A popular application that runs on one phone but not the other increases differentiation in the phone market. This benefits the phone manufacturer that runs the application. For the application provider, the phones provide access to customers. Interoperability increases the size of the market the application provider can reach.

4.2   A Tale of Two Models

A model that is easy to state is not always easy to analyze. This is the case for the models of competition discussed so far. Their analysis becomes difficult when we wish to answer questions that go beyond the basic. For example, is it a good idea to let certain firms merge? If one has a new cost-saving technology, should one sell it or license it to potential users? Should a firm pay for shipping or let the buyer cover the

---

[21] As well as the fact that the phone provider does not have to go through a service provider like Verizon.

cost of transport? To answer questions of this sort, two basic models of competition are used. This section introduces them and illustrates how they can be used.

4.2.1   Cournot Model

Named in honor of Antoine Augustin Cournot (1801–1877), the model supposes two firms producing an identical product. They simultaneously choose a quantity to produce, which can be interpreted as a choice about capacity. They do not pick prices. Rather, the price of their output is determined by impersonal market forces that serve to balance supply with demand. Co-operation between the firms is ruled out.

The model makes most sense in settings where firms must make investments in long-lived assets like hotels and electricity generating plants. While they can certainly choose the size of these (i.e. capacity), it would be foolish to think about the price to be charged in every period during the life of these assets. So, a simplifying assumption is made. Unmodeled market forces will determine the price of, say, hotel rooms. In particular, the market price of a room will decline with the number of available rooms.

Formally, if firm 1 chooses q_1 units of, say, Soma, and firm 2 chooses q_2 units of the same, the market price for each unit will be $\max\{1 - q_1 - q_2, 0\}$. The choice of $1 - q_1 - q_2$ as an expression for inverse demand is arbitrary. What matters about this expression is that the per-unit price declines as the total quantity, $q_1 + q_2$, increases. Both firms have a constant marginal cost of production of c. Given the choice made for the inverse demand curve, the market price can never exceed \$1 a unit. Hence, to ensure that firms have a hope of making a profit, we assume that $c < 1$.

Suppose firm 1 chooses a quantity q_1 and firm 2 chooses a quantity q_2 with $q_1 + q_2 \leq 1$. Then firm 1's profit will be

$$q_1 \max\{0, 1 - q_1 - q_2\} - cq_1$$

while firm 2's profit will be

$$q_2 \max\{0, 1 - q_1 - q_2\} - cq_2.$$

Notice that each firm's profit depends not only on its own quantity choice, but its rival's choice as well. It is this interdependence that will drive the analysis.

Obviously, no firm will choose a quantity exceeding 1. Hence, each firm has as many strategies as there are numbers between 0 and 1. So, writing down a payoff matrix is out of the question. Instead, we determine the profit-maximizing output level a firm should choose given that their opponent has fixed upon a quantity choice. Let's do this for firm 1. Suppose firm 1 believes that firm 2 will choose a quantity $q_2 = 1/4$, say. The profit that firm 1 makes by choosing a quantity q_1 will be

$$q_1 \max\{0, 1 - q_1 - 1/4\} - cq_1.$$

Since firm 1 will never choose $q_1 > 3/4$, we know that $1 - q_1 - 1/4$ will always be larger than or equal to zero. Hence we can write firm 1's profit as

$$q_1(1 - q_1 - 1/4) - cq_1.$$

Firm 1 must now choose q_1 to maximize its profit. In this case the optimal choice[22] for q_1 is $3/8 - c/2$. So, if firm 1 believes that firm 2 will choose $1/4$, firm 1 should choose $3/8 - c/2$.

We want the optimal response of firm 1 not to a specific choice of firm 2's capacity, but as a function of *all* firm 2's possible capacity choices. That is, we want firm 1's **reaction function**. This is the rule that specifies firm 1's optimal quantity choice for each of its rival's quantity choices. If firm 2 chooses q_2, it is clear that firm 1 will choose q_1 so that $q_1 + q_2 \leq 1$. In this case firm 1's profit as a function of q_1 and q_2 will be

$$q_1(1 - q_1 - q_2) - cq_1.$$

We need the revenue-maximizing choice of q_1 given fixed q_2. Notice that the profit-maximizing choice depends on q_2. To determine it, differentiate the profit function with respect to q_1 and set to zero:

$$1 - 2q_1 - q_2 - c = 0 \implies q_1 = \frac{1 - q_2 - c}{2}.$$

The reader can verify that the relevant second-order condition is satisfied and so this is indeed firm 1's profit-maximizing choice of q_1. Notice that, were $c \geq 1$, the expression for q_1 would give us the nonsense result that $q_1 < 0$. Hence the need for the restriction that $c < 1$.

Figure 4.2 shows how q_1 varies with q_2 graphically. Here, q_2 is on the vertical axis and q_1 is on the horizontal.

By symmetry, firm 2 should choose q_2 according to the equation below, assuming that firm 1 has chosen q_1. Firm 2's reaction function is

$$q_2 = \frac{1 - q_1 - c}{2}.$$

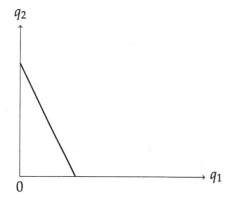

Figure 4.2 Firm 1's reaction function

---

[22] Which you should verify.

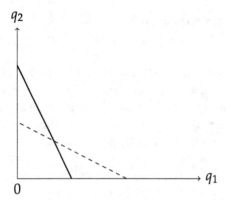

Figure 4.3 Firm 2's reaction function

A graphical representation can be found in Figure 4.3, in which firm 2's reaction function (dashed) is overlaid on the reaction function of firm 1 (solid). A pair of quantity choices (q_1, q_2) form a Nash equilibrium if q_1 is an optimal response to q_2, and vice-versa. Hence, (q_1, q_2) must satisfy the following two equations *at the same time*:

$$q_1 = \frac{1 - q_2 - c}{2},$$

$$q_2 = \frac{1 - q_1 - c}{2}.$$

Solving these equations, we deduce that $q_1 = (1 - c)/3 = q_2$. Graphically, this is where the two reaction functions cross (see Figure 4.3). Firm 1's profits will be

$$\frac{1-c}{3}\left(1 - \frac{2(1-c)}{3}\right) - c\left(\frac{1-c}{3}\right) = \frac{(1-c)^2}{9}.$$

Similarly for firm 2.

First-Mover Advantage

The 1984 Waxman–Hatch Act extended the life of a drug patent by 5 years to compensate for the delays introduced by the Food and Drug Administration's approval process. On the distaff side, the Act reduced the time it took for a generic to gain marketing approval. There is evidence to suggest that the next effect of the legislation was to speed up the entry of generics. Curiously, there was also an increase in the number of patent holders who chose to introduce their own generic version *before* expiration of their patents. Upjohn did this with Xanax, as did Syntax with Naprosyn.[23] Introducing a generic version of one's branded product before its patent expires can only cannibalize sales of one's branded product, so why do it? We can use a variation of the Cournot model to shed light on this.

---

[23] Kamien, M. and I. Zang (1999). Virtual patent extension by cannibalization. *Southern Economic Journal*, 66(1), 117–131.

Suppose in the Cournot model that the firms move sequentially.[24] Specifically, firm 1 moves first. Once it chooses a quantity, this decision is irrevocable. Then firm 2, after observing firm 1's choice, selects a quantity. Is it better to move first or second? How does that compare with moving simultaneously?

If firm 1 chooses the quantity q_1, we know from the analysis above that firm 1 knows that firms 2's best response is to choose a quantity q_2 such that

$$q_2 = \frac{1 - q_1 - c}{2}.$$

Thus, the market price will be

$$1 - q_1 - q_2 = 1 - q_1 - \frac{1 - q_1 - c}{2} = \frac{1 - q_1 + c}{2}.$$

Hence, firm 1's profit will be

$$q_1 \frac{1 - q_1 + c}{2} - c q_1.$$

The value of q_1 that maximizes this profit is $q_1 = (1 - c)/2$. Hence, $q_2 = (1 - c)/4$. Some algebra shows that firm 1's profits will be

$$\frac{1 - c}{2} \left(1 - \frac{3(1 - c)}{4} \right) - c \frac{(1 - c)}{2} = \frac{(1 - c)^2}{8}.$$

Notice that in this scenario firm 1 makes more profit than it did before, because

$$\frac{(1 - c)^2}{9} < \frac{(1 - c)^2}{8}$$

as long as $c < 1$. Firm 1 also makes more profit than firm 2. This follows from the fact that firm 2 has a lower quantity than firm 1. Hence, there is a first-mover advantage in capacity.

Returning now to the matter of patents, we see the possibility of an offsetting benefit. Yes, introducing the generic before expiration of the patent on the branded has a negative effect in that it cannibalizes sales of the branded product. In contrast, doing so gives one a first-mover advantage in the generic market. Whether a firm will introduce a generic before or after expiration will depend on the relative size of these two effects.[25]

Merger

From 1988 through 2005, over 46,000 intentions to merge were filed with the US Federal Trade Commission and Department of Justice in accordance with the Hart–Scott–Rodino Act. In reviewing a merger between two firms in the same industry,

---

[24] This variation of the Cournot model was introduced by Heinrich Freiherr von Stackelberg (1905–1946). For this reason it is often called the Stackelberg model.

[25] This is not, of course, the complete story. There are other benefits from introducing the generic before expiration that we have not accounted for. There is the opportunity to have a monopoly position in the generic segment for 180 days for the first to market and the chance to crowd out others in the distribution network.

anti-trust authorities must trade off the costs of monopoly power with the benefits of efficiency gains, usually lower costs, that may be passed through to consumers. Mergers are blocked if they will result in price increases. The vast majority of these mergers are allowed to pass without modification.

To examine this trade-off formally, suppose two firms, by merging, could reduce their marginal costs of production. How this might happen does not concern us.[26] A merger would result in a single firm, say, allowing it to act like a monopolist. In contrast, it would have lower marginal costs than the firms pre-merger, which might encourage it to set lower prices.

Suppose, pre-merger, each of our firms has constant marginal cost c of production. In equilibrium:

$$q_1 = q_2 = \frac{1-c}{3}.$$

The pre-merger market price will be $1 - q_1 - q_2 = 1 - 2(\frac{1-c}{3}) = \frac{1+2c}{3}$.

Suppose, post-merger, the merged firm will have a constant marginal cost of αc, where $\alpha < 1$. The merged firm will act like a monopolist and choose a quantity q to maximize

$$q(1-q) - \alpha cq.$$

The profit-maximizing choice of q will be $q = \frac{1-\alpha c}{2}$ and the market price will be

$$1 - \frac{1-\alpha c}{2} = \frac{1+\alpha c}{2}.$$

Recall that the pre-merger market price was $\frac{1+2c}{3}$. If

$$\frac{1+\alpha c}{2} < \frac{1+2c}{3},$$

the merger increases consumer surplus. Thus the merger will be beneficial, provided α is small enough (i.e. the efficiency gains from merging are large enough). Hence, simply arguing that costs will be lower post-merger is insufficient to justify a merger. For this reason, the Federal Trade Commission, for example, will rely on a number of empirical methods to estimate the effects of a merger on prices.

4.2.2   Bertrand–Hotelling Model

This is a model of price competition between firms that are differentiated. Unlike the Cournot model, firms do not choose capacities, they choose prices. This makes the model more suitable for understanding competition in prices in the short run.[27]

---

[26] Typically, this happens through the invocation of the magic word "synergies."

[27] Joseph Bertrand was a mathematician whose one foray into economics was prompted by being asked to review Cournot's model. Bertrand thought it unnatural and proposed an alternative. Harold Hotelling (1895–1973) augmented Bertrand's model to incorporate differentiation.

On the line between 0 and 1 are 1000 customers, uniformly distributed. This means that the number of customers in any segment between 0 and 1 is proportional to the length of that segment. For example, the number of customers between 0 and 0.25 will be 250. Each of these customers wants exactly one unit of Soma.

One seller, LEFT, is at the left-hand endpoint (i.e. at 0). The other seller, RIGHT, is at the right-hand endpoint, 1. They make and sell the same product and the marginal cost of production of each firm is c. Differentiation comes not from the product itself, but from geography. Buyers incur a travel cost of $1 per mile.[28] Thus, holding the prices of each firm the same, each buyer will prefer the firm that is closest to them.

While differentiation in this model is geographic, this is a matter of interpretation. The model can accommodate differentiation that is not geographic. For example, suppose the two firms each make a cola drink that differs in the concentration of sugar. Firm LEFT produces a cola with very little sugar, while firm RIGHT produces a cola with a lot of sugar. The "line" between the two firms represents sugar concentration levels intermediate between the offerings of the two firms. The position of a customer on the line is their ideal sugar concentration level. The travel cost represents a psychic cost of consuming a drink with a sugar concentration that differs from one's ideal sugar concentration.

The cost to a customer at distance d from 0 of going to LEFT to purchase a unit of Soma is d. The cost of going to RIGHT is $1 - d$. Given the prices charged by LEFT and RIGHT, customers base their purchase decisions on the relative delivered cost of the product. The delivered cost is the travel cost plus price of the item. For example, the delivered cost of the customer at distance d from LEFT is $d + p_L$, where p_L is the price per unit of Soma being charged by LEFT. If p_R were the selling price of Soma at RIGHT, this customer would buy from LEFT if and only if

$$d + p_L < 1 - d + p_R.$$

If the inequality were reversed, the customer would buy from RIGHT. We'll ignore the case of a tie.

The strategies of the two firms consist of choosing a price for their product. Suppose LEFT chooses the price p_L and RIGHT chooses p_R. The customers who will buy from LEFT must be at a distance d from LEFT, such that

$$p_L + d < 1 - d + p_R.$$

Simplifying:

$$2d < 1 + p_R - p_L \implies d < \frac{1 + p_R - p_L}{2}.$$

---

[28] We assume that buyers only worry about travel in one direction. We can interpret this as a delivery cost, or that the travel cost incorporates a round-trip journey.

Therefore, all customers within distance $\frac{1+p_R-p_L}{2}$ of LEFT will purchase from LEFT. Given the uniformity assumption, a total of $\frac{1000(1+p_R-p_L)}{2}$ customers will go to LEFT.

A customer who is at distance d from LEFT will purchase from RIGHT if

$$d + p_L > 1 - d + p_R,$$

$$1 - d < d + p_L - p_R,$$

$$2(1 - d) < 1 + p_L - p_R \quad 1 - d < \frac{1 + p_L - p_R}{2}.$$

Therefore, all customers within distance $\frac{1+p_L-p_R}{2}$ of RIGHT will purchase from RIGHT. By the uniformity assumption, $\frac{1000(1+p_L-p_R)}{2}$ customers will go to RIGHT.

Since each firm has a continuum of strategies to choose from, working out the equilibrium of the game is a little difficult. As in the quantity game, we will determine each firm's reaction function.

Focus on LEFT. Assume that RIGHT has chosen its price, p_R, and will not change it. What is the profit-maximizing choice of p_L (as a function of p_R) for LEFT? Notice that this would be LEFT's reaction function.

Observe first that we know when LEFT charges a price p_L, the demand for its product will be

$$\frac{1000(1 + p_R - p_L)}{2}.$$

So, the elasticity of demand will be

$$\frac{p_L}{1 + p_R - p_L}.$$

Using the relative markup formula, we know that the profit-maximizing price for LEFT must satisfy

$$\frac{p_L - c}{p_L} = \frac{1 + p_R - p_L}{p_L}.$$

If we solve for p_L, we get

$$p_L = \frac{1 + p_R + c}{2},$$

which is the reaction function we seek.

An exactly symmetrical argument establishes that RIGHT's reaction function is

$$p_R = \frac{1 + p_L + c}{2}.$$

Where the two reaction functions cross is the equilibrium price. To work this out, we need to solve the pair of equations for p_L and p_R, which gives

$$p_L = p_R = 1 + c.$$

So, in equilibrium the firms charge a dollar above marginal cost.

p_R

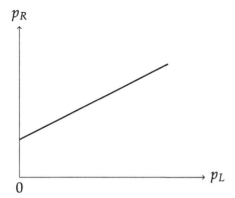

p_L

0

Figure 4.4 RIGHT's reaction function

Notice that the equilibrium prices are $1 above marginal cost. The reason for the 1 above is that the distance between the two firms is 1 mile and travel costs are $1 per mile. Had travel costs been $2 per mile, equilibrium price would have been $2 + c$. Had travel costs been $1 per mile and the distance between the firms been 0.5 miles, equilibrium prices would be $0.5 + c$. Thus the premium above marginal cost that both firms can charge depends on just how separated they are in monetary terms.

Had we done the analysis with different costs for each seller (say c_L for LEFT and c_R for RIGHT), the equilibrium prices would be

$$p_L = 1 + \frac{2c_l + c_R}{3}$$

and

$$p_R = 1 + \frac{2c_R + c_L}{3}.$$

From these two expressions we would conclude that the firm with the higher cost would have the higher price; no surprise.

We summarize the lessons of the numerical example above in a series of graphs. Figure 4.4 displays a graph with p_L on the horizontal axis and p_R on the vertical.

The solid line relates the profit-maximizing price that RIGHT should charge as a function of LEFT's price. For example, if one wants to know what price RIGHT will charge given what LEFT has charged, say $2, we look for $2 on the p_L axis and then zoom vertically up to the solid line and make a left to the p_R axis. Where one hits the p_R axis is the price we are looking for. This line is called a reaction function and what matters about it is not that it is a line, but that it is upward sloping. This means that if LEFT raises (lowers) their price, the best thing for RIGHT to do is raise (lower) theirs.

Figure 4.5 exhibits LEFT's reaction function (dashed). It tells us LEFT's profit-maximizing price as a function of RIGHT's price. The equilibrium pair of prices lie on the intersection of the solid and dotted line. To see why, assume that LEFT picks its equilibrium price. Given this, what is the revenue-maximizing price that RIGHT should pick?

p_R

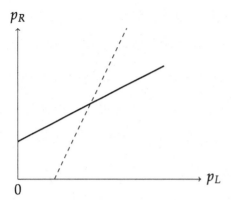

0

Figure 4.5 LEFT's reaction function

Merger

We revisit the merger question but in the context of the Bertrand–Hotelling model. Suppose LEFT and RIGHT each have a constant marginal cost of c per unit. If they merge, their marginal costs would fall to αc per unit, where $0 < \alpha < 1$. Would the merger reduce or increase consumer surplus?

Pre-merger, prices in equilibrium will be

$$p_L = p_R = 1 + c.$$

Post-merger, the merged firm would act like a monopolist. It will choose p_L and p_R to maximize combined profit:

$$\max(p_L - \alpha c)\frac{(1 + p_R - p_L) \times 1000}{2} + (p_R - \alpha c)\frac{(1 - p_R + p_L) \times 1000}{2}.$$

Given the symmetry in the profit expression (interchanging p_L and p_R does not change the expression), we deduce that we can set $p_L = p_R = p$. That is, we can restrict attention to the case where $p_L = p_R$. The monopolist's problem becomes

$$\max(p - \alpha c)\frac{(1) \times 1000}{2} + (p - \alpha c)\frac{(1) \times 1000}{2}.$$

It is straightforward to check that this optimization problem is unbounded. That is, one is free to choose $p_L = p_R = p = \infty$. How can that be?

The reason is that the model does not contain an upper limit on what a buyer will pay. This is easily fixed. Suppose no buyer is prepared to pay more than $U > 1 + c$ (i.e. each buyer's RP is U). In that case, the monopolist would choose $p = U$. Therefore, the merger would make buyers worse off because the merged firm would set its price to the RP of each buyer. This is true no matter the value of α. This contrasts with the Cournot case, where, for α sufficiently large, the merged firm would lower prices. Why is this? Pre-merger, the competitors collectively serve the entire market. Post-merger, the size of the market remains unchanged. Thus, lowering the price cannot possibly increase volume for the merged firm, which is why it has no incentive to lower prices even though costs will fall.

5 Preferences and Utility

Psychologists are irrational, that's all there is to that!
Their heads are full of cotton, hay, and rags!
They're nothing but exasperating, irritating,
vacillating, calculating, agitating,
Maddening and infuriating lags!
Why can't a Psychologist be more like an Economist?[1]

The rational buyer model required an agent's preferences to be denominated on a *common monetary* scale. As your surplus and mine are measured in dollars, we can agree on whether a change in the status quo, for example, makes us collectively better or worse off. However, were Mr. Bumble asked to give a penny to Master Twist, it is not at all obvious that Bumble's loss is commensurate with Twist's gain. There is a sense in which Twist would value the additional penny very differently from Bumble. Furthermore, by focusing on the dollar value of surplus, we ignore ability to pay. One's surplus for option A may exceed one's surplus for option B, but the price of option A may exceed one's budget. For this reason we extend the rational buyer model to a more general model of preferences that allows us to incorporate these concerns. The rational buyer model will turn out to be a special case of this more general model.

We assume that agents have preferences over collections of objects that we call goods. The word "goods" is used in two senses. First, as a synonym for commodity. Second, as something desirable. This could be something as tangible as an apple or as abstract as "free" time. We assume away commodities that we all might want less of, like pungent smells or cancer. This is for convenience only, to avoid having to keep track of "goods" and "bads" separately.

A bundle of n goods will be represented by an n-dimensional non-negative vector x. The ith component of x, denoted x_i, stands for the quantity of good i in the bundle x. Suppose our goods are sugar, salt, and butter (i.e. $n = 3$). Then the vector $(2, 3, 2.7)$ denotes a bundle that contains 2 units of sugar, 3 units of salt, and 2.7 units of butter.[2] Notice that we are assuming that goods are divisible. Problematic if they are not. However, if one is sufficiently imaginative, one can redefine the good to get around

---

[1] Borrowed from Lerner & Lowe.

[2] Had we wanted to include "bads," we could do so by allowing the corresponding components of a bundle x to be negative.

this. For example, one could measure housing by size or length of occupancy rather than number of houses.

Consumers are defined by their *preferences* over bundles of goods. Given a set of bundles to choose from, a consumer will choose their most preferred bundle from the set. Preferences are assumed fixed and innate. Why someone's preferences are the way they are is not, for our purposes, relevant.[3] In this sense economists are among the most tolerant of people as they do not criticize another's preferences so long as they are consistent.[4] Consistency is captured in the four conditions enumerated below.

1. **Completeness**

   For *any* two bundles of goods and services, call them x and y, a consumer should be able to order them in one of the following three ways:
   (a) She prefers x to y, written $x \succ y$.
   (b) She prefers y to x, written $y \succ x$.
   (c) She is indifferent between x and y, written $x \sim y$.
   If the consumer prefers x at least as much as y, this is written $x \succeq y$.

2. **Monotonicity**

   More of a good thing is better (and certainly no worse) than less of it.

3. **Irreflexivity**

   Given two identical bundles, you should never prefer one to the other.

4. **Transitivity**

   If x is preferred to y and y is preferred to z *then* x is preferred to z. If I prefer apples to oranges and oranges to grapefruit, then I prefer apples to grapefruit.

A preference ordering is awkward to write down, so it is useful to have a compact way to represent it. A **numerical representation** of a preference ordering over the set of bundles is a function U such that

$$x \text{ is preferred to } y \text{ if and only if } U(x) \geq U(y)$$

for all bundles x and y. The function U is called a **utility function**. It assigns a numerical score to each bundle so that more preferred bundles receive a higher score. The score assigned to a particular bundle is the utility of that bundle.

Example 30 *Suppose an agent's preferences are represented by the utility function* $U(x_1, x_2) = x_1 x_2$*, where* x_i *represents the quantity of good* $i = 1, 2$ *in the bundle* (x_1, x_2)*. Consider the two bundles* $(3, 2)$ *and* $(2.5, 4)$*. The first bundle has more of good 1 than the second but less of good 2. Which of these two bundles does the agent prefer? The utility of the first bundle is* $U(3, 2) = 3 \times 2 = 6$*, while that of the second is* $U(2.5, 4) = 2.5 \times 4 = 10$*. As the second bundle has a higher utility, she prefers the second bundle to the first.* □

---

[3] Francis Urquhart would describe them as having "no informing principle but the will to survive, just a plump little bag of squirming appetites!"

[4] To see just how tolerant we are, we don't distinguish between preferences and prejudices.

A utility function is called monotone if

$$x \geq y \implies U(x) \geq U(y).$$

As x and y are vectors, $x \geq y$ means $x_i \geq y_i$ for all components $i = 1, \ldots, n$. A utility function is called strictly monotone if

$$x \geq y \& x \neq y \implies U(x) > U(y).$$

Therefore:

1. x is strictly preferred to y if $U(x) > U(y)$.
2. x is weakly preferred to y if $U(x) \geq U(y)$.
3. One is indifferent between x and y if $U(x) = U(y)$.

If a preference ordering satisfies completeness, monotonicity, irreflexivity and transitivity, then it can be represented by a monotone utility function.[5] Hence, a consumer's most preferred bundle from those available is also the bundle that maximizes their utility.

A utility function has no meaning in and of itself. It is merely a succinct way to represent a preference ordering. Different utility functions can represent *exactly* the same preferences. To illustrate, consider the following preference ordering:

$$(3,4) \succ (4, 3.5) \succ (2,3).$$

Here are two different utility functions that can be used to represent this preference ordering:

$$U_1(3,4) = 100, U_1(4, 3.5) = 99.9, U_1(2,3) = 10$$
$$U_2(3,4) = 0, U_2(4, 3.5) = -1, U_2(2,3) = -3000.$$

Therefore, the actual value of the utility assigned to a bundle has no meaning.

Example 31 *Consider the following utility functions over bundles consisting of two goods:*

1. $U(x_1, x_2) = x_1 x_2$
2. $U(x_1, x_2) = 5 x_1 x_2$
3. $U(x_1, x_2) = \ln x_1 + \ln x_2$
4. $U(x_1, x_2) = x_1^2 x_2^2$.

The reader can verify that if bundle (x_1, x_2) is preferred to bundle (y_1, y_2) under the first utility function, it continues to be preferred to (y_1, y_2) under the other three utility functions.

We show that the first and third utility functions represent the same preferences. Denote the first utility function by U_1 and the third by U_3. Consider two bundles

---

[5] The units of the utility function are sometimes called *utils*.

$x = (x_1, x_2)$ *and* $y = (y_1, y_2)$ *and suppose that* $U_1(x_1, x_2) \geq U_1(y_1, y_2)$, *that is bundle* x *is preferred to bundle* y. *Then*

$$x_1 x_2 \geq y_1 y_2$$

$$\Rightarrow \ln(x_1 x_2) \geq \ln(y_1 y_2)$$

$$\Rightarrow \ln x_1 + \ln x_2 \geq \ln y_1 + \ln y_2$$

$$\Rightarrow U_3(x_1, x_2) \geq U_3(y_1, y_2).$$

Hence, x *is preferred to* y *under utility function* U_3. *By reversing the algebra above, we see that if* x *is preferred to* y *under* U_3, *then* x *is preferred to* y *under* U_1. □

The fact that one agent assigns a bundle a utility of 5 while another, different, agent assigns the same bundle a utility of 1 does not mean that the first agent likes this bundle 5 times more than the second agent. The numbers 5 and 1 are an artifact of the utility function used to represent preferences. It would be like comparing 32 degrees Fahrenheit with 0 degrees Centigrade and claiming one is "warmer" than the other.

Casual critics of the idea that individuals maximize their utility dismiss it with the remark that one can explain anything by choosing an appropriate utility function: for any behavior that we observe, choose a utility function which is maximized by that particular behavior. By all means choose your utility function to explain what you want. The challenge is to choose it so that the preferences it represents are consistent (satisfy transitivity, reflexivity, etc.). This severely restricts the kind of utility functions one can select. Not everything can be explained by choosing a utility function that represents consistent preferences.

5.1   Is Money a Good?

You can treat money as a good, in which case one's utility can be a function of money. However, money of the kind commonly used has no intrinsic value. It is a means to an end. Therefore when treated as a good it is employed as a proxy to model some as yet unspecified future end.

The rational buyer model introduced in the first chapter of this book treated money as a good. To illustrate, let x be some quantity of Soma, say, and w some amount of money. Then, in the rational buyer model, the utility an agent enjoys from a bundle consisting of x units of Soma and w units of money is denoted $U(x, w)$ and has a particular functional form:

$$U(x, w) = V(x) + w.$$

We interpret $V(\cdot)$ as the monetary value (i.e. RP) that the agent assigns to x units of Soma. Because $V(\cdot)$ and w are added, they must be measured on the same scale, a monetary one. The technical term for this kind of utility function is **quasi-linear**.

5.2   What is a Good?

No two kernels of corn are alike. One may be entirely yellow and the other have a tinge of red or be white-capped. They may differ in their weight, water content, the blistering displayed, and whether one is weevily or not. If each kernel is a good, then each must have its own price; a proposition so ridiculous as not to be contemplated. Nor can it be that each kernel is treated as if it were identical to another. This problem was solved through the introduction of standards for grains like corn. In the USA, this was effectuated by Act of Congress in 1916. The definition of which two kernels are alike enough to be considered instances of the same good is not given but constructed. Thus, when we refer to types of goods and services we sometimes rely, without realizing it, on an infrastructure of standardization, measurement, and custom. No market can exist without it. How it comes to be is complex and not well understood.

In the case of corn, government action produced this standardization. What if governments disagree? A case in point is champagne. According to the French, champagne is sparkling wine produced from grapes grown in the Champagne region of France.[6] Recognizing that a crisis should never be wasted, the French inserted a clause defining champagne into the Treaty of Versailles that ended the First World War. The USA did not ratify the treaty, which left US producers of sparkling wine free to call their product champagne. However, in 2006, the USA and the European Union signed a wine trade agreement that forbade US producers of sparkling wine from calling their product champagne. *Korbel* (California champagne) and *Miller High Life* (the champagne of beers), among others, were grandfathered in.

Finally, it is not always the case that sellers wish to standardize. If you think shopping for a car is a nightmare, just try buying a mattress. The industry employs a variety of tricks to make it difficult to compare models and dicker for a better price. Mattress manufacturers, for instance, sell identical or nearly identical mattresses to different retailers with exclusive model names. Recall the discussion of price discrimination in Chapter 3.

5.3   Consumer Choice Problem

Suppose the consumer has income I and p_i is the per-unit price of good $i = 1, \ldots, n$. Let x_i denote the quantity of good i that our consumer purchases. This consumer will choose the most preferred bundle she can afford. A bundle $x = (x_1, x_2, \ldots, x_n)$ is affordable if its total price is at most her income (i.e. $\sum_{i=1}^{n} p_i x_i \leq I$). Her most preferred bundle is the affordable bundle that maximizes her utility. Formally, the consumer solves the following problem:

$$\max U(x_1, x_2, \ldots, x_n)$$

---

[6] The French definition also specifies how it is pressed and fermented.

$$\text{s.t. } \sum_{i=1}^{n} p_i x_i \leq I$$

$$x_i \geq 0 \ \forall i = 1, 2, \ldots, n.$$

This is called the consumer choice problem.

Example 32 *Suppose $n = 2$ and our hypothetical consumer has preferences that can be represented using the utility function $U(x_1, x_2) = x_1 x_2$ and income I. Then, the problem she solves to find her most preferred bundle among those she can afford is*

$$\max x_1 x_2$$

$$\text{s.t. } p_1 x_1 + p_2 x_2 \leq I$$

$$x_1, x_2 \geq 0.$$

As discussed in Example 31, her preferences can also be represented using the function $\ln x_1 + \ln x_2$. Hence, an equivalent formulation of her problem is

$$\max \ln x_1 + \ln x_2$$

$$\text{s.t. } p_1 x_1 + p_2 x_2 \leq I$$

$$x_1, x_2 \geq 0.$$

The solutions to the two problems will be the same because the two functions represent the same preferences. The value of the functions being optimized will, of course, differ.   □

To guarantee that the consumer choice problem has a solution, we need to assume that U is continuous. Requiring U to be continuous in turn imposes a condition on the underlying preferences. Roughly speaking, if bundle x is preferred to bundle y, then a bundle z sufficiently "nearby" to bundle x is also preferred to bundle y. To solve the consumer choice problem using only the first-order conditions, we need U to be differentiable and satisfy an additional condition. This condition is called concavity. In fact a weaker notion, called quasi-concavity, will suffice. Their formal definitions appear in the next section and are often justified by an appeal to the **law of diminishing returns**. *The benefit derived from successive units of a particular commodity diminish as total consumption of that commodity increases, the consumption of all other commodities being held constant.* The more salt you have, the less additional salt you want. With a single good, this intuition can be formalized as a statement about the sign of the second derivative of the utility function. If x is the quantity of salt consumed, and $U(x)$ is the relevant utility function which is twice-differentiable, diminishing marginal utility is equivalent to

$$\frac{d^2 U(x)}{dx^2} \leq 0.$$

This is also the condition for concavity of a function of a single variable. Recall that this is also the second-order condition for optimality for a function of a single variable.

The law makes its first appearance in the writings of the eighteenth-century French physiocrat Anne Robert Jacques Turgot:

> The earth's fertility resembles a spring that is being pressed downwards by the addition of successive weights. If the weight is small and the spring is not very flexible, the first attempts will have no results. But when the weight is enough to overcome the first resistance then it will give to the pressure. After yielding a certain amount it will again begin to resist the extra force put upon it, and weights that formerly would have caused a depression of an inch will now scarcely move it by a hair's breadth. And so the effect of additional weights will diminish.

This is charming but confused. Diminishing marginal utility is a condition on how the *cardinal* value of a utility function behaves. However, the value of a utility function, as noted earlier, has no meaning. We care only if the utility of x exceeds that of y. The magnitude of the utility difference has no meaning.

The honest, but unsatisfying, justification for the law of diminishing marginal utility in the single-good case is that it allows one to avoid verifying the second-order conditions when solving optimization problems. A more reasonable justification will be offered later in this chapter.

5.3.1 Concavity and Quasi-concavity

A set C of vectors is called **convex** if for every $\lambda \in [0, 1]$ and pair of $x, y \in C$, the following is true:

$$\lambda x + (1 - \lambda)y \in C.$$

Geometrically, a set is convex if any two points within it can be joined by a straight line that lies entirely within the set. Equivalently, the weighted average of any two points in C is also in C. The quintessential convex set is the region enclosed by a circle. Figure 5.1 displays another example of a convex set.

Figure 5.2 shows an example of a non-convex set.

A function U whose domain is a convex set is called **concave** if for each $\lambda \in [0, 1]$ and for any two vectors x and y in the domain of U:

$$U(\lambda x + (1 - \lambda)y) \geq \lambda U(x) + (1 - \lambda)U(y).$$

Figure 5.1 Convex set

Figure 5.2 Non-convex set

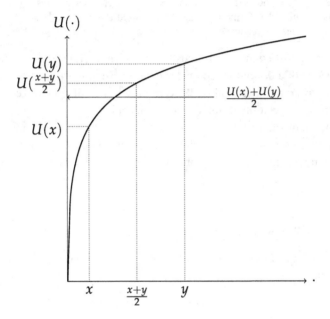

Figure 5.3 Concave $U(x)$

Informally, the utility of the "average" is larger than the "average" of the utility. A graphical illustration of a concave function in one real variable is shown in Figure 5.3.

If $x = (x_1, x_2)$ and the second-order partials of $U(x)$ exist, concavity of U is verified by a determinant test involving the Hessian:

$$\frac{\partial^2 U}{\partial x_1^2}, \frac{\partial^2 U}{\partial x_2^2} \le 0,$$

$$\left(\frac{\partial^2 U}{\partial x_1^2}\right)\left(\frac{\partial^2 U}{\partial x_2^2}\right) - \left(\frac{\partial^2 U}{\partial x_1 x_2}\right)\left(\frac{\partial^2 U}{\partial x_2 x_1}\right) \ge 0.$$

If U is a function of just one variable [i.e. $U(x_1)$], then concavity reduces to the familiar second-derivative test for a maximum.

If a consumer's utility function is continuous and concave, then the optimal solution to her consumer choice problem is given by the solutions to the first-order conditions of the Lagrangian, when they exist.[7] In fact, a weaker condition than concavity, called quasi-concavity, can be used in place of concavity. Call the **indifference curve** $I_q(U)$ of function U at threshold q the set of non-negative vectors that deliver utility exactly q:

$$I_q(U) = \{x \geq 0 : U(x) = q\}.$$

Example 33 *Consider the function $U(x) = \log x$. Pick a threshold q. The indifference curve at threshold q will be $\{x \geq 0 : \log x = q\}$. This is just one point, e^q.*   □

Example 34 *Consider the utility function $U(x_1, x_2) = x_1 x_2$. Pick a threshold q, then the indifference curve at threshold q is the set of bundles (x_1, x_2) such that $x_1 x_2 = q$. Figure 5.4 displays a sketch of the curve $x_2 = \frac{q}{x_1}$ for three values of q.*
Consider the indifference curve at threshold $q = 1$ and $q = 2$. Clearly, $I_1(U) = \{(x_1, x_2) \geq 0 : x_1 x_2 = 1\}$ and $I_2(U) = \{(x_1, x_2) \geq 0 : x_1 x_2 = 2\}$. Each bundle on the curve $I_2(U)$ delivers a utility of exactly 2. Every bundle on $I_1(U)$ delivers a utility of exactly 1. Therefore, any agent whose preferences can be represented by the utility function of this example strictly prefers every bundle on $I_2(U)$ to every bundle on $I_1(U)$. One can see this visually from the fact that $I_2(U)$ lies above $I_1(U)$, a fact the reader should verify.   □

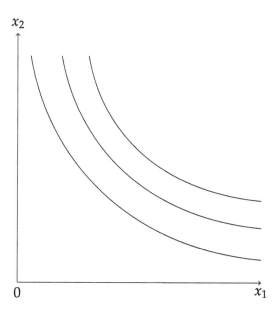

Figure 5.4 Indifference curves at various thresholds

---

[7] The first-order conditions need not have a solution and therefore one must still check the boundaries.

Call the **upper contour** set of a function U at threshold q the set of vectors

$$C_q(U) = \{x \geq 0 : U(x) \geq q\}.$$

In words, $C_q(U)$ is the set of bundles that deliver a utility of *at least* q. The "lower" boundary of the upper contour set at threshold q is the indifference curve at threshold q.

Example 35 *Consider the function $U(x) = \log x$. Pick a threshold q. The upper contour set at threshold q will be $\{x \geq 0 : \log x \geq q\}$. This is just the set of numbers that are at least as large as e^q.*   □

A function U is called **quasi-concave** if $C_q(u)$ is a convex set for each value of q.

Example 36 *Consider the utility function $U(x_1, x_2) = x_1^{0.7} x_2$. Pick a threshold q. The indifference curve at threshold q is the set of bundles (x_1, x_2) such that $x_1^{0.7} x_2 = q$. In Figure 5.5 we sketch the curve $x_2 = q x_1^{-0.7}$. The region above and to the right of the indifference curve is the upper contour set at threshold q. Visually, we see that this region is convex, so the utility function is quasi-concave.*   □

If we restrict ourselves to functions of just two variables (i.e. two goods), there is an algebraic condition that can be used to verify quasi-concavity of a utility function.

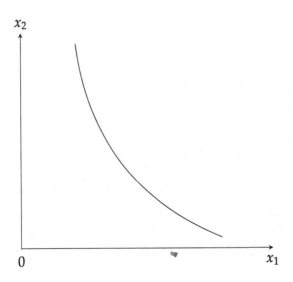

Figure 5.5 Upper contour set

Formally, $U(x_1, x_2)$ is quasi-concave if and only if

$$\left(\frac{\partial U}{\partial x_1}\right)^2 \frac{\partial^2 U}{\partial x_2^2} - 2\frac{\partial U}{\partial x_1}\frac{\partial U}{\partial x_2}\frac{\partial^2 U}{\partial x_1 \partial x_2} + \left(\frac{\partial U}{\partial x_2}\right)^2 \frac{\partial^2 U}{\partial x_1^2} \leq 0. \qquad (5.1)$$

In Section 5.7 we will use this condition to provide a justification for the assumption of quasi-concavity.

A concave function is quasi-concave but the converse is false. The following example illustrates this.

Example 37 *Consider the function $U(x) = -\log x$. The second derivative is positive, so it is clearly not concave. However, the upper contour set is just an interval and so is clearly convex. Hence, this function is quasi-concave.* ☐

Next is an example of a specific utility-maximization problem.

Example 38 *Suppose we have two goods 1 and 2 and denote by x_i the quantity of good $i = 1, 2$ purchased for consumption. The utility function of our agent is $U(x_1, x_2) = 16x_1^4 x_2^8$. If p_i is the price per unit of good i, this agent's utility-maximization problem is*

$$\max 16x_1^4 x_2^8$$

$$\text{s.t. } p_1 x_1 + p_2 x_2 \leq I$$

$$x_1, x_2 \geq 0.$$

Because the utility function is monotone, at optimality the budget constraint holds at equality (i.e. $p_1 x_1 + p_2 x_2 = I$). Dropping the non-negativity restriction on the x_i variables (we must remember to check that the resulting solution satisfies the omitted non-negativity constraints), the problem becomes

$$\max 16x_1^4 x_2^8$$

$$\text{s.t. } p_1 x_1 + p_2 x_2 = I.$$

This problem can be solved using the method of Lagrange multipliers. The Lagrangian is

$$L(x_1, x_2, \lambda) = 16x_1^4 x_2^8 + \lambda(I - p_1 x_1 - p_2 x_2).$$

The relevant first-order conditions are the following:

$$\frac{\partial L}{\partial x_1} = 64x_1^3 x_2^8 - \lambda p_1 = 0,$$

$$\frac{\partial L}{\partial x_2} = 128x_1^4 x_2^7 - \lambda p_2 = 0,$$

$$\frac{\partial L}{\partial \lambda} = I - p_1 x_1 - p_2 x_2 = 0.$$

This is a system of three equations and three variables: x, x_2, and λ. Solving for x_1 and x_2, we find that

$$x_1 = \frac{I}{3p_1}, \quad x_2 = \frac{2I}{3p_2}.$$

Quasi-concavity of the utility function allows us to conclude that this is indeed an optimal solution. Notice that the utility-maximizing bundle depends on the unit prices and the income of the agent. □

Next we give an example of a function that is not a quasi-concave function.

Example 39 *Consider the utility function $U(x_1, x_2) = x_1^2 + x_2^2$. To see that it is not quasi-concave, consider the indifference curve at threshold 1:*

$$\{(x_1, x_2) \geq 0 : x_1^2 + x_2^2 = 1\}.$$

This is just the quarter circle. The upper contour set of the area above this quarter circle in the non-negative orthant. Figure 5.6 shows the indifference curves at three different thresholds. The quarter circle farthest from the origin is the indifference curve at threshold 1. If we choose $x' = (1, 0)$, $x'' = (0, 1)$, and $\lambda = 1/2$ (i.e. the midpoint of the line segment joining x' and x''), then $\frac{1}{2}x' + \frac{1}{2}x'' = (0.5, 0.5) = \bar{x}$, lies outside the upper contour set. □

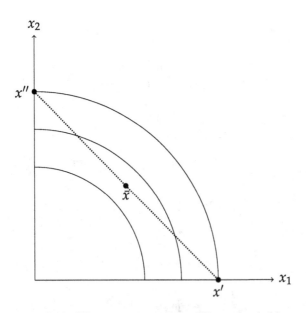

Figure 5.6 Indifference curves at three different thresholds

The next example shows why the first-order conditions are insufficient for optimality when the utility function is not quasi-concave.

Example 40 *Consider the following constrained utility-maximization problem:*

$$\max x_1^2 + x_2^2$$
$$\text{s.t. } p_1 x_1 + p_2 x_2 = I.$$

Notice that the budget constraint has been expressed as an equality. This follows from monotonicity of the utility function. To maximize utility, one spends all one's income. The non-negativity constraints on x_1 and x_2 have been omitted. We can check after the fact if they are satisfied.
The Lagrangian function is

$$\mathcal{L}(x_1, x_2, \lambda) = x_1^2 + x_2^2 + \lambda(I - p_1 x_1 - p_2 x_2),$$

and the first-order conditions are

$$2x_1 - \lambda p_1 = 0,$$
$$2x_2 - \lambda p_2 = 0,$$
$$I - p_1 x_1 - p_2 x_2 = 0.$$

In Figure 5.7 the middle one of the three indifference curves is tangent to the budget line at x^*. However, there is another bundle, y on the budget line, which lies on an indifference curve with higher threshold (the indifference curve farthest from the origin) and therefore delivers a higher utility than x^*. Therefore, the solution to the first-order conditions does not yield a maximum. □

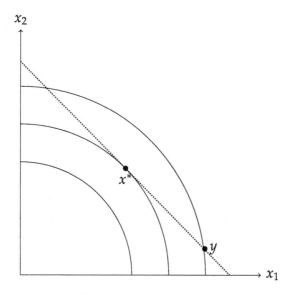

Figure 5.7 Indifference curves

In the remainder of this chapter we restrict ourselves to the case of just two goods. The insights obtained carry over to three or more goods. With two goods, the generic consumer choice problem will be

$$\max U(x_1, x_2)$$

$$\text{s.t. } p_1 x_1 + p_2 x_2 \leq I$$

$$x_1, x_2 \geq 0.$$

Denote an optimal solution/bundle to this problem by $(x_1(p_1, p_2, I), x_2(p_1, p_2, I))$. This highlights the dependence of the optimal bundle on prices and income. The utility an agent enjoys at her utility-maximizing bundle is called her **indirect** utility function. It depends on p_1, p_2, and I and is denoted $V(p_1, p_2, I)$. Therefore:

$$V(p_1, p_2, I) = U(x_1(p_1, p_2, I), x_2(p_1, p_2, I)).$$

Example 41 *Recall Example 38. In that example:*

$$V(p_1, p_2, I) = 16x_1(p_1, p_2, I)^4 x_2(p_1, p_2, I)^8 = 16 \left(\frac{I}{3p_1}\right)^4 \left(\frac{2I}{3p_2}\right)^8. \qquad \square$$

5.4   Utility and Consumption

Knowing an agent's utility function and their income allows one to predict how they will allocate their income amongst different goods. To illustrate, suppose we have a rational agent and two goods: sugar and salt. The agent's income is \$12. So as to establish a connection between income and the two commodities, let \$2 be the price per unit of sugar and \$1 the price per unit of salt.[8] How does the agent choose between the two commodities? From among all combinations of salt and sugar with a total cost of no more than \$12 she chooses the combination with highest utility.

If x_1 and x_2 represent the amount of sugar and salt she buys, respectively, then the amount she spends is $2x_1 + x_2$. If her total wealth is \$12, then

$$2x_1 + x_2 \leq 12.$$

In order to decide which combination of salt and sugar she likes best, we need her utility function. For illustrative purposes suppose her utility function is $U(x_1, x_2) = x_1 x_2$. For example, her utility from consuming 2 pounds of sugar ($x_1 = 2$) and 5 pounds of salt ($x_2 = 5$) will be $2 \times 5 = 10$. Her utility from consuming 3 pounds of sugar ($x_1 = 3$) and 2 pounds of salt ($x_2 = 2$) will be $3 \times 2 = 6$. In a choice between the first combination ($x_1 = 2$, $x_2 = 5$) and the second ($x_1 = 3$, $x_2 = 2$), she would prefer the first.

---

[8] We assume that the agent's choices do not affect prices and that she will live no more than a day.

Given this utility function, our fictional rational agent would choose $x_1 \geq 0$ and $x_2 \geq 0$ so that $2x_1 + x_2 \leq 12$ and $x_1 x_2$ is maximized. Formally, she needs to solve the following kind of optimization problem:

$$\max x_1 x_2$$

$$\text{s.t. } 2x_1 + x_2 \leq 12$$

$$x_1, x_2 \geq 0.$$

Monotonicity of the utility function means that she will spend *all* her wealth on sugar and salt. Therefore, we can assume that her budget constraint will hold at equality:

$$2x_1 + x_2 = 12.$$

Hence, her utility-maximization problem becomes

$$\max x_1 x_2$$

$$\text{s.t. } 2x_1 + x_2 = 12$$

$$x_1, x_2 \geq 0.$$

Let's try to solve this problem using common sense. I have \$12 to spend and since I have no sugar and no salt, my current utility is zero. Where should I spend the **first** dollar of that \$12? Suppose I use it to buy sugar. At \$2 a pound I can buy half a pound. If I do this, I will own half a pound of sugar ($x_1 = 1/2$) and no salt ($x_2 = 0$) and so my utility will be $1/2 \times 0 = 0$. No improvement in utility!

Suppose I use it to buy salt instead. Then I will own no sugar ($x_1 = 0$) and 1 pound of salt ($x_2 = 1$) and my utility will be $0 \times 1 = 0$ as well. So it does not matter where I spend my first dollar. The increase in utility is the same. For no reason at all I'll spend my first dollar on salt. My utility is still zero after this purchase.

Now, how should I spend my **second** dollar? If I spend it on sugar, I can acquire half a pound ($x_1 = 1/2$) and since ($x_2 = 1$) from my previous purchase, my utility will be $1/2 \times 1 = 1/2$. So my utility increases by $1/2$ from what it was before.

Perhaps I could get more of a boost by spending the second dollar on salt. Let's see what happens. If I do this, $x_1 = 0$ because I still have no sugar and $x_2 = 2$. So, utility is $0 \times 2 = 0$. No improvement. Clearly I should spend the second dollar on sugar. I now have half a pound of sugar and 1 pound of salt, giving me a utility of $1/2$.

How should I spend my **third** dollar? If I spend it on sugar I would now own 1 pound of sugar ($x_1 = 1$) and 1 pound of salt ($x_2 = 1$), giving me a utility of $1 \times 1 = 1$. An increase from my previous utility by $1/2$.

If I spend the third dollar on salt, $x_1 = 1/2$ and $x_2 = 2$, yielding a utility of $1/2 \times 2 = 1$, an increase of $1/2$ over my previous utility. So, a dollar's worth of sugar and a dollar's worth of salt yield the same improvement in my utility. For no reason at all, I will break the tie in favor of sugar. So, I spend the third dollar on sugar. I now own 1 pound of sugar, 1 pound of salt, and have a utility of 1.

How should I spend my **fourth** dollar? If I spend it on sugar, $x_1 = 1.5$ and $x_2 = 1$, yielding a utility of 1.5. If I spend it on salt, $x_1 = 1$ and $x_2 = 2$, yielding a utility of 2. Since buying salt produces the largest increase in utility, I will spend the fourth dollar on salt. I now have 1 pound of sugar and 2 pounds of salt.

The reasoning should be clear by now. At each stage I spend my money on that good which will increase my utility the most. What is interesting is that this commonsense principle will guide one to the allocation that maximizes utility in this case. You are urged to complete the analysis. You will find, barring arithmetical errors, that the utility-maximizing allocation is $x_1 = 3$ and $x_2 = 6$, yielding a utility of 18.

Thus, in choosing how to divide her \$12 between sugar and salt, our rational agent keeps her eyes on two things. The first is the incremental benefit (the bang) to be had from one more unit of the commodity and the second its price. This idea is formalized as the marginal utility principle and discussed next.

5.5   Marginal Utility

The satisfaction a player receives from consumption is called his utility, because we measure it with a utility function.[9] The **marginal utility** of a commodity is the increase in utility which results from increasing the consumption of that commodity by an infinitesimal amount.[10] It is the derivative of the utility function with respect to the variable that represents the amount of the relevant commodity (the amount of the other commodity being held constant). Thus, the marginal utility for good i is $\frac{\partial U}{\partial x_i}$.

It is important to distinguish between *total* utility and *marginal* utility. Consider the following choice: if you had to give up one of the following (altogether), salt or sugar, which would it be? In this choice you compare the utility of your total consumption of salt with that of sugar to decide. In other words, you compare the *total* utility of salt consumption with the *total* utility of sugar consumption.

Now consider the following choice: increase the consumption of salt by 1 pound a year or increase the consumption of sugar by half a pound a year. In this case you are comparing a small increase in salt consumption to a small increase in sugar consumption. You are comparing the *marginal* utility of salt to the *marginal* utility of sugar.

Why is the distinction important? Because choices are determined by marginal utilities and not total utilities. Alfred Marshall (1842–1924), among the first to make this observation, put it this way:

... good management is shown by so adjusting the margins of suspense on each line of expenditure that the marginal utility of a shillings worth of goods on each line shall be the same. And this result each one will attain by constantly watching to see whether there is anything on which he is spending so much that he would gain by taking a little away from that line of expenditure and putting it on some other line.

---

[9] I know, this is circular.
[10] A better term would be *incremental* utility, but it is not what economists use.

In other words, choose your salt and sugar combination so that a dollar's worth of salt yields the same increase in utility as a dollar's worth of sugar. To express Marshall mathematically, let p_1 and p_2 be the unit price of sugar and salt, respectively. Marshall says that the following must be true at a utility-maximizing bundle:

$$\frac{\frac{\partial U}{\partial x_1}}{p_1} = \frac{\frac{\partial U}{\partial x_2}}{p_2}.$$

If we think of the marginal utilities as the bang to be had from an additional unit, then the above says that to maximize utility we should allocate our expenditures so as to equalize the bang per buck on each good. This is the equimarginal principal. The principle is not always valid. It requires a qualifier: the utility-maximizing bundle must lie in the *interior* of the budget line. This is discussed in greater detail below.

Let us verify the **equimarginal principle** with the problem that began this section:

$$\max x_1 x_2$$

$$\text{s.t. } 2x_1 + x_2 \leq 12$$

$$x_1, x_2 \geq 0.$$

As mentioned before, the optimal solution was $x_1 = 3$ and $x_2 = 6$. Total utility at this allocation is 18. Now we compute the marginal utility of sugar (holding the amount of salt fixed). Increase the current amount of sugar by 1 pound. The new utility is $(3 + 1) \times 6 = 24$. So, the *increase* in utility from an additional pound of sugar is $24 - 18 = 6$. Similarly, the increase in utility from an additional pound of salt is $3 \times (6 + 1) - 18 = 3$. So, the marginal utility of sugar is 6 and the marginal utility of salt is 3. Now examine the marginal utility (benefit) to the price (cost) ratio of each product. For sugar it is 6/2 and for salt it is 3/1 (i.e. equal).

The most important implication of the equimarginal principle is that demand for a commodity depends not just on its price, but on the price of *all other* commodities. Customers will buy more of a particular commodity only if its perceived value relative to price exceeds the perceived value relative to price of *all* their other spending options.[11]

5.5.1   Deriving the Equimarginal Principle

The equimarginal principle is a consequence of the method of Lagrange multipliers. To see why, consider the utility-maximization problem for our hypothetical consumer choosing quantities of sugar and salt:

$$\max U(x_1, x_2)$$

$$\text{s.t. } p_1 x_1 + p_2 x_2 = I$$

$$x_1, x_2 \geq 0.$$

---

[11] I do mean all. When deciding to buy ice-cream, say, I don't just make a comparison with other ice-creams. I can spend my money on chocolate mousse, coffee, tiramisu, or the laundry.

Notice that the income constraint is set at equality rather than inequality. Once again, we rely on the monotonicity of the utility function to assert that the consumer will spend all her income on goods. The Lagrangian is

$$L(x_1, x_2, \lambda) = U(x_1, x_2) + \lambda(I - p_1x_1 - p_2x_2).$$

The first-order conditions for optimality are

$$\frac{\partial U}{\partial x_1} - \lambda p_1 = 0$$

and

$$\frac{\partial U}{\partial x_2} - \lambda p_2 = 0.$$

Divide the one by the other to arrive at the equimarginal principle.

Figure 5.8 is a graphical representation of the equimarginal principle. Here U_0 is the maximum level of utility achieved subject to the budget constraint. In the graph, the indifference curve at threshold $q = U_0$ is displayed. The point (x_1^*, x_2^*) is the utility-maximizing bundle [i.e. $U(x_1^*, x_2^*) = U_0$]. It must lie both on the indifference curve as well as the budget line, $p_1x_1 + p_2x_2 = I$. Notice that it is the point where the budget line is tangent to the indifference curve, which is a geometric restatement of the equimarginal principle.

Keep in mind that the first-order conditions for optimality don't always have a solution. To see why, consider the following consumer choice problem:

$$\max U(x_1, x_2) = 3x_1 + x_2$$

$$\text{s.t. } p_1x_1 + p_2x_2 = I$$

$$x_1, x_2 \geq 0.$$

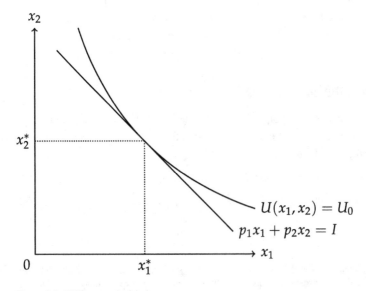

Figure 5.8 Utility maximization

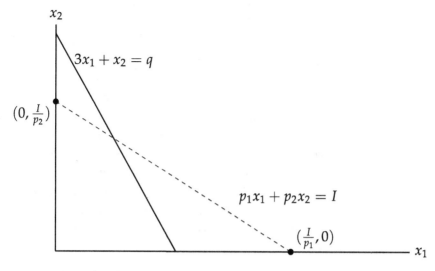

Figure 5.9 A non-interior optimal

The Lagrangian is

$$L(x_1, x_2, \lambda) = 3x_1 + x_2 + \lambda(I - p_1x_1 - p_2x_2).$$

The first-order conditions for optimality are

$$\frac{\partial U}{\partial x_1} - \lambda p_1 = 3 - \lambda p_1 = 0$$

and

$$\frac{\partial U}{\partial x_2} - \lambda p_2 = 1 - \lambda p_2 = 0.$$

This requires $\lambda = \frac{3}{p_1} = \frac{1}{p_2}$ which cannot always be true unless p_1 and p_2 take on very specific values. In this case, the utility-maximizing bundle must occur at one of the corners of the budget line, which violates the equimarginal principle. This can be seen in Figure 5.9. The indifference curve (solid black line) at any threshold is a straight line. In the figure it is shown crossing the budget (dashed) line at a point that is clearly not utility maximizing. There is clearly room to push the indifference curve farther out and still intersect the budget line. For this figure, the point $(\frac{I}{p_1}, 0)$, marked in the lower right-hand side of the budget line, is clearly the utility-maximizing bundle. The complete analysis can be found in Example 42.

Example 42 *Consider*

$$\max U(x_1, x_2) = 2x_1 + x_2$$

$$\text{s.t. } p_1x_1 + p_2x_2 = I$$

$$x_1, x_2 \geq 0.$$

The reader can verify that the utility function is quasi-concave.
  If

$$\frac{2}{p_1} = \frac{1}{p_2} \Rightarrow p_1 = 2p_2,$$

then any combination of x_1, x_2 such that the budget constraint holds,
$p_1 x_1 + p_2 x_2 = I$, is utility maximizing. Whenever $p_1 \neq 2p_2$ we are at a corner
solution. If $p_1 < 2p_2$ it will be optimal to spend all income on good 1. To see this
more clearly, note that if $p_1 < 2p_2$ we can spend all income on good 1 to get $\frac{I}{p_1}$ units
of good 1 or all income on good 2 to get $\frac{I}{p_2}$ units of good 2. In terms of utility, we
either have $\frac{2I}{p_1}$ if we only buy good 1 or $\frac{I}{p_2}$ if we only buy good 2. As $p_1 < 2p_2$ we will
strictly prefer to buy only good 1. By a similar reasoning, if $p_1 > 2p_2$ we will spend
all of our income on good 2. Thus, the optimal bundles are given by

$$x_1^*(p_1, p_2, I) = \begin{cases} I/p_1 & \text{if } p_1 < 2p_2, \\ 0 & \text{if } p_1 > 2p_2, \end{cases}$$

$$x_2^*(p_1, p_2, I) = \begin{cases} 0 & \text{if } p_1 < 2p_2, \\ I/p_2 & \text{if } p_1 > 2p_2, \end{cases}$$

and if $p_2 = 2p_1$, any combination of $x_1 \geq 0$ and $x_2 \geq 0$ such that the budget
constraint holds at equality is optimal.   □

5.6   Changing Price

If the price of just one commodity, say sugar, rises, and all other prices stay the same,
we expect the demand for sugar to decrease.[12] Does the theory developed thus far
predict this? Yes, as we illustrate with our running example.

   Suppose the price of sugar rises to $3. Before the price rise, the agent's utility-
maximizing bundle consisted of 3 pounds of sugar and 6 pounds of salt. If she
attempted to purchase the same quantities after the price increase, she would exceed
her budget of $12. Thus she has to give up some sugar or some salt or a combination
of the two.

   To decide what she has to give up, let us ask the following question: should she
give up a dollar's worth of sugar or a dollar's worth of salt? If she gives up a dollar's
worth of sugar (remember we are working with the new prices now), she gives up a

---

[12] Sir Robert Giffen thought that there were goods that violated this law of demand (i.e. their demand
increased as the price increased). He had observed that among the laboring classes, demand for bread
rose with price. Giffen neglected, though, to check whether income was constant during the rise in
bread prices. You should think about how one can use a change in income and the theory of demand
described in this section to explain Giffen's observation.

third of a pound of sugar. Her utility before the sacrifice was $3 \times 6 = 18$. Her utility after she gives up a third of a pound of sugar is $(3 - 1/3) \times 6 = 16$, a drop of 2 in her total utility.

If she gives up a dollar's worth of salt, she reduces salt consumption by a pound. If we go through the same arithmetic, her total utility goes down by $18 - 3 \times (6 - 1) = 3$.

Which should she give up? Obviously sugar, it reduces her utility by a smaller amount. Notice that to answer this question we examined the ratio of marginal utility to price. If, after reducing her expenditures by \$1, she is still above her budget, she can repeat the process. What is important is that she has responded to the price increase on sugar by consuming less of it.

If one does the calculations exactly, after the price increase she will purchase 2 pounds of sugar and 6 pounds of salt. Notice that the demand for sugar dropped from 3 to 2. The demand for salt stayed at 6.

5.7   Substitutes and Complements

Good 1 is a **substitute** for good 2 if $\frac{dx_1(p_1,p_2,I)}{dp_2} > 0$. In words, if the price of good 2 rises, the demand for good 1 rises, holding the price of good 1 fixed. As the price of good 2 rises, the consumer "fights" to maintain the same level of utility as before by compensating for the reduction in the quantity of good 1 consumed by increasing the consumption of good 2. The rate at which the consumer is ready to give up good i in exchange for good j, while holding the consumption of other goods fixed and maintaining the same level of utility, is called the **marginal rate of substitution** (MRS) between good i and j. Formally, it is

$$MRS(i,j) = \frac{\frac{\partial U}{\partial x_i}}{\frac{\partial U}{\partial x_j}}.$$

$MRS(i,j)$ is the negative of the slope of the indifference curve.

Example 43 *This can be seen most easily with the following utility function,* $U(x_1, x_2) = 2x_1 + 4x_2$. *The indifference curve at threshold q is the set of points* (x_1, x_2) *such that*

$$2x_1 + 4x_2 = q.$$

The graph of this indifference curve (x_1 on the horizontal and x_2 on the vertical) is a straight line with slope $-1/2$.

Suppose the initial bundle being consumed is $(2, 3)$. The utility of this bundle is $2 \times 2 + 4 \times 3 = 16$. If our consumer gives up y units of good 1, her utility goes down to $16 - 2y$. However, she can recover the original level of utility by increasing consumption of good 2 by $y/2$ units. Thus, this consumer is willing to trade off one unit of good 1 for half a unit of good 2 [i.e. $MRS(1, 2) = 1/2$].   □

Quasi-concavity of the utility function for two goods can be justified by an appeal to the property of **diminishing marginal rates of substitution**. Fix an indifference curve $I_q(U)$ at some threshold, q say. Now increase the amount of good 1 consumed (i.e. increase x_1), but staying on the indifference curve $I_q(U)$. The slope of the indifference curve becomes less negative, implying that the marginal rate of substitution of good 1 for good 2 falls. As the agent moves to the right along $I_q(U)$, she is consuming more of good 1 and less of good 2, so the marginal value of good 1 in terms of good 2 is falling. That is, as the individual has more of good 1 and less of good 2, the individual is willing to give up less of good 2 to get another unit of good 1. Formally:

$$\frac{\partial MRS(1,2)}{\partial x_1} \leq 0.$$

If you unpack this condition it is equivalent to inequality (5.1).

Good 1 is a **complement** for good 2 if $\frac{dx_1(p_1,p_2,I)}{dp_2} < 0$. An example of a utility function that exhibits such complementarity is $U(x_1,x_2) = \min\{x_1,x_2\}$.

Example 44 *Consider the following consumer choice problem:*

$$\max \min\{x_1, x_2\}$$

$$\text{s.t. } p_1 x_1 + p_2 x_2 \leq I$$

$$x_1, x_2 \geq 0.$$

The utility function $U(x_1,x_2) = \min\{x_1,x_2\}$ is not differentiable, so the method of Lagrange multipliers will not work. Now we argue that in an optimal solution, $x_1 = x_2$. To see why, suppose $x_1 > x_2$. Then $U(x_1,x_2) = x_2$. Now decrease the amount of good 1 bought by a tiny amount δ, so that $x_1 - \delta > x_2$. In words, we decrease the amount of good 1 purchased but still purchase more units of good 1 than good 2. Notice that $U(x_1 - \delta, x_2) = x_2$ (i.e. utility remains unchanged, even though we are consuming less!). In fact, we could increase δ to $x_1 - x_2$ and this would still be true. Hence, we can assume utility is maximized by purchasing an equal amount of the two goods. The utility function is monotone, so we know that at an optimal solution the budget constraint will hold at equality (i.e. $p_1 x_1 + p_2 x_2 = I$). As $x_1 = x_2 = x$, say, it follows that

$$p_1 x_1 + p_2 x_2 = I \implies (p_1 + p_2)x = I \implies x = \frac{I}{p_1 + p_2}.$$

Hence, $x_1(p_1, p_2, I) = \frac{I}{p_1 + p_2}$. It is straightforward to verify that $\frac{dx_1(p_1,p_2,I)}{dp_2} < 0$.   □

5.8   Changing Income

A question we were unable to answer with the rational buyer model is how demand changes with income. Let's first tackle the problem of how utility changes with income. The consumer choice problem is restated below:

$$\max U(x_1, x_2)$$

$$\text{s.t. } p_1 x_1 + p_2 x_2 \leq I$$

$$x_1, x_2 \geq 0.$$

The marginal utility of income will be $\frac{\partial V(p_1,p_2,I)}{\partial I}$. It is the incremental change in utility from an infinitesimally small change in income.

Let λ^* be the optimal Lagrange multiplier that we would obtain if we solved this problem using the method of Lagrange multipliers. Then

$$\frac{\partial V(p_1, p_2, I)}{\partial I} = \lambda^*.$$

This identity can be derived in the following way. Recall

$$V(p_1, p_2, I) = U(x_1(p_1, p_2, I), x_2(p_1, p_2, I)).$$

When we differentiate the left-hand side with respect to I, we must do the same to the right-hand side. However, keep in mind that the quantity of good 1 and 2 consumed is also a function of I. Hence, we have to use the chain rule:

$$\frac{\partial V}{\partial I} = \left(\frac{\partial U}{\partial x_1}\right)\left(\frac{\partial x_1}{\partial I}\right) + \left(\frac{\partial U}{\partial x_2}\right)\left(\frac{\partial x_2}{\partial I}\right).$$

Now, from the first-order conditions of optimality (or the equimarginal rule) we know that $\frac{\partial U}{\partial x_i} = \lambda^* p_i$. Hence:

$$\frac{\partial V}{\partial I} = \lambda^* p_1 \frac{\partial x_1(p_1, p_2, I)}{\partial I} + \lambda^* p_2 \frac{\partial x_2(p_1, p_2, I)}{\partial I}$$

$$= \lambda^*(p_1 \frac{\partial x_1(p_1, p_2, I)}{\partial I} + p_2 \frac{\partial x_2(p_1, p_2, I)}{\partial I}) = \lambda^*.$$

The last equality follows from differentiating both sides of

$$p_1 x_1(p_1, p_2, I) + p_2 x_2(p_1, p_2, I) = I$$

with respect to I.

The graph of $x_i(p_1, p_2, I)$ against I is called the Engel curve for product i. It records how the demand for good i changes with income. The **income elasticity of demand** is the percentage change in demand for an infinitesimally small percentage change in income. Formally:

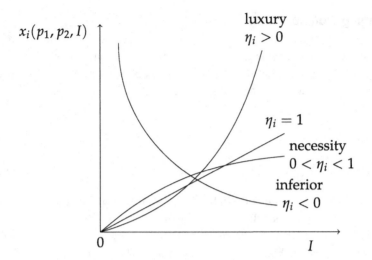

Figure 5.10 Engel curves

$$\eta = \frac{\% \text{ change in quantity demanded}}{\% \text{ change in income}}$$

$$= \frac{\partial x_i(p_1, p_2, I)}{\partial I} \frac{I}{x_i(p_1, p_2, I)}.$$

A **normal good** is one whose demand increases as income increases. A normal good is called a **luxury good** if its demand rises faster than income (i.e. $\eta > 1$). It is called a **necessity** if demand rises slower than income (i.e. $0 \leq \eta \leq 1$). An **inferior good** is one whose demand declines as income increases (i.e. $\eta < 0$). Beer might be an example of an inferior good for some. As income rises, a consumer may spend less on beer and more on, say, wine. Figure 5.10 displays the Engel curve for each of the possibilities just discussed.

Example 45 *Suppose* $U(x_1, x_2) = x_1^{0.4} x_2^{0.6}$. *Then the demand for good 1 will be*

$$x_1(p_1, p_2, I) = \frac{0.4I}{p_1}.$$

This is good 1's Engel curve. The income elasticity of good 1 is

$$\frac{0.4}{p_1} \times \frac{I}{\frac{0.4I}{p_1}} = 1. \qquad \Box$$

5.9   Inflation

Is inflation a bad thing? Stories of the German hyperinflation of 1922–3 suggest so. At its zenith, waiters would climb on tables to call out new menu prices every half hour to keep up with the inflation rate. Banknotes replaced toys as playthings because they were cheaper. The hyperinflation of Zimbabwe was worse. Its peak month of inflation was estimated at 79.6 billion percent. The government of Zimbabwe even introduced a \$100,000,000,000,000 note before abandoning its own currency.

To think through the issue, suppose you own a home. If the price of every home, including yours, doubled in price but all other prices are unchanged, would you be better or worse off? To deduce the consequences of a doubling in home prices, let p_1 be the price per unit of home before the change and p_2 the current price per unit of a composite good that represents consumption of other things, assumed to be consumables which cannot be resold.[13] The distinction is important because a durable good, like a house, can be resold.[14] Food purchased for consumption typically cannot.[15]

If I is income in the current period and $U(x_1, x_2)$ the utility from consuming the bundle (x_1, x_2), one should choose a bundle to solve the following:

$$\max U(x_1, x_2)$$

$$p_1 x_1 + p_2 x_2 \leq I$$

$$x_1, x_2 \geq 0.$$

Let (x_1^*, x_2^*) be a utility-maximizing bundle. By monotonicity of the utility function, $p_1 x_1^* + p_2 x_2^* = I$.

In the next period, the unit price of housing is now $2p_1$ and one receives another income payment of I. The price per unit of the composite good remains at p_2 per unit. In this period, the utility-maximization problem is

$$\max U(x_1, x_2)$$

$$2p_1 x_1 + p_2 x_2 \leq I + 2p_1 x_1^*$$

$$x_1, x_2 \geq 0.$$

The right-hand side of the budget constraint is *not* I. This is because, in the second period, one can sell the home back into the market for $2p_1$ per unit. We rely on the fact that housing is durable and that one can buy and sell any quantity of housing at the going price without penalty.[16]

If we purchase bundle (x_1^*, x_2^*) again, the total amount spent is only

$$2p_1 x_1^* + p_2 x_2^* = (p_1 x_1^* + p_2 x_2^*) + p_1 x_1^* = I + p_1 x_1^*.$$

---

[13] A consumable is a good intended for immediate consumption.

[14] A durable is a good that is long lasting. It can be enjoyed without literally consuming it.

[15] The distinction is neither hard nor fast because a supermarket buys food for resale.

[16] We are ignoring, for example, the very real transaction costs such as taxes and fees.

This is less than the amount of money available. In particular, $p_1 x_1^*$ units of money are left over. This can be spent on additional housing or the composite good, which results in increased utility. Hence, the price of housing doubling makes us better off.

What if the price of housing halved in the next period? The utility-maximization problem becomes

$$\max U(x_1, x_2)$$
$$0.5 p_1 x_1 + p_2 x_2 \leq I + 0.5 p_1 x_1^*$$
$$x_1, x_2 \geq 0.$$

If we purchase the original bundle (x_1^*, x_2^*), the total amount spent is

$$0.5 p_1 x_1^* + p_2 x_2^* = (p_1 x_1^* + p_2 x_2^*) - 0.5 p_1 x_1^* = I - 0.5 p_1 x_1^*.$$

Again, there is money left over that can be spent on additional consumption. Again, we are better off!

In both cases one responds to the price change by reselling the house. In the first case, one is left with additional cash that can be used to buy more of the composite or a larger house. In the second case, one can buy more house because housing costs less than before. Clearly, the fact that the good whose price changed was a durable is important. Durability allowed one to resell the good at the new price. This "trick" would not work with consumables.

Suppose instead we have two goods, each of which is a consumable. Assume the price of everything doubles. This is inflation. By everything we do mean everything, including wages, which are the price of labor. Before inflation hits, the utility-maximization problem is

$$\max U(x_1, x_2)$$
$$p_1 x_1 + p_2 x_2 \leq I$$
$$x_1, x_2 \geq 0.$$

After the doubling in prices and income, the utility-maximization problem becomes

$$\max U(x_1, x_2)$$
$$2 p_1 x_1 + 2 p_2 x_2 \leq 2I$$
$$x_1, x_2 \geq 0.$$

Notice that the budget constraints are identical in the two cases. Therefore, a doubling of all prices does not change consumption. In other words, inflation is not a problem!

Wait, you say. This is because all prices change simultaneously. Surely the problem is that not all prices adjust at the same speed. Recall the story of the German waiters. If inflation is a problem because not all prices adjust at the same speed, then it is an information technology problem not an economic one. It is easy to imagine a world equipped with smart displays in which prices of hundreds of stock-keeping units can be changed in the blink of an eye. In fact, if we switched to a cashless world, pensions, salaries, and all manner of monetary transactions could be inflation adjusted in the blink of an eye.

To understand why the end of inflation is not around the corner, one must know how the inflation rate is determined. In the USA, two indices are computed – one for consumers and the other for producers. In each case the prices of a large number of goods and services (around 80,000) are tracked. The price changes on these items are weighted and averaged together to determine an inflation rate. The weighting is an attempt to construct a standardized bundle.

Thus, the inflation rate is based on a standardized bundle. However, the bundle you consume to maximize your utility is unlikely to be the same as the standardized bundle used to calculate the inflation rate. The price of higher education, for example, is not included in the bundle used by the US government to determine the inflation rate. Nevertheless, you are very likely to have consumed higher education at some point. When the prices of individual goods change, the percentage change in the cost of your utility-maximizing bundle will not coincide with the percentage change in the cost of the standardized bundle. Thus, the government-calculated inflation rate does not reflect the actual inflation rate that any one person faces. It suggests that we should not rely on a single inflation rate, but on a personalized one. Each of us should face an inflation rate customized to our *own* consumption. How would this be determined? Just track what one consumes and calculate the inflation rate accordingly. Why not do this? If you knew that today's consumption would affect tomorrow's inflation rate, you would have an incentive to distort current consumption to exaggerate future inflation.

5.10 Income vs. Sales Tax

Governments raise money through taxes in at least two ways. One via an income tax and the other via a sales tax. The income tax as we currently understand it was introduced by Pitt the Younger in 1798 to finance a war against France.[17]

The sales tax is older. Among the earliest was the *centesima rerum venalium* levied by the Emperor Augustus to fund his army. It amounted to 1% of the value of anything sold. Tiberius lowered it to 0.5% and Caligula abolished it entirely. In the USA, the first attempt at a sales tax was a tax on whiskey, which prompted the Whiskey Rebellion of 1794.

Is there a reason to prefer one kind of tax over the other? To ensure an apples-with-apples comparison, fix the sales tax, say. Then compare that with an income tax that would raise an equivalent amount of money. This comparison would leave the government indifferent, assuming it cares only about the money raised. So we examine the effect in the utility of the agent being taxed.

Let's begin with a particular instance involving two goods and a consumer whose utility function is given by $U(x_1, x_2) = x_1 x_2$. This utility function is quasi-concave.

---

[17] It was abolished by Henry Addington (1757–1844) during the Peace of Amiens, the exception to the rule that taxes are inevitable. Addington was compelled to reintroduce it with a new war. It was abolished a year after Waterloo. On that occasion the Chancellor of the Exchequer publicly burnt all tax records. Copies, however, were retained in the basement of the tax court.

Suppose first income is taxed at a fraction t. Then the consumer's utility-maximization problem is

$$\max x_1 x_2$$

$$p_1 x_1 + p_2 x_2 \leq (1 - t)I$$

$$x_1, x_2 \geq 0.$$

The utility-maximizing bundle, denoted (x_1^t, x_2^t) satisfies

$$x_1^t = \frac{(1 - t)I}{2p_1}, \quad x_2^t = \frac{(1 - t)I}{2p_2}.$$

The utility of the agent at this bundle is $\frac{(1-t)^2 I^2}{4p_1 p_2}$.

Now consider a sales tax on good 2 only that charges a fraction r of the selling price.[18] The consumer's utility-maximization problem is

$$\max x_1 x_2$$

$$p_1 x_1 + (1 + r)p_2 x_2 \leq I$$

$$x_1, x_2 \geq 0.$$

The utility-maximizing bundle, denoted (x_1^r, x_2^r), is given by

$$x_1^r = \frac{I}{2p_1}, \quad x_2^r = \frac{I}{2(1 + r)p_2}.$$

The utility of the consumer at this bundle is $\frac{I^2}{4(1+r)p_1 p_2}$.

To compare the utility of the consumer under these two scenarios, we need to set t and r so as to generate the same revenue for the taxing authority. Let's fix r and determine t so that the income and sales tax raise the same dollar amount.

The income tax raises tI. The sales tax raises $rp_2 x_2^r$. Hence:

$$tI = rp_2 x_2^r = \frac{rI}{2(1 + r)}$$

$$\Rightarrow t = \frac{r}{2(1 + r)}.$$

For the choice of t given above, we can compare the utility of the consumer between the two scenarios. Under the income tax, the utility of the consumer is $\frac{(1-t)^2 I^2}{4p_1 p_2}$. Under the sales tax, her utility is $\frac{I^2}{4(1+r)p_1 p_2}$. We now verify that the first is larger than the second:

$$\frac{(1 - t)^2 I^2}{4p_1 p_2} > \frac{I^2}{4(1 + r)p_1 p_2}$$

$$\Rightarrow (1 - t)^2 > \frac{1}{1 + r}$$

[18] Why don't we consider a sales tax on all goods?

$$\Rightarrow (1 - \frac{r}{2(1+r)})^2 > \frac{1}{1+r}$$

$$\Rightarrow \frac{(2+r)^2}{4(1+r)} > 1$$

$$\Rightarrow 4 + 4r + r^2 > 4 + 4r$$

$$\Rightarrow r^2 > 0.$$

The left-hand side of the last inequality is clearly larger than the right-hand side, so the consumer will prefer the income tax to the sales tax.

Does this comparison depend on the particular utility function chosen? No. To see why, let's consider a more general problem where the utility function of the agent is denoted $U(x_1, x_2)$. Under the sales tax, she solves

$$\max U(x_1, x_2)$$

$$\text{s.t. } p_1 x_1 + (1+r)p_2 x_2 \leq I$$

$$x_1, x_2 \geq 0.$$

Denote by (x_1^r, x_2^r) an optimal solution to this problem. Let R be the amount of revenue raised by the sales tax (i.e. $R = rp_2 x_2^r$). Choose an income tax rate t so that

$$tI = R \Rightarrow t = \frac{rp_2 x_2^r}{I}. \tag{5.2}$$

Under an income tax, the consumer solves

$$\max U(x_1, x_2)$$

$$\text{s.t. } p_1 x_1 + p_2 x_2 \leq (1-t)I = I - tI = I - R$$

$$x_1, x_2 \geq 0.$$

Let (x_1^t, x_2^t) be an optimal solution to this problem.

Observe that (x_1^r, x_2^r) is a feasible solution to the optimization problem involving an income tax because

$$p_1 x_1^r + p_2 x_2^r = p_1 x_1^r + (1+r)p_2 x_2^r - rp_2 x_2^r = I - R,$$

hence $U(x_1^t, x_2^t) \geq U(x_1^r, x_2^r)$.

Does it follow that we should immediately abolish all sales taxes and rely on an income tax alone? As tempting as that might be, no. The analysis above began with an arbitrary sales tax rate r and then selected an income tax rate t to generate the same revenue. The choice of t in equation (5.2) depended on x_2^r. In other words, the equivalent income tax rate depended on the amount of good 2 consumed when subjected to a sales tax. However, the amount of good 2 consumed depends on the agent's utility function. Thus, a choice of t obtained from one person's consumption choices will not be appropriate for another. More generally, the revenue generated via a sales tax on some good from an individual will depend on the amount of that good consumed. An individual who consumes very little of good 2 will not generate much revenue via a sales tax on good 2. The equivalent income tax rate will be correspondingly small. An individual who consumes great quantities of good 2 will generate more revenue via the sales tax. The equivalent income tax rate will be higher.

To really understand the impact of a sales tax (a price increase or decrease) on a consumer, we must understand what is known as the income and substitution effect.

5.11   Hunger

It is generally believed that hunger declines as a country's wealth increases. However, by some measures hunger in China and India has increased with income. One could blame the unequal distribution of wealth, inefficient or indifferent governments and aid agencies, and increases in world food prices. Another possibility is that we are measuring hunger incorrectly.

The standard approach compares the number of calories eaten to the number needed, with "need" defined by a population average. Therefore, hunger is determined by whether the amount of calories ingested matches an exogenous standard. Most of us are not average. To know how many calories a person needs, one must know their age, sex, activity level, and so on. It's also hard to know how many calories a person is actually ingesting, as poor health means not all calories consumed are absorbed by the body.

What if we track the food they eat and not just the calories consumed? Hunger is unpleasant, making the marginal utility from calories extremely high. Hungry people, therefore, will be prompted to spend a larger share of their budget on staples like rice, which are a cheap source of calories. Once the hunger pangs are blunted, they spend their incremental cash on choices that provide variety and taste. Hence the share of calories that comes from staples declines once a person is no longer famished. Therefore, an unusually high share of calories coming from staples indicates that a person is hungry.[19]

To see how this works, suppose Bunter cares not just about the total calories consumed, but their source. Bunter likes beef more than rice, holding the amount of calories they provide equal to each other. This is captured in his utility function, which is given by $U(b, r) = b^{0.8} r^{0.2}$, where b is the calories of beef consumed and r is those from rice. To survive, Bunter must consume at least 2000 calories per day. The price per unit of calories from beef is given by $p_b = 2$. The price per unit of calories from rice is given by $p_r = 1$. Both rice and beef provide 1 calorie per unit.

Initially, Bunter's income is \$2020. His utility-maximization problem is

$$\max_{b,r} b^{0.8} r^{0.2}$$

$$\text{s.t. } 2b + 1r \leq 2020$$

---

[19] Jensen, R. and N. Miller (2010). A revealed preference approach to measuring hunger and undernutrition. NBER Working Paper 16555.

$$b + r \geq 2000$$

$$b, r \geq 0.$$

We will be interested in the ratio of calories from rice to calories from beef (i.e. $\frac{r}{b}$). The optimal solution to the above problem has $r/b = 99$. The derivation may be found in Example 46.

Example 46 *First, the budget constraint has to bind ($2b + r = 2020$) because if not, Bunter can increase either b or r (or both) and increase his utility without violating any constraint. Now, ignore for the moment the calorie constraint. Through the method of Lagrange multipliers, say, one can derive at optimality $r/b = 1/2$. If we substitute this into the budget constraint, we get $r = 404$ and $b = 808$. This solution has a total calorie count of 1212, which is smaller than 2000. Hence, our solution violates the ignored calorie constraint. Therefore, in the optimal solution the calorie constraint will hold at equality. Thus, we have two equations and two unknowns to be solved for:*

$$2b + r = 2020,$$

$$b + r = 2000.$$

The solution is $b = 20$, $r = 1980$ (i.e. $r/b = 99$).   □

Now suppose Bunter's income increases to \$3000. His utility-maximization problem becomes

$$\max_{b,r} b^{0.8} r^{0.2}$$

$$\text{s.t. } 2b + 1r \leq 3000$$

$$b + r \geq 2000$$

$$b, r \geq 0.$$

The optimal solution to this problem has $r/b = 1$. The total calories consumed continues to be 2000.

In this example, the total amount of calories consumed is unchanged after an increase in income. Thus, if hunger is measured by calories consumed, Bunter is as hungry after an increase in income as before. However, the share of calories Bunter derives from rice has fallen dramatically.[20] This suggests that Bunter is less hungry.

---

[20] In this example, rice is an inferior good.

5.12   Income and Substitution Effect

When the price of a good like sugar rises, perhaps because of a sales tax, a consumer will react in two ways. First, she will reduce her consumption of sugar. Second, she may compensate for the reduction by increasing consumption of a substitute good. For example, if the price of sugar rises, the consumer will reduce her consumption of sugar and increase her consumption of alternative sweeteners. This is called the substitution effect. It works up to a point. Thereafter, the effect of the sales tax acts like an income tax. This is called the income effect.

When the price of a good rises, demand for that good (other prices held fixed) will fall. We decompose the drop in consumption into an income and a substitution component. After describing the decomposition, we discuss its interpretation. As a warmup, we consider a "pure" income effect.

Example 47 *Consider a one-good consumer choice problem. Let x denote the quantity of the good purchased, let p be its unit price, and I the consumer's income. The utility the consumer derives from x units of the good is denoted $U(x)$. To determine the quantity of the good she will purchase to maximize her utility, we must solve*

$$\max U(x)$$

$$\text{s.t. } px \leq I$$

$$x \geq 0.$$

As utility is monotone, the optimal quantity will be $x = I/p$. Now raise the unit price to $p + \Delta$. The utility-maximizing quantity of the good is now

$$x = \frac{I}{p + \Delta} = \frac{\frac{pI}{p+\Delta}}{p}.$$

In words, the effect of the price increase is equivalent to a reduction in income by a factor of $\frac{p_1}{p_1+\Delta}$.   □

When there are two or more goods, an increase (or decrease) in the price of one of the goods cannot always be mimicked by a change in income alone. To see why, it is useful to have a specific example in mind. Suppose we have the utility function $U(x_1, x_2) = x_1^{0.4} x_2^{0.6}$, where x_i denotes the quantity of good $i = 1, 2$ purchased. A straightforward calculation shows that the utility-maximizing demand for each good is given by

$$x_1(p_1, p_2, I) = 0.4I/p_1 \text{ and } x_2(p_1, p_2, I) = 0.6I/p_2.$$

Initially, suppose $p_1 = 0.5$, $p_2 = 1$, and $I = 30$, and consider an increase in the unit price of good 1 to $1.

First, compute the utility-maximizing bundle at the initial prices and call it e_1^*. The coordinates of e_1^* are

$$x_1 = \frac{0.4 \times 30}{0.5} = 24, \; x_2 = \frac{0.6 \times 30}{1} = 18.$$

In Figure 5.11, the budget line at the initial prices is labeled BC1. The bundle e_1^* is displayed, as well as the indifference curve, denoted IC$_1$, going through e_1^*.

Next, compute the utility-maximizing bundle at the new prices. Call it e_2^*. It is

$$x_1 = \frac{0.4 \times 30}{1} = 12, \; x_2 = \frac{0.6 \times 30}{1} = 18.$$

In Figure 5.11, the budget line at the new prices is labeled BC2. The bundle e_2^* is displayed, as well as the indifference curve, denoted IC$_2$, going through e_2^*.

The demand for good 1 has dropped from 24 units to 12. We will apportion the 12-unit decrease in demand between an income and a substitution effect.

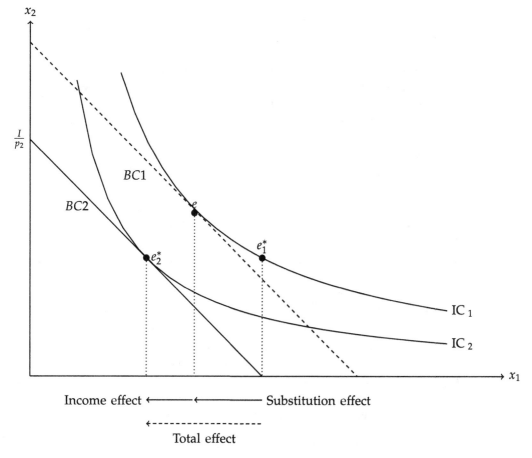

Figure 5.11 Income and substitution

Consider the consumer at the new, higher prices. Their utility is lower than before. We now ask how much extra income they must receive so that at the new prices, they can enjoy the same level of utility as before. Algebraically, we seek an income Y such that the utility achieved by the following optimization problem equals $U(24, 18)$:

$$\max U(x_1, x_2)$$

$$1 \times x_1 + 1 \times x_2 \le Y$$

$$x_1, x_2 \ge 0.$$

The optimal solution to this problem is

$$x_1(p_1, p_2, I) = 0.4Y \text{ and } x_2(p_1, p_2, I) = 0.6Y.$$

Call this bundle e. The utility of this bundle is $(0.4)^{0.4}(0.6)^{0.6}Y$. We need to choose Y so that this utility is equal to the utility enjoyed at e_1^*:

$$(0.4)^{0.4}(0.6)^{0.6}Y = (24)^{0.4}(18)^{0.6} \implies Y = 10 \times 6^{0.4} \times 3^{0.6}.$$

Therefore, e is the bundle

$$(0.4 \times 10 \times 6^{0.4} \times 3^{0.6}, 0.6 \times 10 \times 6^{0.4} \times 3^{0.6}) = (15.83, 23.75).$$

Notice that by design the bundle e lies on the indifference curve IC_1 and the dotted budget line parallel to BC2. The bundle e is called **compensated demand**. By raising the price of good 1, we have lowered the utility enjoyed by the consumer. The amount $Y - I$ represents the amount of cash needed to compensate the consumer for this drop in utility. The bundle e is the bundle she will consume with this extra cash (at the new higher price for good 1), hence the term "compensated demand."

The difference between the x_1 coordinates of e_1^* and e is called the substitution effect of good 1. The agent responds to the increase in the price of good 1 by switching from e_1^* to e. This keeps her utility the same. It reduces the amount of good 1 consumed but increases the amount of good 2. However, the bundle e costs an amount $Y > I = 30$ (i.e. it is unaffordable at the new prices). Now the consumer must adjust by shifting consumption to e_2^*. The difference between the x_1 coordinates of e and e_2^* is the income effect for good 1. It represents the drop in demand for good 1 that can be directly imputed to a drop in income.

If the substitution effect is large relative to the income effect, the consumer can adjust to a price increase by substituting another good for the one whose price has risen. If the income effect is large relative to the substitution effect, the sales tax on the good acts like an income tax. As an illustration, consider the imposition of a sales tax on sugary drinks. Suppose also that the tax has been imposed to discourage the consumption of such drinks for health reasons. If the substitution effect is large, it means that consumers will respond to the sales tax in the desired manner by reducing their consumption of sugary drinks and increasing their consumption of substitutes, which hopefully are healthier. In contrast, if the income effect dominates, the sales tax acts like an income tax.

5.13 Measuring Benefits

An advantage of the rational buyer model is that one could measure the effect of a change like a merger or a price ceiling by comparing total surplus before and after. This was possible because each agent's utilities were denominated on a common monetary scale. This is not possible in general because utils are a scale-free measure. Scaling one's utility function by 10 or 100 does not change the underlying preferences, only the magnitude of the utils. Hence, we cannot determine if a change that reduces one person's utility but raises another's is, on balance, a good thing. Rather than focus on utilities, we must focus on monetary amounts.

Given a target level of utility q, we can determine the minimum cost bundle needed to achieve this level of utility. This problem can be formulated as follows:

$$E(p_1, p_2, q) = \min p_1 x_1 + p_2 x_2$$

$$\text{s.t. } U(x_1, x_2) = q$$

$$x_1, x_2 \geq 0.$$

This is called the expenditure problem, and $E(p_1, p_2, q)$ is called the expenditure function. In fact, we solved such an expenditure problem in our analysis of the income and substitution effect. Recall the problem of finding the least amount of income Y needed to achieve the level of utility enjoyed before the price increase. Denote the optimal solution to the expenditure problem by $(x_1^c(p_1, p_2, q), x_2^c(p_1, p_2, q))$. Here, $x_i^c(p_1, p_2, U)$ is called **compensated demand**. This is to distinguish it from $x_i(p_1, p_2, I)$, actual demand.

Suppose the prices are initially (p_1, p_2) and the consumer's maximum utility at these prices is q. Subsequently, the price of good 1, say, changes to $p_1' > p_1$. Clearly, this will reduce our consumer's utility. How much extra does one have to pay the consumer to leave them with the utility they had before the price increase? The answer to this question is called **compensating variation**, denoted CV:

$$CV = E(p_1', p_2, q) - E(p_1, p_2, q).$$

I will now argue that CV behaves very much like consumer surplus. First, note that

$$E(p_1, p_2, q) = p_1 x_1^c(p_1, p_2, q) + p_2 x_2^c(p_1, p_2, q).$$

Differentiating both sides with respect to p_1 (using the chain rule), we see that

$$\frac{\partial E(p_1, p_2, q)}{\partial p_1} = x_1^c(p_1, p_2, q) + p_1 \frac{\partial x_1^c(p_1, p_2, q)}{\partial p_1} + p_2 \frac{\partial x_2^c(p_1, p_2, q)}{\partial p_1}. \tag{5.3}$$

From the first-order conditions for optimality of the expenditure problem, we know that $p_i = \frac{1}{\lambda^*} \frac{\partial U}{\partial x_i}$ for $i = 1, 2$, where λ^* is the optimal Lagrange multiplier of the expenditure problem. Substituting this into the right-hand side of equation (5.3):

$$x_1^c + \lambda^* \left[\frac{\partial U}{\partial x_1} \frac{\partial x_1^c}{\partial p_1} + \frac{\partial U}{\partial x_2} \frac{\partial x_2^c}{\partial p_1} \right] = x_1^c(p_1, p_2, q).$$

How do we know that

$$\frac{\partial U}{\partial x_1}\frac{\partial x_1^c}{\partial p_1} + \frac{\partial U}{\partial x_2}\frac{\partial x_2^c}{\partial p_1} = 0?$$

Recall that $U(x_1^c(p_1, p_2, q), x_2^c(p_1, p_2, q)) = q$. Differentiating both sides with respect to p_1:

$$\frac{\partial U}{\partial x_1}\frac{\partial x_1^c}{\partial p_1} + \frac{\partial U}{\partial x_2}\frac{\partial x_2^c}{\partial p_1} = 0.$$

Therefore:

$$\frac{\partial E(p_1, p_2, q)}{\partial p_1} = x_1^c(p_1, p_2, q).$$

By the fundamental theorem of calculus:

$$CV = E(p_1', p_2, q) - E(p_1, p_2, q) = \int_{p_1}^{p_1'} x_1^c(t, p_2, q) dt. \qquad (5.4)$$

Notice that if we replaced $x_1^c(t, p_2, q)$ in the right-hand side of equation (5.4) by $x_1(t, p_2, I)$, we would have consumer surplus. Alas, there is nothing that says $x_1^c(t, p_2, q) = x_1(t, p_2, I)$. Furthermore, we never observe $x_1^c(t, p_2, q)$ because agents do not minimize expenditure to achieve some target level of utility. However, if the income effect of the increased price of good 1 is small, we can assert that $x_1(t, p_2, I)$ is close to $x_1^c(t, p_2, q)$. To see why, examine Figure 5.11. If the income effect is small, the x_1 coordinate of bundle e (this is the bundle that corresponds to compensated demand), is close to the x_1 coordinate of e_2^*. Hence, if the income effect is small, consumer surplus is a good approximation to compensating variation.

6 Perfect Competition

The northernmost mosque in the world lies in Norilsk, population 175,000, inside the Arctic Circle. Inhabitants endure an average temperature (summer included) of −9 degrees centigrade, ensconced within a wasteland the size of Germany, bathed in acid rain caused by the annual discharge of 900,000 tons of sulfur dioxide from three giant nickel furnaces.

Norilsk and her "dark satanic" mills were planted in the permafrost by prison labor in the 1930s. By 1950, over 100,000 political prisoners were employed in its furnaces to ensure Soviet self-sufficiency. Norilsk and other cities like her turned Russia from an agrarian backwater into an industrial behemoth and military superpower. What had taken the West generations to achieve through capitalism, the Soviets achieved in one, through control of the "commanding heights" of the economy.

At this remove it is hard to ken the grip that a dream of plenty, wrought by central planning, had over so many. What was the alternative? A decentralized economy propelled by the greed of individuals pursuing different and possibly contradictory ends. How could the result be anything but chaos? Francis Spufford, in his book *Red Plenty*, captures the essence of it:

Marx had drawn a nightmare picture of what happened to human life under capitalism, when everything was produced only in order to be exchanged; when true qualities and uses dropped away, and the human power of making and doing itself became only an object to be traded. Then the makers and the things made turned alike into commodities, and the motion of society turned into a kind of zombie dance, a grim cavorting whirl in which objects and people blurred together till the objects were half alive and the people were half dead. Stock-market prices acted back upon the world as if they were independent powers, requiring factories to be opened or closed, real human beings to work or rest, hurry or dawdle; and they, having given the transfusion that made the stock prices come alive, felt their flesh go cold and impersonal on them, mere mechanisms for chunking out the man-hours. Living money and dying humans, metal as tender as skin and skin as hard as metal, taking hands, and dancing round, and round, and round, with no way ever of stopping; the quickened and the deadened, whirling on . . . And what would be the alternative? The consciously arranged alternative? A dance of another nature, Emil presumed. A dance to the music of use, where every step fulfilled some real need, did some tangible good, and no matter how fast the dancers spun, they moved easily, because they moved to a human measure, intelligible to all, chosen by all.

Yet, there is a tradition, older than Marx, that argued otherwise. The economists Kenneth Arrow and Frank Hahn explain:

The immediate 'common sense' answer to the question 'What will an economy motivated by individual greed and controlled by a very large number of different agents look like?' is probably: There will be chaos. That quite a different answer has long been claimed true and has permeated the economic thinking of a large number of people who are in no way economists is itself sufficient ground for investigating it seriously. The proposition having been put forward and very seriously entertained, it is important to know not only whether it *is* true, but whether it *could* be true.

This is the task we take up in this chapter.

6.1   The Setting

Our analysis will be conducted within a stylized setting conceived by Leon Walras (1834–1910), called an **exchange economy**:

1. A finite number of agents and firms.
2. Each agent is characterized by their utilities and endowments.
3. Utility is a monotone, quasi-concave function of own consumption only.
4. A finite number of commodities.

There is no production in this economy. The available set of goods is fixed, agents can only exchange them among themselves.

An example will help to fix ideas. Suppose we have two agents, called A and B, and two goods, labeled 1 (sugar) and 2 (salt). Agent A has an endowment of 7 units of good 1 and 3 units of good 2, denoted $w^A = (7, 3)$. Agent B has an endowment of 0 units of good 1 and 4 units of good 2, denoted $w^B = (0, 4)$. There is no production for the moment.

Agent A's utility function is $U_A(x_1, x_2) = x_1^2 x_2$, while agent B's utility function is $U_B(y_1, y_2) = 3 \ln y_1 + 2y_2$. Here x_i is the quantity of good $i = 1, 2$ consumed by agent A and y_i is the quantity of good $i = 1, 2$ consumed by agent B.

6.1.1   The Benevolent Central Planner

What will a benevolent central planner do? It depends on the powers at her disposal and her objectives. Assume the planner can dictate how the total endowment of the two agents is to be allocated, but she would like to allocate the endowment in a way that benefits each of the agents.

The simplest thing the planner can do is to tell each agent to consume their own endowment. If each agent does so, agent A will enjoy a utility of $U_A(7, 3) = 7^2 \times 3 = 147$. Agent B will enjoy a utility of $U_B(0, 4) = -\infty$.

If agent B exchanges 2 units of good 2 for 1 unit of good 1 from agent A, agent A will be left with the bundle $(6, 5)$, while agent B will have the bundle $(1, 2)$. A's utility will now be $U_A(6, 5) = 6^2 \times 5 = 180$. As this exceeds the utility earned on the endowment, agent A is clearly better off after the trade. What about agent B? Agent B's utility after the trade is $U_B(1, 2) = 2$, which clearly exceeds the utility enjoyed from the endowment. Hence, there is a mutually beneficial exchange the agents can make. Is it the only one? No. As the reader can verify, B giving up 1.5 units of good 2 for 1 unit of good 1 is also mutually beneficial. Is it always the case that there will be a mutually beneficial exchange? No. One can easily see this if one agent's endowment consists of all the goods and the other none.

If there is a mutually beneficial exchange, how could the central planner find it? This problem can be expressed algebraically as finding (x_1, x_2, y_1, y_2) such that

$$x_1 + y_1 = 7, \tag{6.1}$$

$$x_2 + y_2 = 7, \tag{6.2}$$

$$x_1, x_2, y_1, y_2 \geq 0, \tag{6.3}$$

$$U_A(x_1, x_2) \geq U_A(7, 3), \tag{6.4}$$

$$U_B(y_1, y_2) \geq U_B(0, 4). \tag{6.5}$$

The conditions (6.1)–(6.3) taken together constitute feasibility. In words, the total amount of each good to be allocated must exactly equal the amount available. Conditions (6.4) and (6.5) require that each agent receives at least as much utility as they enjoy from consuming their endowment. The set of solutions to this system, provided it is non-empty, describes the set of mutually beneficial exchanges. Call these the set of **individually rational allocations**. By any reasonable definition of benevolent, a central planner should choose an allocation that is individually rational.

We can visualize the set of mutually beneficial exchanges using an Edgeworth box (see Figure 6.1). The length of its horizontal side is the total endowment of good 1. The length of its vertical side is the total endowment of good 2.[1] Each point in the box represents the allocation of the combined endowments between the two agents. Consider the point q marked in the interior of the box. Its coordinates (x_1, x_2), when

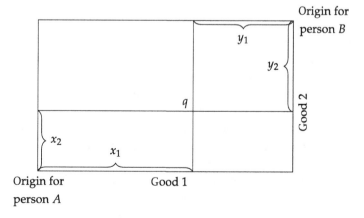

Figure 6.1 An Edgeworth box

---

[1] In our example above, this corresponds to 7 units each.

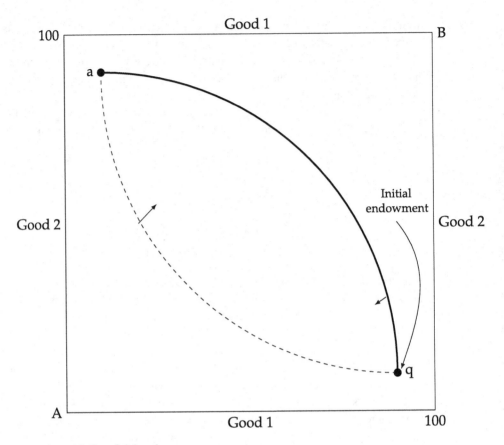

Figure 6.2 Beneficial exchanges

using the lower left-hand corner as the origin, give us the bundle assigned to agent A. The coordinates of the same point (y_1, y_2), but using the upper right-hand corner as the origin, give us agent B's bundle.

Consider the Edgeworth box displayed in Figure 6.2. It corresponds to an economy with a total of of 100 units of each good. The endowment of each agent is represented by the point marked q. Its coordinates when using the lower left-hand corner give agent A's endowment. Its coordinates when measured from the upper right-hand corner give agent B's endowment.

Now, consider all bundles that give agent A exactly as much utility as A's endowment does. These bundles lie on the indifference curve of A that passes through q, shown as dashed. Similarly, all bundles that give B exactly as much utility as B's endowment lie on B's indifference curve that passes through q. This is the solid curve. Every point in the box above the dashed curve (see the nearby arrow) corresponds to a bundle that gives agent A strictly more utility than their endowment. Every point in the box below the solid curve (see the nearby arrow) corresponds to a bundle that gives agent B strictly more utility than their endowment. Therefore, every point in the region bounded by the dashed and solid curves corresponds to a mutually beneficial trade. As this figure shows, there can be many different possible mutually beneficial trading opportunities in this instance.

How would a central planner find these mutually beneficial exchanges? As we did. Inquire after each agent's utility function and endowments and then trace out the possibilities. From these many possibilities, which should the planner pick?

6.2 Pareto Optimality

If there are many individually rational allocations, which one should the central planner pick? The one that maximizes total utility? Perhaps. But utility functions are simply a device for representing an ordering and have no cardinal meaning. Recall that two distinct utility functions can represent the same preference ordering. So, the choice of representation will affect which allocation is selected to maximize total utility. Is there a criterion we can use that is not sensitive to the representation of preferences? Yes, it's called Pareto optimality.

Let X denote some allocation of commodities to two (for simplicity) agents. Let Y be some other allocation. The allocation Y is said to be **Pareto superior** to X if each agent is at least as well off under Y as they are under X and at least one agent is strictly better off. We measure whether someone is better off using their utility function. By way of an example, suppose that in X, agent A gets a utility of 3 and agent B a utility of 5. Suppose that in Y, agent A gets a utility of 7 and agent B a utility of 5. This is summarized in Table 6.1.

Table 6.1 Table of utilities

	Allocation X	Allocation Y
Utility A	3	7
Utility B	5	5

In choosing between X and Y, agent B is indifferent. However, agent A would clearly prefer Y to X. In this case, Y is said to be Pareto superior to X. If, instead, agent B enjoyed a utility of 4 in allocation Y (see Table 6.2), then Y would not be Pareto superior to X. Although agent A is better off under Y, agent B is not.

Table 6.2 Table of utilities

	Allocation X	Allocation Y
Utility A	3	7
Utility B	5	4

The feasible allocation X is **Pareto optimal** if there is no feasible allocation Y that is Pareto superior to X. The set of Pareto-optimal allocations (sometimes there can be more than one) represent the set of allocations that cannot be altered without decreasing some agent's utility.

In Figure 6.2, any point between the red and black indifference curves is Pareto superior to the endowment q as well as the point a. This is because such a point is "above" the indifference curve of both agents. The reader should convince themselves that a Pareto-optimal point will be one where the two indifference curves are tangent to each other.

Example 48 *Consider the exchange economy introduced earlier in this section. If there is no trade, each agent simply derives utility from their endowment. Agent A enjoys a utility of $7^2 \times 3$, while agent B enjoys a utility of $3 \ln 0 + 2 \times 4$.*

Consider the allocation X^* that gives to agent A the bundle $(6, 4.5)$ and to agent B the bundle $(1, 2.5)$. Then

$$U_A(6, 4.5) = 6^2 \times 4.5 > 7^2 \times 3 = U_A(7, 3)$$

and

$$U_B(1, 2.5) = 3 \ln 1 + 2 \times 2.5 > U_B(0, 4).$$

In words, both are strictly better off than the status quo of no trade. Thus, the allocation X^* is Pareto superior to the status quo. Is there a feasible allocation that can do even better for both agents?

*X^* is **Pareto optimal** if there is no other **feasible** allocation that gives each agent at least as much utility as they enjoy under X^* and at least one agent gets strictly higher utility. If X^* is not Pareto optimal, we should be able to find a new allocation (x_1, x_2, y_2, y_2) such that*

$$x_1 + y_1 = 7,$$
$$x_2 + y_2 = 7,$$
$$x_1, x_2, y_1, y_2 \geq 0,$$
$$U_A(x_1, x_2) \geq U_A(6, 4.5),$$
$$U_B(y_1, y_2) \geq U_B(1, 2.5),$$

with at least one of the last two inequalities being strict. You should convince yourself that this is simply not possible. Hence, X^* is Pareto optimal.   □

How can one find a Pareto-optimal allocation? It turns out that any feasible allocation that maximizes a non-negative weighted sum of the agent's utility is Pareto optimal. Specifically:

$$\max w_A U_A(x_1, x_2) + w_B U_B(y_1, y_2)$$

$$\text{s.t. } x_1 + y_1 = 7$$

$$x_2 + y_2 = 7$$

$$x_1, x_2, y_1, y_2 \geq 0.$$

Here, $w_A, w_B \geq 0$ are non-negative weights. Let $(x_1^*, x_2^*, y_1^*, y_2^*)$ be an optimal solution to this problem. I will now argue that $(x_1^*, x_2^*, y_1^*, y_2^*)$ is Pareto optimal.

Suppose, for a contradiction, that it is not. Then there must be another feasible allocation $(\bar{x}_1, \bar{x}_2, \bar{y}_1, \bar{y}_2)$ that is Pareto superior to $(x_1^*, x_2^*, y_1^*, y_2^*)$. This means that

$$U_A(x_1^*, x_2^*) \leq U_A(\bar{x}_1, \bar{x}_2), \tag{6.6}$$

$$U_B(y_1^*, y_2^*) \leq U_B(\bar{y}_1, \bar{y}_2). \tag{6.7}$$

At least one of the inequalities (6.6) and (6.7) must hold strictly. Now multiply the first inequality through by w_A and the second by w_B and add them:

$$w_A U_A(x_1^*, x_2^*) + w_B U_B(y_1^*, y_2^*) < w_A U_A(\bar{x}_1, \bar{x}_2) + w_B U_B(\bar{y}_1, \bar{y}_2). \tag{6.8}$$

Inequality (6.8) contradicts the assumption that $(x_1^*, x_2^*, y_1^*, y_2^*)$ was chosen to maximize the weighted sum of utilities.

Pareto-optimal allocations need not be equitable. Consider a cake to be divided between two people. Each agent prefers more cake to less. The allocation where one gets 99% of the cake and the other 1% is Pareto optimal. So is the 50–50 split. Indeed, each division of the cake is Pareto optimal.

To summarize, the central planner can find an allocation that is feasible, individually rational, and Pareto optimal. Can a decentralized market do this?

6.3 Perfectly Competitive Market

To determine what allocation, if any, will be selected in a decentralized market, we must describe what each agent knows and how each will behave.

1. Each agent is aware of the price of every good.
2. The transaction costs of a sale, purchase, and so on are zero.
3. Agents can buy and sell as much or as little as they want at the going price. They assume that their individual transactions do not affect the going price. This is called the **price-taking** assumption.
4. Agents will maximize utility.

This economy is called a perfectly competitive market (without production).

6.3.1 Walrasian Equilibrium

In a perfectly competitive market, is there a set of prices, one for each good, at which consumer demands will balance the total supply of goods? Remarkably, under the conditions set forth at the very beginning of this section, yes. To see why, imagine an auctioneer (called the Walrasian auctioneer) who sets prices.[2]

1. The auctioneer announces a price vector $p = (p_1, p_2, \ldots, p_n)$ of prices, one for each good.
2. At the announced prices, each consumer reports the quantity of each good they wish to buy or sell to maximize their utility. Some consumers will wish to increase the amount of good j, say, they consume above their endowment of that good. These are the "demanders" for good j. Others will want to reduce the supply of good j from their endowment. These are the suppliers of good j. They do so because they wish to use the money earned from the sale of good j to purchase more of some other good.
3. The auctioneer gathers up these reports and determines the excess demand for each good (i.e. the difference between the quantity demanded and the quantity offered).[3]

If the excess demand for each good is zero, we have discovered the price we are looking for. Suppose the excess demand for good 1, say, is positive. That is, at the announced price the demand for good 1 exceeds the supply of good 1. What should the auctioneer do? Raising the price of good 1 (holding other prices fixed) will cause two things to happen. Those demanding good 1 will moderate their demands, while those willing to sell good 1 will increase the amount they wish to offer. If we are lucky (and we are), if we raise the price just enough demand will match supply. What does luck have to do with it? As the price on good 1 rises, demand may shift to another good. To maintain a balance between supply and demand for the second good, one may have to increase the price of the second good. However, this may cause a shift in demand back to good 1. Thus, prices may oscillate in vain trying to find an equilibrating point.

The price vector at which supply equals demand (i.e. excess demand is zero) for all goods is called the **Walrasian equilibrium price**. The associated utility-maximizing bundles are called a **Walrasian allocation**. The important point is this: under the right prices, agents acting *independently* to maximize their utility will choose bundles so that the excess demand of each good is zero. It says that an economy can be run by prices, but it does not say how they emerge.

Example 49 *Consider the exchange economy of Example 48. Recall that agent A has an endowment of 7 units of good 1 and 3 units of good 2, denoted $w^A = (7, 3)$. Agent B has an endowment of 0 units of good 1 and 4 units of good 2, denoted $w^B = (0, 4)$. This is an example of a pure exchange economy as there is no production.*

---

[2] The auctioneer need not be human. It could be a piece of code that adjusts prices.
[3] If this difference is positive for some good, it means that demand exceeds supply for that good. If negative, supply exceeds demand.

Agent A's utility function is $U_A(x_1, x_2) = x_1^2 x_2$, while agent B's utility function is $U_B(y_1, y_2) = 3 \ln y_1 + 2y_2$. Suppose unit prices p_1, p_2 are set by the Walrasian auctioneer.

1. Auctioneer announces (p_1, p_2).
2. Each agent reports their utility-maximizing bundle at announced prices.
3. Auctioneer chooses (p_1^*, p_2^*) to "clear" the market (i.e. the demand for good 1 is equal to the total supply of good 1 and the demand for good 2 is equal to the total supply of good 2).

At the announced prices, each agent engages in the following thought experiment. First, sell my endowment into the market at the announced prices to get cash. With the cash available, go back and purchase the mix of goods that will maximize my utility.

At the announced prices (p_1, p_2), agent A solves

$$\max x_1^2 x_2$$

$$\text{s.t. } p_1 x_1 + p_2 x_2 \leq 7p_1 + 3p_2$$

$$x_1, x_2 \geq 0.$$

At the announced prices (p_1, p_2), agent B solves

$$\max 3 \ln y_1 + 2y_2$$

$$\text{s.t. } p_1 y_1 + p_2 y_2 \leq 0 \times p_1 + 4p_2$$

$$y_1, y_2 \geq 0.$$

Now we can arbitrarily select one of the goods, good 1 say, and set its price to 1. Why? Multiplying all prices through by the same number (i.e. a scale change) does not change anyone's budget constraint and therefore the utility-maximizing bundle is unchanged. When we set the price of good 1 to 1, we make good 1 the numeraire in the sense that p_2, the price of good 2, represents the number of units of good 1 that must be exchanged for 1 unit of good 2. For example, $p_2 = 2$ would mean that 2 units of good 1 can be exchanged for 1 unit of good 2.

Setting $p_1 = 1$ means that agent A solves

$$\max x_1^2 x_2$$

$$\text{s.t. } x_1 + p_2 x_2 \leq 7 + 3p_2$$

$$x_1, x_2 \geq 0.$$

The solution to this is

$$x_1 = \frac{2(7 + 3p_2)}{3}, \quad x_2 = \frac{7 + 3p_2}{3p_2}.$$

Similarly, agent B solves

$$\max 3 \ln y_1 + 2y_2$$

$$\text{s.t. } y_1 + p_2 y_2 \leq 0 \times 1 + 4p_2$$

$$y_1, y_2 \geq 0,$$

yielding a solution of

$$y_1 = \frac{3p_2}{2}, \ y_2 = 2.5.$$

Our Walrasian auctioneer wishes to choose $(1, p_2)$ so that the demand for each good exactly meets the supply of each good:

$$\frac{2(7 + 3p_2)}{3} + \frac{3p_2}{2} = 7 \ \Rightarrow p_2 = \frac{2}{3},$$

$$\frac{7 + 3p_2}{3p_2} + 2.5 = 7 \ \Rightarrow p_2 = \frac{2}{3}.$$

Hence, the Walrasian equilibrium prices are $p_1 = 1$, $p_2 = \frac{2}{3}$ and the equilibrium allocation is for agent A to consume $(6, 4.5)$ while agent B consumes $(1, 2.5)$. □

Let us examine where the assumptions of a perfectly competitive market were used in Example 49. Clearly, we used the fact that consumers were aware of the price and we ignored transaction costs of any kind. We also assumed that the agents would *truthfully* report their endowments and demands at the announced prices. Should they? The next example shows that it is possible for an agent to gain by misreporting their demand.

Example 50 *Suppose we have two agents (called A and B) and two goods. Agent A's utility function is denoted $u_A(x_1, x_2) = x_1 x_2$, where x_i denotes the quantity of good $i = 1, 2$ consumed by A. Agent A is endowed with 0.5 units of good 1 and no units of good 2. Agent B's utility function is denoted $u_B(y_1, y_2) = 2y_1 + y_2$, where y_i is the quantity of good $i = 1, 2$ consumed by B. Agent B is endowed with 0.5 units of good 1 and 1 unit of good 2. Set good 1 as the numeraire and let p be the unit price of good 2.*
  The reader can verify that the utility-maximizing demands for agent A are

$$x_1 = \frac{1}{4}, \ x_2 = \frac{1}{4p}.$$

The utility-maximizing demands for the second agent depend on whether p is larger or smaller than 1/2 (recall Example 42). If $p > 1/2$, then

$$y_1 = \frac{1}{2} + p, \ y_2 = 0.$$

If $p < 1/2$, the utility-maximizing demand for B is

$$y_1 = 0, \quad y_2 = 1 + \frac{1}{2p}.$$

If $p = 1/2$, then all points on B's budget line, $y_1 + py_2 = \frac{1}{2} + p$, give her the same utility and so they are all utility maximizing.

The reader can verify directly that for $p > 1/2$, the demand for good 1, say, does not match its supply:

$$\frac{1}{4} + \frac{1}{2} + p \neq 1.$$

The same is true for $p < 1/2$.

So, we must check the case $p = 1/2$. At this price, agent A's demand for good 1 is 1/4. This leaves 3/4 of a unit of good 1 for agent B. Agent A's demand for good 2 is $\frac{1}{4 \times 1/2} = \frac{1}{2}$, which leaves half a unit of good 2 for agent B. If the bundle $(3/4, 1/2)$ lies on agent B's budget line, this will be utility maximizing for her and we have an equilibrium allocation. Let's verify this:

$$3/4 + p \times 1/2 = 3/4 + 1/2 \times 1/2 = 1.$$

Agent B's utility for the bundle $(3/4, 1/2)$ is $2 \times 3/4 + 1/2 = 2$.

Now, let us examine what happens if agent B were to pretend to have the utility function $y_1 y_2$. At a price of p per unit for good 2, agent B would claim to have a demand for good 1 of $\frac{1}{4} + \frac{p}{2}$ and for good 2 of $\frac{1}{4p} + \frac{1}{2}$. These are obtained by solving the following maximization problem:

$$\max y_1 y_2$$

$$\text{s.t. } y_1 + py_2 = \frac{1}{2} + p.$$

Using agent A's demand reports and the demand that agent B is now reporting, a new equilibrium value for p will be determined. As before, it suffices to check market clearing for good 1:

$$\frac{1}{4} + \frac{1}{4} + \frac{p}{2} = 1 \implies p = 1.$$

At this price agent B would receive $\frac{1}{4} + \frac{1}{2} = \frac{3}{4}$ units of good 1 and $\frac{1}{4} + \frac{1}{2} = \frac{3}{4}$ units of good 2. Her utility (evaluated using her actual utility function rather than her pretended one) for this bundle would be $2 \times \frac{3}{4} + \frac{3}{4} = \frac{9}{4}$, which exceeds 2. In words, by misreporting her demands, agent B was able to increase her utility, making her better off.

Notice that B's advantage was secured by pushing up the price of good 2. Recall that agent B was the only agent to possess good 2. She has exploited this monopoly power to better herself. □

Given that one's reported demand affects the price, one has an incentive to mis-report it. The price-taking assumption rules this out by presuming that each agent believes that a change in their demand reports cannot influence the price. This is the crucial assumption that makes all that is to follow in this chapter true. Is it reasonable? The next example suggests conditions under which the answer is "yes."

Example 51 *Consider a variation of Example 50 with 2N agents. There are N clones of agent A and N clones of agent B. The N clones of agent A share the same utility function and endowment as agent A did. The same is true of the N clones of agent B. It is easy to see that the equilibrium price of good 2 will continue to be $\frac{1}{2}$ (good 1 is the numeraire).*

Now, suppose one of the clones of agent B misreports its demand in order to push p above $\frac{1}{2}$. The combined demand of the clones of agent A for good 1 is $\frac{N}{4}$. Because $p > \frac{1}{2}$, the combined demand of all the clones of agent B (except the one misreporting her demand) for good 1 is $(N-1)(\frac{1}{2}+p)$. The demand for good 1 by the "deviant" clone of agent B is $\frac{1}{4} + \frac{p}{2}$. Thus, the total demand for good 1 is

$$\frac{N}{4} + (N-1)\left(\frac{1}{2}+p\right) + \frac{1}{4} + \frac{p}{2}.$$

This must equal the total supply of good 1:

$$\frac{N}{4} + (N-1)\left(\frac{1}{2}+p\right) + \frac{1}{4} + \frac{p}{2} = N$$

$$\Rightarrow p = \frac{1}{2} + \frac{1}{2N}.$$

Notice that if N is very large, the equilibrium price will be close to 1/2. In words, the ability of the one deviant B clone to push the price of good 2 above 1/2 declines as the number of clones increases. This is to be expected as the deviant B clone no longer has a monopoly position in the ownership of good 2.   □

One might wonder whether the existence of a Walrasian equilibrium is an artifact of Example 49. No, as illustrated in the Edgeworth box of Figure 6.3. The Walrasian allocation is marked. It was obtained by shifting A's indifference curve up (northeast direction) and B's indifference curve down (southwest direction). A "simulation" of the trajectories of each indifference curve is displayed using the dashed curves.

The curves move towards each other until they touch at *exactly* one point. This is the pair of solid indifference curves. At this point the two indifference curves share a common tangent line (not displayed). That common line of tangency is the budget line for each agent. Its slope gives us the ratio of Walrasian equilibrium prices. The point where they meet is the Walrasian allocation. As can be verified in Example 49 and from Figure 6.3, the Walrasian allocation enjoys three properties:

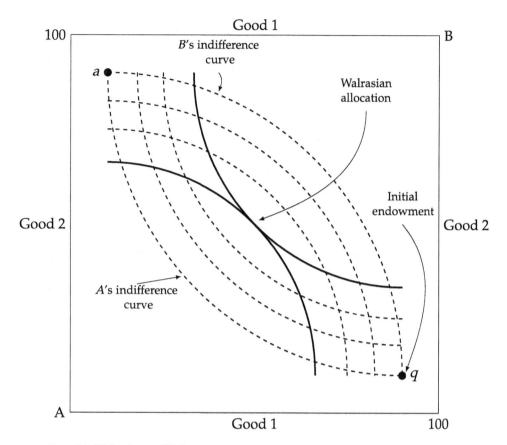

Figure 6.3 Walrasian equilibrium

1. It is feasible (i.e. the total amount of each good allocated is equal to the amount available).
2. It is individually rational.
3. It is Pareto optimal. This follows from the fact that the solid indifference curves are tangent to each other at the point that corresponds to the Walrasian allocation. Any other point in the box must be below A's solid indifference curve or above B's solid indifference curve, making at least one agent worse off compared to the Walrasian allocation.

The second property ensures that each agent has an incentive to participate in the market because they are guaranteed to achieve at least as much utility from consuming their endowment only. The third property shows that the Walrasian allocation cannot be improved upon without making someone worse off. This conclusion goes under the name of the first welfare theorem of economics. Let's restate this for future reference:

Under the conditions set forth at the beginning of this section, a Walrasian equilibrium allocation is feasible, individually rational, and Pareto optimal.

The first welfare theorem is the basis for statements of the following form: the free market generates an allocation of goods that cannot be improved upon. One must interpret this statement with care. While the equilibrium allocation cannot be improved upon in a Pareto sense, that does not mean it is equitable.

6.4   Production and Invisible Hand

To incorporate production, assume the existence of factories with production technologies that exhibit decreasing returns to scale. Further, each firm maximizes profit and the profits are shared among the agents in the economy. Finally, agents and firms act as price-takers.

In this setting, an agent may sell some of its endowment to a factory, which in turn converts it into a good that the agent may consume. As the agent may earn a share of the firm's profit, this sets up a potential spiral. The more sales the factory makes, the more income the agent earns, which, in turn, can be spent on more of the output. What is to prevent this spiraling off into infinity?

Example 52 *This example includes the possibility of production. There are two agents, each endowed with a unit of a good we will call "input" that can be interpreted as labor.*

There is a factory that uses input to produce two outputs called good 1 and good 2. The utility of each agent depends on the quantity of goods 1 and 2 consumed. No utility is derived from the consumption of input. Each agent owns a half share of the factory's profits.

Let x_i denote the quantity of good i purchased by agent 1. Let y_i denote the quantity of good i purchased by agent 2. Let p_1 be the unit price of good 1, p_2 the unit price of good 2, and p the unit price of input.

Agent 1's utility as a function of the bundle (x_1, x_2) is $U_1(x_1, x_2) = x_1 x_2$. Agent 2's utility as a function of the bundle (y_1, y_2) is $U_2(y_1, y_2) = y_1 y_2$.

The production function of good 1 is $\sqrt{z_1}$, where z_1 is the number of units of input used in the production of good 1. The production function of good 2 is $\frac{\sqrt{z_2}}{2}$, where z_2 is the number of units of input used in the production of good 2.

Given the price vector (p_1, p_2, p), the factory will choose z_1, z_2 to maximize its profit. This profit-maximization problem is given below:

$$\Pi = \max p_1 \sqrt{z_1} + p_2 \frac{\sqrt{z_2}}{2} - p(z_1 + z_2)$$

$$\text{s.t. } z_1, z_2 \geq 0.$$

Its optimal solution can be found in the usual way:

$$z_1 = \left(\frac{p_1}{2p}\right)^2, \quad z_2 = \left(\frac{p_2}{4p}\right)^2.$$

This is the factory's demand curve for goods 1 and 2, respectively. The factory's supply of good 1 will be $\sqrt{z_1} = \frac{p_1}{2p}$. The supply of good 2 will be $\frac{\sqrt{z_2}}{2} = \frac{p_2}{8p}$. The factory's profits will be

$$\Pi = \frac{4p_1^2 + p_2^2}{16p}.$$

Agent 1's utility-maximization problem is

$$\max x_1 x_2$$

$$\text{s.t. } p_1 x_1 + p_2 x_2 \leq p \times 1 + \frac{\Pi}{2}$$

$$x_1, x_2 \geq 0.$$

The right-hand side of the budget constraint consists of the money earned from selling input and the half share in the profit of the factory. The utility-maximization bundle is given by

$$x_1 = \frac{p + \frac{\Pi}{2}}{2p_1}, \quad x_2 = \frac{p + \frac{\Pi}{2}}{2p_2}.$$

These are agent 1's demand curve for goods 1 and 2. Notice that agent 2's utility function is identical to that of agent 1 and has the same income. Hence, agent 2 has exactly the same demand curves as agent 1.

To determine the Walrasian equilibrium, we need the market clearing conditions (supply equals demand) for goods 1, 2 and input:

$$\frac{p + \frac{\Pi}{2}}{2p_1} + \frac{p + \frac{\Pi}{2}}{2p_1} = \frac{p_1}{2p},$$

$$\frac{p + \frac{\Pi}{2}}{2p_2} + \frac{p + \frac{\Pi}{2}}{2p_2} = \frac{p_2}{8p},$$

$$\left(\frac{p_1}{2p}\right)^2 + \left(\frac{p_2}{4p}\right)^2 = 2.$$

Recall that we can always set the price of one of the goods to 1. In this case we set $p = 1$. The market clearing conditions become

$$2 \times \frac{1 + \frac{\Pi}{2}}{2p_1} = \frac{p_1}{2},$$

$$2 \times \frac{1 + \frac{\Pi}{2}}{2p_2} = \frac{p_2}{8},$$

$$\left(\frac{p_1}{2}\right)^2 + \left(\frac{p_2}{4}\right)^2 = 2.$$

Simplifying:

$$2 + \Pi = p_1^2,$$

$$8 + 4\Pi = p_2^2,$$

$$\left(\frac{p_1}{2}\right)^2 + \left(\frac{p_2}{4}\right)^2 = 2.$$

The solution is $p_1 = 2$ and $p_2 = 4$.   □

Example 53 *This example introduces a wrinkle that arises when the production functions of factories are linear in input. In this case, as will be seen, the equilibrium prices will be such that the factory makes zero profit.*

As before, there are two agents, with endowments and utilities as in Example 52. The production function of good 1 is z_1, where z_1 is the number of units of input used in the production of good 1. The production function of good 2 is $\frac{z_2}{2}$, where z_2 is the number of units of input used in the production of good 2.

Given the price vector (p_1, p_2, p), the factory will choose z_1, z_2 to maximize its profit. This profit-maximization problem is given below:

$$\Pi = \max p_1 z_1 + p_2 \frac{z_2}{2} - p(z_1 + z_2)$$

$$\text{s.t. } z_1, z_2 \geq 0.$$

If $p_1 > p$, the reader can verify that the optimal solution would set $z_1 = \infty$. This would be inconsistent with a Walrasian equilibrium allocation because the agent cannot possibly supply ∞ units of labor. If $p_1 < p$, the factory would never produce any of good 1. Similarly, if $\frac{p_1}{2} > p$, the factory would produce ∞ units of good 2. Again, this would be inconsistent with a Walrasian equilibrium outcome. Hence, at a Walrasian equilibrium it must be the case that $p_1 = p$ and $\frac{p_2}{2} = p$. However, at this specification the factory makes zero profit. Furthermore, any non-negative pair of z_1 and z_2 would be profit maximizing. This is because the marginal profit of each good is zero.

Let's set $p = 1$. Then $p_1 = 1$ and $p_2 = 2$. Agent 1's utility-maximization problem becomes

$$\max x_1 x_2$$

$$\text{s.t. } x_1 + 2x_2 \leq 1$$

$$x_1, x_2 \geq 0.$$

The right-hand side of the budget constraint consists of the money earned from selling input. As the factory makes no profit, there is no profit share to account for on the income side. The utility-maximization bundle is given by

$$x_1 = \frac{1}{2}, \quad x_2 = \frac{1}{4}.$$

These are agent 1's demand curve for goods 1 and 2. Notice that agent 2's utility function is identical to that of agent 1 and has the same income. Hence, it has exactly the same demand curves as agent 1.   □

6.4.1   Cost Minimization

With production, it is still the case that a Walrasian allocation is Pareto optimal. However, we can say even more. The mix of goods produced must have been produced at lowest possible cost. To see why, consider an economy consisting of just two firms (firm 1 and firm 2), each producing a single commodity (Soma). Suppose that the total demand for Soma is 100 units.

Imagine you are a central planner charged with meeting the demand for Soma at minimum cost. The government has nationalized the two firms, so they are at your disposal. You must decide how much Soma to make at each firm and minimize total production costs as well. How? Parcel out Soma production one unit at a time to whichever firm currently has the lower marginal cost. Stop once all 100 units of it are assigned. This clearly is the cheapest way to produce the 100 units of Soma.[4] Now, in the end, both firms must have the same marginal cost. If not, we could lower costs by transferring some Soma production from the firm with higher marginal costs to the one with lower marginal costs.[5]

Instead of deciding how much each firm should produce, you could announce a price that the firms will be paid for their output of Soma. Suppose you announce the price p. If the firms are profit maximizing, they will each produce to the point that their marginal cost equals p. Their marginal production costs are identical! The only problem is that the total amount of Soma produced may not equal 100. No problem. If it exceeds 100, lower p. If it is less than 100, raise p.

Under both regimes, production of the 100 units will be allocated so as to equalize the marginal costs of the two firms. In the second case, neither firm is concerned with minimizing overall costs. Their only goal is to minimize their firm-specific costs. Nevertheless, they end up producing so as to minimize the *total* costs of production. This is the basis of Adam Smith's (1723–1790) memorable passage about the invisible hand:[6]

As every individual, therefore, endeavors as much as he can both to employ his capital in the support of domestic industry, and so to direct that industry that its produce may be of greatest value; every individual necessarily labors to render the annual revenue of the society as great

---

[4] Since both firms exhibit decreasing returns to scale, as the amount of Soma each firm produces increases, their marginal costs rise.

[5] This is not quite true. One firm could have a marginal cost of production so large compared to the other that no production would ever be assigned to it. In this case all 100 units would be made by one firm and the marginal costs of the two firms would not be equal. The conclusion of the story would still be true in this case.

[6] The invisible hand works like Goethe's Mephisto in the way that it conjures up *"part of that power, not understood, Which wills the bad, and always works the good."*

as he can. He generally, indeed, neither intends to promote the public interest, nor knows how much he is promoting it. By preferring the support of domestic to that of foreign industry, he intends only on his own security; and by directing that industry in such a manner as its produce may be of greatest value, he intends only his own gain, and he is in this as in many other cases, led by an invisible hand to promote an end which was no part of his own intention.

Our illustrative example is one-sided in that demand was given and fixed. What if we did not know the demand ahead of time? Not a problem. Simply announce a price p. Consumers tell you what they demand at that price (that's the demand) so as to maximize their utility. The firms will tell you what they can produce so as to maximize profit (that's the supply). If supply exceeds demand, lower p. If not, raise p. We know that as price increases, demand drops. Also, as price increases, supply increases. With demand going down and supply going up, they must meet somewhere. Bingo!

6.5 Planning vs. Markets

> *Comrade. I've been fascinated by your Five-Year Plan for the last fifteen years.*
> Count Leon d'Algout

A perfectly competitive market can replicate the outcomes generated by a benevolent central planner. So, why bother with markets? One reason is informational.[7] To allocate resources through central planning imposes an enormous informational burden on the planner. She needs to know all the resources available, all the production functions, and everyone's utility function. Prices allow one to avoid the headache of collecting all this information. It combines all this information into a single number. The price tells everything.[8] The argument is summarized by Kenneth Arrow:

Not only is it [price system] capable of achieving efficient allocations in the sense just described, but it requires of the participants in an economy relatively little knowledge. They need only know their own needs. The individual need not worry about the social effects of his actions. According to the system, if he does something which affects somebody else, he pays the price. If he withdraws resources that somebody else could use, he is made aware through the price he has to pay, but he does not have to further consider others as individuals. They are compensated through the prices he has to pay.

Even Leon Trotsky (1879–1940) acknowledged this fact:

The innumerable living participants in the economy, state and private, collective and individual, must serve notice of their needs and of their relative strength not only through the statistical determinations of plan commissions but by the direct pressure of supply and demand.

But not Stalin (1878–1953).[9] Under Uncle Josef, the Soviet Union eschewed prices and relied solely on central planning. This "mania" was exported to the countries

---

[7] The other reason (political) is that one cannot trust the planner to be benevolent.

[8] This observation is credited to Friedrich Hayek (1899–1992).

[9] Who ordered Trotsky's assassination in 1940.

that entered the Soviet orbit at the end of the Second World War. Jo Langer, who worked for a Czech export company in 1948, gave the following "workers' eye view" of central planning:[10]

... in December the head of the planning department asked me to make out a table showing exactly how many toothbrushes (what sort of bristles, what colors, etc) I was planning to deliver to Switzerland, England, Malta, Madagascar and so on during the first half of the coming year. I said that I couldn't possibly know, as our agents in various places were ordinary mortals and as such were subject to illness and death ... My objections were waved aside and I was told to draw up my forecast without delay.

6.6   Free Trade

Glasgow's main cemetery is called the City of the Dead. At the foot of the hill upon which it sits, you will find Glasgow's cathedral. It lacks the pomp of St. Paul's or the majesty of Westminster, that is as it should be. It is, strictly speaking, not a cathedral because it hasn't served as a bishop's seat since 1690. The interior is spare but beautiful. Buried within are the expected complement of worthy divines, doctors, and burghers. Upon its flagstones, walls, and stained glass are memorials to Scots whose bones lie uncoffined elsewhere: Afghanistan, Belgium, China, Egypt, India, and South Africa. Conrad wrote of them being borne on the Thames:

Hunters for gold or pursuers of fame, they all had gone out on that stream, bearing the sword, and often the torch, messengers of the might within the land, bearers of a spark from the sacred fire. What greatness had not floated on the ebb of that river into the mystery of an unknown earth! ... The dreams of men, the seed of commonwealths, the germs of empires.

Scotland supplied not just soldiers to the empire, but teachers, doctors, nurses, engineers, and civil servants. Other than whiskey and golf, Scotland's chief export to the world has been its people. This would have been impossible without the *Pax Britannica*. Empires encourage, sometimes by force, the flow of people across borders.

Between 1500 and 1800, for example, 2 million Europeans and 8 million Africans, in chains, made their way to the New World. At the same time, on the other side of the world, 4 million Chinese moved to Sichuan, the southwest frontier of the Chinese empire. Over a million went to Manchuria and about the same number traversed the waters to Taiwan.[11]

In our own time, one of the largest movements of people since the end of the Second World War is underway. From Afghanistan, Bangladesh, Somalia, Syria, Honduras, and China, hundreds of thousands of individuals and families are crossing borders to great consternation and angst. Should one allow them in? The question is a variant of

---

[10] Jo Langer was born in Budapest but moved to Bratislava upon marrying Oscar Langer, a prominent Slovakian communist. Oscar Langer was sentenced to a 22-year prison term during one of the Stalinist purges. The quote comes from her memoirs (*Convictions: My Life With a Good Communist*) of that period.

[11] Pomerantz, K. and S. Topik (1999). *The World That Trade Created,* 1st edn, New York, Routledge.

whether "free trade" is a good thing. If it is a good idea to reduce tariffs and barriers on the trade of apples, cheese, and cars, why not labor? Why can't a hairdresser in Poland export their labor to the UK? Why shouldn't an Englishman, if he wishes, have his hair dressed by a Pole?

Perhaps the best way to understand the *standard* economic argument for free trade is with a provocative framing due to David Friedman. He observes that there are two technologies for manufacturing automobiles in the USA. One is well known and, historically, has been centered in Detroit. The other, often overlooked, is in Iowa. Detroit *makes* cars but Iowa *grows* them. Yes, grows them. Plant seeds, wait till they become wheat, harvest it, put it on a boat to Japan. In time, the boat returns with cars.

The two ways of producing automobiles are like the two Soma manufacturers of Section 6.4. In a perfectly competitive market, each, acting independently, will choose output to minimize the total cost of producing them. The resulting mix of foreign and domestic vehicles will be the cost-minimizing one. Now, suppose a tariff is imposed on imported vehicles (i.e. Iowa-produced vehicles). This reduces the demand for Iowa-made vehicles as it raises their price. Thus, less production is allocated to the Iowa manufacturer than otherwise would have been the case. In particular, the resulting mix will no longer be the one that minimizes total cost. What is the impact of all this?

1. Because fewer Iowa-made vehicles are produced, Iowa farmers make less than before.
2. Detroit manufacturers sell more cars than they did before. This means that the marginal cost of the last car produced is higher than it was before. Recall that the price is set by the marginal cost of the last vehicle, so prices are higher. Hence, the Detroit manufacturers see higher total profits.
3. Consumers pay higher prices for cars and will be worse off.
4. Using arguments that we have deployed before, it is easy to see that total surplus will go down. Thus, we are collectively worse off.

Therefore, the imposition of such a tariff favors Detroit auto workers at the expense of Iowa farmers and consumers. A subsidy to the Iowa farmers has the opposite effect.

To summarize, *assuming* trade between nations resembles a perfectly competitive market, imposing a barrier to trade can only reduce the total surplus of the countries involved. However, there will be constituents within one of the countries that will be better off.

In June 2016, close to half a century after joining the European Union, the citizens of the UK voted to depart. The vote shocked the world and exposed a class and generational divide that had hitherto been papered over by good manners and English reserve. The central concern of "Leavers" was immigration. Membership of the Union meant, among other things, the elimination of trade barriers between member states. This applied to goods, services, *and* people. It was possible to be born in France, educated in Germany, find employment in the UK, and retire in Spain. For the UK it meant Polish contractors, Spanish waiters, Austrian professors, and Greek nurses entering the country. It also meant increased mobility for UK citizens', with younger UK nationals relocating to the continent.

Assuming the labor market in the European Union resembled a perfectly competitive one, an exit by Britain from the Union would be equivalent to a tariff on imported labor and goods. Collectively, by the argument above, the UK would be worse off. So, why did a majority vote to exit the Union? Did they not know which side their bread was buttered?

Yes, total surplus for the UK will decline with an exit. However, the distribution of that surplus also matters. Those who benefit from lower barriers will vote to remain, while those who don't will vote to exit. An analysis of the distribution of the votes highlights clearly that the large swaths of England and Wales that voted for exit were also the areas that had seen a decline in economic activity since the UK's entry into the Union. Some of this decline was inevitable. The passage into Imperial twilight had quieted the Lancastrian mills, shuttered the Clydeside shipyards, and darkened the Newcastle furnaces. By the 1970s, the UK had replaced Turkey as the sick man of Europe.[12] Membership of the Union brought huge benefits, but these were concentrated in London and the South East.

Thus far, we have discussed imposing a trade barrier when there was none. What if a trade barrier is present, and we contemplate removing it. Does the argument work in reverse? There will be a constituency that is made worse off by elimination of the barrier. Total surplus, however, will increase. Hence, there is sufficient additional surplus generated to compensate those who are worse off.

We conclude this section with three caveats to bear in mind when contemplating this argument for free trade.

1. When we apply it to justify removing a trade barrier, we are assuming that it will bring us closer to the perfectly competitive outcome. However, if there are other restrictions in place (labor laws, pollution regulation), removing just one barrier need not have the intended effect. One must account for how the different restrictions currently in place interact with each other.
2. While one can, *in principle*, compensate those who are made worse off by elimination of the barrier, it doesn't mean that one can do so in practice. Who should be compensated? How should they be compensated? Who should pay for the compensation?
3. Within a representative democracy, how would the elimination of such a barrier be enacted? Recall the Iowa–Detroit example. The benefits of the tariff are concentrated among the Detroit producers but the costs are shared by a wider and more diffuse group: Iowa farmers and consumers. If participation in the democratic process is costly, it is unclear that those who bear the cost of such barriers will have the incentive to overturn them.

What about the argument for restricting trade? It is logically incoherent. Any argument for restricting trade between nations would apply with equal force to trade between provinces and states within the same country. Further, even if free trade were

---

[12] The term is attributed to Tsar Nicholas I of Russia. In the run up to the Crimean War he is reported to have described the Ottoman Empire as "a sick man, a very sick man."

a bad idea, it is unclear that we know enough to manage trade so as to do better. American sugar policy from the early 1980s is instructive. To maintain high domestic prices for sugar, the US government restricted the volume of sugar that could be imported, a sugar quota. As worldwide sugar prices declined, the quota shrank. Domestic sugar prices rose. So much so that US firms found it cheaper to buy cake mix, iced tea, and other goods with a high sugar content to extract the sugar contained within. Coke and Pepsi, two major consumers of sugar, switched to corn syrup, gutting domestic demand. Sugar farmers in Central America, unable to sell their product to the USA, switched to narcotics.

6.7   Automation Redux

In Section 2.8.1 we showed that if labor and automation were substitutes for each other, a drop in the price of automation would encourage a shift away from labor. To conclude from this that automation will make workers worse off is to be guilty of the fallacy of composition.[13]

To trace out the effect of automation, we use a simple model involving two agents and one factory. The factory takes labor (measured in units of time) as input and outputs a product, say Soylent Green, for consumption by two agents.[14] Each agent is endowed with one unit of time, which they can use for either leisure or labor. Agents derive utility from the consumption of leisure and Soylent. If x is the amount of leisure consumed and z the amount of Soylent Green, the utility will be xz. The two agents differ in their share of the profits of the factory. Agent 1 owns a share μ while agent 2 owns a share $1 - \mu$.

We consider two scenarios corresponding to two choices of a production function for the factory. In the first, which is the benchmark, $f(L) = 2\sqrt{L}$ is the amount of Soylent produced from L units of labor (measured in units of time).

Let w denote the unit price of labor and p the unit price of Soylent Green. An outline of the derivation of the equilibrium prices and quantities appears below. Equilibrium prices are $w = 1$ and $p = \sqrt{\frac{2}{3}}$. The quantities of each of the goods consumed in equilibrium are $x_1 = \frac{1+\mu(\frac{2}{3})}{2}$, $z_1 = \frac{1+\mu(\frac{2}{3})}{2\sqrt{\frac{2}{3}}}$, $x_2 = \frac{1+(1-\mu)(\frac{2}{3})}{2}$, and $z_2 = \frac{1+(1-\mu)(\frac{2}{3})}{2\sqrt{\frac{2}{3}}}$.

Example 54 *Given w and p, the factory will choose L to maximize $2p\sqrt{L} - wL$. The profit-maximizing choice of L is $(\frac{p}{w})^2$. Therefore, the factory's profit will be $\frac{p^2}{w}$.*

Suppose agent i chooses an amount x_i of leisure to consume and z_i units of Soylent to consume. This will leave agent 1 with $1 - x_1$ units of labor that can be sold to the factory. This allows the agent obtaining an income of $w(1 - x_1) + \mu(\frac{p^2}{w})$. Agent 1 will

---

[13] To infer that something is true of the whole from the fact that it is true of some part of the whole.
[14] A green wafer advertised to contain high-energy plankton.

then choose x_1 and z_1 to solve

$$\max x_1 z_1$$

$$\text{s.t. } pz_1 \leq w(1 - x_1) + \mu\left(\frac{p^2}{w}\right)$$

$$0 \leq x_1 \leq 1$$

$$z_1 \geq 0.$$

The optimal solution is $x_1 = \frac{w + \mu(\frac{p^2}{w})}{2w}$ and $z_1 = \frac{w + \mu(\frac{p^2}{w})}{2p}$, provided of course that $\frac{w + \mu(\frac{p^2}{w})}{2w} \leq 1$.

Agent 2 will choose an amount of leisure (x_2) and Soylent (z_2) to solve

$$\max x_2 z_2$$

$$\text{s.t. } pz_2 \leq w(1 - x_2) + (1 - \mu)\left(\frac{p^2}{w}\right)$$

$$0 \leq x_2 \leq 1$$

$$z_2 \geq 0.$$

The optimal solution is $x_2 = \frac{w + (1 - \mu)(\frac{p^2}{w})}{2w}$ and $z_2 = \frac{w + (1 - \mu)(\frac{p^2}{w})}{2p}$, provided of course that $\frac{w + (1 - \mu)(\frac{p^2}{w})}{2w} \leq 1$.

We can choose $w = 1$ (i.e. labor is the numeraire). To determine p, we balance the supply and demand for Soylent:

$$\frac{1 + \mu p^2}{2p} + \frac{1 + (1 - \mu)p^2}{2p} = 2p$$

$$\Rightarrow p = \sqrt{\frac{2}{3}}.$$

Hence, $x_1 = \frac{1 + \mu(\frac{2}{3})}{2} = z_1$ and $x_2 = \frac{1 + (1 - \mu)(\frac{2}{3})}{2} = z_2$. □

We model the introduction of automation by having the factory switch to a new production function in which the same amount of Soylent can be produced using less labor. While convenient, we are suppressing the fact that automation must be provided by someone.

Suppose the new production function is $f(L) = 4\sqrt{L}$. Our goal is to see if the two agents are better or worse off. The equilibrium prices will be $w = 1$, $p = \sqrt{\frac{1}{2}}$. The equilibrium quantities are $x_1 = \frac{1 + 2\mu}{2}$, $z_1 = \frac{1 + 2\mu}{\sqrt{2}}$, $x_2 = \frac{1 + 2(1 - \mu)}{2}$, and $z_2 = \frac{1 + 2(1 - \mu)}{\sqrt{2}}$.

The utility of agent 1 in the benchmark case is $[\frac{1+2\mu}{2}]^2(\sqrt{\frac{3}{2}})$. Her utility in the second case is $[\frac{1+2\mu}{2}]^2(\frac{2}{\sqrt{2}})$. Notice that her utility has increased! The same is true for agent 2 as well. How can that be? The new technology requires *less* labor to produce the same level of output of Soylent. In fact, as can be verified, the total amount of labor supplied goes down. Notice what happened to the equilibrium price of Soylent. It declined as well. Automation lowered the factory's production costs, which allowed it to produce more Soylent using less labor. This Soylent subsequently sold for a lower price. The profit of the factory goes up after the switch in production functions. This benefits the agents, because each owns some share of the profits. Keep in mind that this example ignores the benefits that should accrue to the sellers of automation. Therefore, it cannot be used to argue that automation will be an unalloyed good. However, it is useful in alerting us to the knock-on effects of automation. Yes, automation will displace labor if it is more cost effective. However, this will result in more output and lower prices. This benefits the sellers of inputs that are combined with labor to generate the output. Owners of shares in the profits of the factory also benefit. Unanswered is the effect on those who are endowed only with labor.

6.8   Minimum Wage Redux

Raises in the minimum wage generally face opposition from business lobbies. The arguments against can be extreme. In a 1937 Congressional hearing, Guy Harrington of the National Publishers Association asserted that the minimum wage caused the decline of the Roman Empire. The subsequent exchange between Harrington and Committee Chairman, Congressman William Connery (D-MA) is delightful.

Chairman: Would you object to telling us from what bibliography this information was obtained?
Mr. Harrington: As a matter of fact, a man who wrote a book and became an authority on Roman history was my source of information. If I am not mistaken, he was a member of the United States Senate at one time and he came from Missouri and was prominent in the political affairs of the State of Missouri.
Chairman: What was his name?
Mr. Harrington: I don't recall his name now, but at that time he became considered an authority on Roman history, and particularly on the economic situation in Rome.
Chairman: Did you ever read Ferrara's economic history of Rome?
Mr. Harrington: No; I never did.
Chairman: Did you ever read any of the other economic histories except this one that some man that used to serve in the Senate from Missouri wrote?
Mr. Harrington: He was considered an authority. That is the reason I mentioned him.
Chairman: Did you read Gibbon at that time?
Mr. Harrington: Yes; I have read Gibbon.
Chairman: Do you recall whether he referred to the fixing of prices?
Mr. Harrington: At the moment, I cannot.
Chairman: You make the direct and positive statement that Rome fell on that account, and I have heard and read some conflict of ideas as to the real reason that Rome fell.
Mr. Harrington: Yes.

Chairman: It may have fallen for this reason, but I really had not heard that reason assigned before. But you make the direct and positive statement that the reason that Rome fell was because several hundred years after Augustus Caesar they began to fix prices and services.

Mr. Harrington: That was one of the contributing causes. I am only expressing an opinion.

Chairman: What were some of the other reasons?

Mr. Harrington: The attacks from without, the degeneration of its social system and social life, and that sort of thing, probably were contributory factors. No question about that.

Chairman: Could you give us the name of that man that wrote the book?

Mr. Harrington: Yes, sir; I would be very glad to do that. I will do that as soon as I get back to my house.

Let's review the customary model used to illustrate the folly of imposing a minimum wage found in economics textbooks. It takes as a primitive two curves. One a demand curve for labor, denoted $D(w)$, where w is the wage per unit of labor. Two a labor supply curve, denoted $S(w)$.

$D(w)$ is assumed to decline with an increase in w $\left[\text{i.e. } \frac{dD(w)}{dw} < 0 \text{ while } \frac{dS(w)}{dw} > 0\right]$. These are both sensible assumptions. Furthermore, there is a high enough wage $\bar{w}$, say, such that $D(\bar{w}) < S(\bar{w})$ and a low enough wage w' such that $D(w') > S(w')$. In words, there is a wage where the demand for labor will be less than the supply and conversely. In addition, $D(w)$ and $S(w)$ are assumed to be continuous. Under these assumptions, there will be a wage w^* where $D(w^*) = S(w^*)$ (i.e. a wage where labor supply meets labor demand). This will be the equilibrium or market-clearing wage. This is illustrated in Figure 6.4. The quantity of labor is displayed on the vertical while wage is on the horizontal.

Suppose a minimum wage $\hat{w} > w^*$ is imposed. As the wage is raised from w^* to $\hat{w}$, the demand for labor falls. This follows from the assumption that the derivative of

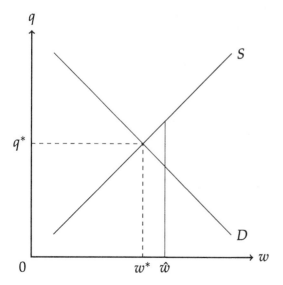

Figure 6.4 Labor supply and demand

$D(w)$ is negative. Therefore, $D(\hat{w}) < D(w^*)$. At the same time, because the derivative of $S(w)$ is positive, it follows that $S(\hat{w}) > S(w^*)$. Hence, $D(\hat{w}) < S(\hat{w})$. Thus, less labor is demanded. Always. No matter how small the increase. This is to be contrasted with the monopsony case of Section 2.9.1. There, a sufficiently small increase resulted in the monopsonist acquiring more labor.

While fewer workers are employed (or fewer hours are worked), these workers get higher wages. Thus, to see if imposing a minimum wage above the equilibrium wage is a bad idea, we must evaluate the change in total surplus, say. A straightforward calculation (as in Section 2.6) shows that total surplus (buyer and labor) declines after the imposition of a minimum wage.

This simple analysis is seductive but incomplete. For example, couldn't a higher wage cause the workers who earn it to spend more on goods? Thus, a rise in labor costs would be offset by a rise in demand. Also, if agents' preferences cannot be denominated in a common monetary scale, how could we tell that imposing a minimum wage (above the equilibrium level) makes everyone worse off?

To examine these possibilities we use the same model as in Section 6.7. A number of steps in the analysis will be skipped under the assumption that the reader can fill them in.

Suppose we have two agents and one factory. The factory takes labor (measured in units of time) as input and outputs Soylent Green. Each agent is endowed with one unit of time, which they can use for either leisure or labor. Agents derive utility from the consumption of leisure and Soylent. If x is the amount of leisure consumed and z the amount of Soylent Green, the utility will be xz. Agents 1 and 2 each own a 50% share of the profits of the factory. Let $f(L) = 2\sqrt{L}$ be the amount of Soylent produced from L units of labor (measured in units of time).

Let w denote the unit price of labor and p the unit price of Soylent Green. The reader can verify that equilibrium prices are $w = 1$ and $p = \sqrt{\frac{2}{3}}$. In words, $\sqrt{\frac{2}{3}}$ units of labor are needed to purchase one unit of Soylent. Forcing the wage to be $1 + \delta$ will only cause the price of Soylent to become $(1+\delta)\sqrt{\frac{2}{3}}$. This is because prices are relative not absolute. Therefore, a minimum wage should be interpreted as restricting the ratio of the price of Soylent to wages. In particular, we want that ratio to be smaller than $\sqrt{\frac{2}{3}}$. The smaller the ratio, the less labor is required to buy a unit of Soylent. In effect, labor becomes more valuable, which is presumably the intended effect of a minimum wage. So, suppose we require that

$$\frac{p}{w} = \alpha\sqrt{\frac{2}{3}}, \tag{6.9}$$

where $0 < \alpha < 1$ is a variable whose value we will determine later. The smaller α is chosen, the higher the minimum wage.

At a price ratio of $\alpha\sqrt{\frac{2}{3}}$, the factory will choose $\frac{2\alpha^2}{3}$ units of labor to maximize profit. The total output of Soylent will be $2\alpha\sqrt{\frac{2}{3}}$.

Recall the utility-maximization problem for agent 1:

$$\max x_1 z_1$$

$$\text{s.t. } pz_1 \leq w(1 - x_1) + 0.5\left(\frac{p^2}{w}\right)$$

$$0 \leq x_1 \leq 1$$

$$z_1 \geq 0.$$

If we divide the budget constraint through by w and impose condition (6.9), agent 1's utility-maximization problem becomes

$$\max x_1 z_1$$

$$\text{s.t. } \alpha\sqrt{\frac{2}{3}}z_1 \leq (1 - x_1) + 0.5\frac{2\alpha^2}{3}$$

$$0 \leq x_1 \leq 1$$

$$z_1 \geq 0.$$

The optimal solution is

$$x_1 = \frac{1 + 0.5\frac{2\alpha^2}{3}}{2}, \quad z_1 = \frac{1 + 0.5\frac{2\alpha^2}{3}}{2\alpha\sqrt{\frac{2}{3}}}.$$

For agent 2 we have

$$x_1 = \frac{1 + 0.5\frac{2\alpha^2}{3}}{2}, \quad z_1 = \frac{1 + 0.5\frac{2\alpha^2}{3}}{2\alpha\sqrt{\frac{2}{3}}}.$$

The total amount of labor supplied is

$$1 - x_1 + 1 - x_2 = 1 - \frac{\alpha^2}{3}.$$

This exceeds the amount demanded, because

$$1 - \frac{\alpha^2}{3} > \frac{2\alpha^2}{3}.$$

This is as expected. The total demand for Soylent is

$$z_1 + z_2 = \frac{2 + \frac{2\alpha^2}{3}}{2\alpha\sqrt{\frac{2}{3}}} = \frac{1 + \frac{\alpha^2}{3}}{\alpha\sqrt{\frac{2}{3}}}.$$

This does not match the supply of Soylent, because

$$\frac{1 + \frac{\alpha^2}{3}}{\alpha\sqrt{\frac{2}{3}}} \neq 2\alpha\sqrt{\frac{2}{3}}.$$

The mismatch between supply and demand of labor is expected. Why the mismatch for Soylent? Because each agent chooses a utility-maximizing bundle under the assumption that his or her labor will be consumed by the factory. In effect, each agent overestimates his or her income.

To deal with the imbalance between the demand for labor and its supply, we assume that the factory will ration between the two agents. One can imagine a variety of rationing rules. For example, get as much labor from agent 1 first, and then agent 2. We will assume the factory is even-handed and splits its labor demand between the two agents.

At the current prices, agent 1 is willing to provide

$$1 - x_1 = \frac{1 - \frac{\alpha^2}{3}}{2}$$

units of labor. This exceeds the total labor demand of the factory, because $\frac{1 - \frac{\alpha^2}{3}}{2} > \frac{2\alpha^2}{3}$. Thus, agent 1 will be willing to supply $\frac{\alpha^2}{3}$ units of labor. This is half the factory's demand for labor. Similarly for agent 2. Agent 1's leisure consumption will be $1 - \frac{\alpha^2}{3}$ units. Given this, agent 1's utility-maximization problem becomes

$$\max \left(1 - \frac{\alpha^2}{3}\right) z_1$$

$$\text{s.t. } \alpha\sqrt{\frac{2}{3}} z_1 \leq \frac{\alpha^2}{3} + 0.5\frac{2\alpha^2}{3}$$

$$z_1 \geq 0.$$

The solution to this is $z_1 = (\frac{2\alpha}{3})(\sqrt{\frac{3}{2}})$. The utility that agent 1 enjoys is

$$\left(1 - \frac{\alpha^2}{3}\right)\left(\frac{2\alpha}{3}\right)\left(\sqrt{\frac{3}{2}}\right).$$

The utility that agent 1 enjoyed before the imposition of the minimum wage was

$$\left(\frac{4}{9}\right)\left(\sqrt{\frac{3}{2}}\right).$$

As can be verified, agent 1's utility was higher before the imposition of the minimum wage. The same is true for agent 2.

To summarize, the minimum wage reduces the hours worked by each agent. This reduces the output of the factory, resulting in less Soylent available for consumption. Thus, while the agents earn more per unit of labor, this is not enough to offset the drop in hours and decrease in Soylent.

6.9   The Specter of Costs

> *An economic specter haunts the democratic governments of the world's most pros-*
> *perous economies. The rising cost of health care and education casts a shadow*
> *over virtually any election ... ever more of gross national product will have to be*
> *channeled through the public sector, with all the problems we know that to entail.*
> William Baumol

In 1908, the average American had to work approximately 4700 hours to earn enough
to buy a Model T Ford. In 2008, a typical car could be obtained for only 1365 hours
of labor. The 2008 car would be sleeker, faster, safer, and have cup holders. Therefore,
the price of a car has fallen over time and its quality has risen. As another example,
between December 1997 and August 2015, the Consumer Price Index for personal
computers and peripheral equipment declined 96%. The price index for TVs decreased
94% in the same period. In fact, personal electronics of every kind have dropped in
price and increased in quality over time.[15] This downward trend is not universal.

In education, for example, the total (inflation-adjusted) cost of K-12 education in
the USA has increased since 1970. However, test scores of various kinds, which we
can interpret as measures of quality, have moved hardly at all.[16] Tertiary education is
no different. In 1980, the average inflation-adjusted cost of a university education was
approximately $2000 a year. It is now about $20,000 a year.[17] It's less obvious how
one measures quality, but one can frame the issue in the following way: does college
today provide $18,000 a year greater value than when one's parents went to college?

For the same period, the cost of medical care increased by 250%.[18] By way of
comparison, average price and wage increases were 110% and 150%, respectively, for
the same period. As a share of GDP, US spending on health care is growing approximately 1.4% a year. At this rate, a century from now, health-care spending will be
60% of GDP. This is not just an American problem. Health-care spending per person
in Japan grew by 5.7% a year in real terms between 1960 and 2006. In the UK it rose
by 3.5% a year over the same period. Was there a corresponding increase in quality? Much harder to say in this case. Life expectancy has increased, but some would
attribute that to low-cost interventions like sanitation, nutrition, and quitting smoking.

Such dramatic cost increases demand explanations and concomitant fixes. By way
of illustration, the various explanations for the rise of college costs are listed below,
along with their attendant cures.

1. It is a consequence of reduced government support for tertiary education. The
   obvious solution is to increase subsidies for college. Free college anyone?

---

[15] Based on data from the Bureau of Labor Statistics, US Department of Labor at www.bls.gov/
opub/ted/2015/long-term-price-trends-for-computers-tvs-and-related-
items.htm.
[16] See www.cato.org/blog/public-school-spending-theres-chart.
[17] See https://nces.ed.gov/programs/digest/d07/tables/dt07_320.asp.
[18] See www.kff.org/report-section/health-care-costs-a-primer-2012-report/.

2. It is a consequence of greater regulations that force colleges to hire more apparatchiks to ensure compliance. Remove these government shackles.
3. Increased federal student aid (Pell grants, loans) encourages rapacious university presidents to raise fees.[19] Alternatively, given college's tremendous return on investment, it was underpriced in the past. Colleges were unaware of how valuable their product was until recently. Today's price reflects the actual value of what is being offered.[20] Shall we regulate fees and how endowments are spent?
4. Education is defined too narrowly. If we include on-line courses and other resources, the cost of education is actually dropping. No problem here, move along.

What if rising college and health costs are as inevitable as death? In which case, attempts to bend the cost curve are in vain.

Consider an economy with two factories, each representing a different sector. One is indexed by the letter m to denote manufacturing and the other by the letter s, denoting service. Think of factory m as producing a manufactured product like a car or mobile phone. Given y units of labor, factory m will generate $a_m y$ units of manufactured output. Factory s provides a service, like education. Given y units of labor, factory s will generate y units of service output. Notice that the production functions for each of the factories are linear in input. The parameter a_m measures how productive factory m is. The larger a_m is, the more productive factory m is. If $a_m > 1$, it means that factory m is more productive than factory s.

There is one agent (who is a stand-in for an entire population), endowed with a unit of labor and interested in consuming both manufactured goods and services. If this agent consumes x_m units of the output of factory m and x_s units of service, she enjoys a utility of $x_m x_s$.

Set the price per unit of the manufactured good to $1 and let the price per unit of service be p. Let w_m be the wage paid per unit of labor by factory m and w_s be the wage paid per unit of labor by factory s. If the agent allocates α units of labor to factory m and the remainder to factory s, her consumer choice problem is

$$\max x_m x_s$$

$$\text{s.t. } x_m + p x_s \leq w_m \alpha + w_s (1 - \alpha)$$

$$x_m, x_s, \alpha \geq 0.$$

As the two factories have production functions that are linear in labor, at equilibrium they must each make zero profit. This happens when $1 \times a_m = w_m$ and $p = w_s$.

If $w_m > w_s$, our one agent would never choose to work for factory s. This would mean the output of factory s would be zero. If $w_m < w_s$, our one agent would never choose to work for factory m. This would mean the output of factory m would be

---

[19] This explanation is often credited to William Bennett, US Secretary of Education under Ronald Reagan: "Federal student aid makes it easier for colleges to do what they're going to do anyway, which is raise tuition." Mr. Bennett does not explain why competition evaporates in the face of increased student aid.

[20] Non-profit does not mean zero profit.

zero. Observe that in both these cases, the agent will always choose to consume a positive amount of the output of m as well as s. Another way to phrase this is that both industries must pay the same or else get no workers! Hence, at a Walrasian equilibrium it must be that $w_m = w_s$.

Therefore, at equilibrium the unit price of the manufactured good will be \$1 and the wage paid by m will be $w_m = a_m$. Hence, the wage paid by factory s will also be $w_s = a_m$. Finally, the price of service will be $p = w_s = a_m$. At these prices, the agent's utility-maximization problem becomes

$$\max x_m x_s$$

$$\text{s.t. } x_m + a_m x_s \le a_m$$

$$x_m, x_s, \alpha \ge 0.$$

The optimal solution is $x_m = \frac{a_m}{2}$ and $x_s = \frac{1}{2}$.

Now, increase a_m above 1. This makes the manufacturing sector of our hypothetical economy more productive relative to the service sector. Notice the wages paid by each sector increase. Thus, in the service sector we see rising wages but *no increase* in output per unit of labor! The unit price of service also rises as manufacturing becomes more productive. The total amount spent on service, $\frac{a_m}{2}$, is also increasing.

Why does an increase in the productivity of the manufacturing sector make labor in the service sector more expensive? How do we know that this is not just an artifact of the functional forms of the model we have built? To answer this we need to trace out what is happening in the model.

As productivity in the manufacturing sector increases, the wage paid to labor in this sector also increases. This makes intuitive sense. As workers become more productive, their pay should increase. This need not be the case if the employer were a monopsony, and so the assumption that we have a perfectly competitive economy has bite. As workers can switch between sectors, it follows that the service sector will have to raise wages to retain workers. This argument does not depend on the particular functional forms selected.

The model also says that while the total amount of services consumed remains fixed at $\frac{1}{2}$, the total amount of spending on services will increase. Invariance in the quantity of services consumed is an artifact of the choice of utility function. The increasing expenditure on services is not, as can be verified by reworking the model with a different utility function. In fact, one will see an increase in the consumption of services.

If we accept the explanation of rising costs given by this analysis, it follows that health costs, say, are destined to consume an increasing share of our GDP. We are doomed, therefore, to become a nation of health-care workers and their clients. Well, no. Health care is not the only service sector in which productivity is stagnant. There is education, the arts, and sports. A music quartet cannot be formed from fewer than four musicians and a rugby team needs 15 players. These sectors will also consume more labor and that is as one would expect. If manufacturing enjoys an increase in productivity, it means that less labor is needed to produce the same output. That labor is freed to be deployed elsewhere.

7 Externalities and Public Goods

The effect on you from an action I take is called an **externality**. It is difficult to conceive of a case where an externality is absent, because "No man," as John Donne observed, "is an Iland, intire of it selfe; every man is a peece of the Continent, a part of the maine." If the action I take confers a benefit upon you, it is called a **positive externality**. Politeness, on my part, in my dealings with you, would be a positive externality. If the action I take imposes a cost upon you, it is called a **negative externality**. Breaking wind in your presence would be a negative externality.[1]

It's been rumored that smelling farts could prevent cancer, making flatulence a positive externality.[2] This is, of course, false, but just the thing to cover one's embarrassment when needed.

An externality that has dominated our discussion thus far is the one that is generated when I purchase a good. My purchase of the good prevents you from owning the same, imposing a negative externality upon you, assuming you have an interest in the good. If the price paid to acquire the good was set to clear the market, then that price accounts for the negative externality I impose on you. To illustrate, suppose the good is unique, say a painting. The opportunity cost to the seller of the painting is $1000. My RP for the painting is $2000, while yours is $1500. Each of our outside options delivers zero surplus. Let us find a Walrasian price for this simple economy. For any price strictly below $1000, the demand will be 2 (you and I are both willing to purchase at such a price), but supply is 0 because the seller is unwilling to part with it. For any price at or above $1000, but strictly below $1500 (inclusive), demand will be 2 but supply is exactly 1. So, the market does not clear. For any price above $1500 up to and including $2000, the market does clear (i.e. supply equals demand).[3] At any of the market clearing prices, the total surplus (sum of producer and consumer

---

[1] On June 22, 2016 a Swedish footballer, Adam Lindin Ljungkvist, was sent off for breaking wind during a match. The referee Dany Kako accused him of "deliberate provocation" and "unsportsmanlike behavior." Ljungkvist said "I asked the referee, 'What, am I not allowed to break wind a little?' 'No,' he replied … I don't get it but maybe he thought I farted in my hand and threw the fart at him. But I did not." Kako confirmed that Ljungkvist had received the second yellow card for breaking wind, explaining: "He did it on purpose and it was inappropriate. Therefore, he received a yellow card."

[2] *TIME*, July 11, 2014.

[3] At a price of $1500 you would be exactly indifferent between buying and not. Thus, allocating the good to me would clear the market.

surplus) is equal to $2000 - 1000 = \$1000$. This is the maximum possible. Notice that a market clearing price must be at least as large as $1500, your RP. In this sense a market clearing price must be large enough to cover the cost of the negative externality I impose on you. Notice also that while I pay for the externality I impose on you, you do not receive this. It goes to the seller. However, ensuring that the price I pay covers the externality imposed on you produces the outcome that maximizes total surplus.

An explicit price is not always needed to inhibit an externality. A proxy may suffice. For example, a promise of future beneficial interactions serves to reward politeness. The threat of withholding such interactions discourages bad behavior.

Introducing externalities into a model must be done carefully to ensure that we don't produce preference orderings that violate the assumption of consistency. In the next section we explore the consequences of an externality that is mispriced. Subsequently, we examine possible remedies.

7.1   Pigweed and Dicamba

In the fall of 2016, Michael Wallace, an Arkansas farmer, drove across the Arkansas–Missouri border to meet a farmhand, Allan Curtis Jones. The subject of their meeting was pigweed and Dicamba. Jones brought along his cousin and a gun.

A single pigweed plant can produce more than a million seeds that grow into new plants that choke fields and kill crops like cotton and soybeans. Until the mid-1990s, weedkillers that would eliminate pigweed also destroyed crops. This inspired the development of genetically engineered crops to resist certain kinds of herbicide, like Monsanto's Roundup. They allowed farmers to spray their fields with weedkillers without damaging crops. Monsanto sold the genetically modified seeds and Roundup as a bundle.

A decade after the introduction of Roundup, pigweed evolved into a Roundup-resistant strain. This caused a switch to the herbicide Dicamba, and in 2015 Monsanto introduced a new seed that was resistant to Dicamba. Unfortunately, when Dicamba is sprayed improperly (or an unapproved version of Dicamba is used), the particles drift in the wind and damage neighboring crops that are not resistant to it. The genetically modified seeds allow Dicamba to be sprayed after crops emerge from the ground when it is hotter and more humid. This increases the volatility of Dicamba, turning it into a gas, making it easier to drift onto nearby crops. Even a small percentage of drift can cause widespread damage, which is what prompted the meeting between Wallace and Jones. That meeting escalated into an argument. Wallace, who was not carrying a weapon, grabbed Jones by the arm. Jones pulled away and emptied his magazine into Wallace's body. Wallace bled out on the side of the road, leaving behind a wife and child.

Pesticide drift is an example of mispriced externality. Imagine two neighboring farms called 1 and 2. Farm 1 produces soybeans and x_1 denotes the quantity of soybeans it produces. The production of soybeans on farm 1 uses Dicamba. Let z be the amount of Dicamba that farm 1 employs. Some portion of this drifts onto farm 2, which will raise farm 2's production costs.

Denote by x_2 the quantity of soybeans generated by farm 2. Dicamba drift lowers farm 2's yield and so pushes up farm 2's production costs. Hence, farm 1 imposes a negative externality on farm 2.

Farm 1's total cost as a function of the amount of soybeans produced and Dicamba used is denoted $C_1(x_1, z)$. We assume that $C_1(\cdot, \cdot)$ has the following properties:

1. Total cost should increase with the quantity of soybeans, holding the amount of Dicamba fixed: $\frac{\partial C_1}{\partial x_1} > 0$.
2. Total cost (for a fixed amount of Dicamba) should exhibit decreasing returns to scale: $\frac{\partial^2 C_1}{\partial x_1^2} > 0$.
3. The total cost of producing each fixed amount of soybeans declines with an increase in the use of Dicamba, up to a point. After this point, the total costs increase: $\frac{\partial C_1}{\partial z} < 0$ for small z and $\frac{\partial C_1}{\partial z} > 0$ for large z.
4. Diminishing returns to scale in Dicamba use: $\frac{\partial^2 C_1}{\partial z^2} > 0$.
5. Dicamba use affects the total cost of production but not the marginal cost of production with respect to soybeans: $\frac{\partial^2 C_1}{\partial x_1 \partial z} = 0$.

Farm 2's cost function, denoted $C_2(x_2, z)$, satisfies the following:

1. Total cost should increase with soybean output, holding the amount of Dicamba fixed: $\frac{\partial C_2}{\partial x_2} > 0$.
2. Total costs (for fixed amount of Dicamba) should exhibit decreasing returns to scale: $\frac{\partial^2 C_2}{\partial x_2^2} > 0$.
3. The more Dicamba that farm 1 uses, the higher farm 2's total cost of production: $\frac{\partial C_2}{\partial z} > 0$.

Suppose the market is such that any amount of soybeans from farm 1 can be sold for p_1 per unit and any amount of soybeans from farm 2 can be sold for p_2 per unit. We are allowing for the output of the two farms to fetch different prices, but that is not essential. Given these assumptions we determine what output level each firm will choose when operating independently of the other. For simplicity, we assume that farm 1 moves first, followed by farm 2.[4]

Farm 1 will choose x_1 and z to maximize $p_1 x_1 - C_1(x_1, z)$. By the first-order conditions, the profit-maximizing choice of x_1 and z must satisfy

$$\frac{\partial C_1}{\partial x_1} = p_1, \quad \frac{\partial C_1}{\partial z} = 0. \tag{7.1}$$

The assumptions imposed on $C_1(\cdot, \cdot)$ ensure that the second-order condition holds. Let (x_1^*, z^*) be the profit-maximizing choice for farm 1.

---

[4] The simultaneous-move case would involve the analysis of Nash equilibrium choices without changing the qualitative outcome.

Farm 2 chooses x_2 to maximize $p_2 x_2 - C_2(x_2, z^*)$. Note that farm 2 does not choose the amount of Dicamba employed by farm 1. That is controlled by farm 1. The profit-maximizing choice of x_2 must satisfy the usual first-order condition:

$$\frac{\partial C_2}{\partial x_2} = p_2. \tag{7.2}$$

Again, one can verify that the second-order condition holds. Let x_2^* be the profit-maximizing choice of x_2.

We now compare the output choices made above with the output choice of a central planner whose goal is to maximize the total profit of both farms. The central planner chooses x_1, x_2, and z to solve

$$\max p_1 x_1 + p_2 x_2 - C_1(x_1, z) - C_2(x_2, z)$$

$$\text{s.t. } x_1, x_2, z \geq 0.$$

The first-order conditions for optimality are:

$$\frac{\partial C_1}{\partial x_1} = p_1, \frac{\partial C_2}{\partial x_2} = p_2, \tag{7.3}$$

$$\frac{\partial C_1}{\partial z} + \frac{\partial C_2}{\partial z} = 0. \tag{7.4}$$

Let $(\bar{x}_1, \bar{x}_2, \bar{z})$ be the optimal solution to the central planner's problem. From equation (7.4) and the properties of $C_2(\cdot, \cdot)$, we see that

$$\frac{\partial C_1}{\partial z} = -\frac{\partial C_2}{\partial z} < 0.$$

Because the second derivative of C_1 with respect to z is positive, this implies that $\bar{z} < z^*$. Thus, the optimal solution to the planner's problem does not coincide with (x_1^*, x_2^*, z^*) [i.e. $(\bar{x}_1, \bar{x}_2, \bar{z}) \neq (x_1^*, x_2^*, z^*)$]. Therefore, the total profit of the farms when operating independently is *less* than the total profit generated in the central planner's solution. This is the inefficiency caused by the negative externality that farm 1 imposes on farm 2.[5]

To interpret (7.4), recall that $\frac{\partial C_1}{\partial z}$ and $\frac{\partial C_2}{\partial z}$ have opposite signs for small z. Increasing z decreases farm 1's costs *but* elevates farm 2's costs. Thus, (7.4) shows that the central planner increases z, the amount of Dicamba used, to the point where any further cost savings to farm 1 are exactly offset by the cost increases to farm 2. When the farms act independently of each other, farm 1 (unsurprisingly), in pursuit of its own profits, ignores the impact of its actions on farm 2. In other words, farm 1 does not compare its cost savings from an increase in Dicamba with the increase in farm 2's costs.

The presence of the externality (Dicamba) and the fact that it is not "priced" results in an inefficient mix of outputs. How might we correct it? There are three traditional remedies and we consider each in turn. Under the right conditions, they all produce the same outcome! Thus, which remedy one selects depends on which conditions hold at the time.

---

[5] This should remind you of double marginalization.

7.1.1   Merger

One solution is to merge the farms.[6] The merged farm will choose (x_1, x_2, z) to maximize joint profits just as the central planner would. While this solves the problem posed by the externality, it may create another. As the outputs of farms 1 and 2 are substitutes for each other, merging them would decrease competition in the downstream market that they supply.

7.1.2   Regulation

A second solution is to regulate the amount of Dicamba used by farm 1.[7] In this setting, the regulator would mandate that farm 1 is not permitted to use more than $\bar{z}$ units of Dicamba. Farm 1's optimization problem becomes

$$\max p_1 x_1 - C_1(x_1, z)$$

$$\text{s.t. } 0 \leq z \leq \bar{z}$$

$$x_1 \geq 0.$$

It is straightforward to argue that the solution to this problem will have $z = \bar{z}$.

There are two drawbacks, and the first is that the regulator must know *each* farm's cost curves to determine $\bar{z}$. Farm 1 clearly has an incentive to dissemble when asked to disclose its cost curve. Even if the regulator has a truth serum that could compel honest disclosure, it must be able to monitor farm 1's compliance with the regulation.

Regulation is used to limit the externalities generated by behavior considered anti-social. In 1998, the UK introduced anti-social behavior orders (ASBOs) to be used against persons engaging in such behavior. Examples include spitting, swearing, and public drunkeness.[8]

7.1.3   Taxes

A third solution is to tax farm 1 for Dicamba usage. This is consistent with a common-law principle that a person causing a nuisance, negative externality in our jargon, should be made to pay damages. Is there a tax that would incentivize farm 1 to choose $\bar{z}$ as the amount of Dicamba to use? To find out, suppose we tax farm 1 t units per unit of Dicamba used. Under this tax, farm 1 will choose x_1 and z to solve

$$\max p_1 x_1 - C_1(x_1, z) - tz$$

$$\text{s.t. } x_1, z \geq 0.$$

---

[6] Recall the discussion of double marginalization.

[7] The type of Dicamba used and the manner in which it is sprayed is regulated.

[8] ASBO is used as a term of derision for a person who is rude and disruptive: "Chumley's such an ASBO, I saw him peeing in the fountain the other day."

The first-order conditions for optimality are

$$\frac{\partial C_1}{\partial x_1} = p_1,$$

$$\frac{\partial C_1}{\partial z} + t = 0.$$

If we set $t = \frac{\partial C_2}{\partial z}|_{x_1 = \bar{x}_1, z = \bar{z}}$, then

$$\frac{\partial C_1}{\partial z} + \frac{\partial C_2}{\partial z} = 0.$$

This is precisely (7.4).

Taxation suffers the same drawbacks as regulation. The taxing entity must know enough about farm 1's costs to determine the correct tax. It must also monitor farm 1's Dicamba use so as to collect the tax. Also, what happens to the money raised in taxes?

7.1.4   Externality and Empire

> *Oh! A dreadful man! A Scotchman, richer than Croesus, one McDruggy, fresh from Canton, with a million of opium in each pocket, denouncing corruption, and bellowing free trade.*
>
> Benjamin Disraeli

If one travels north on line number 4 of the Beijing subway, one will arrive at the Yuanmingyuan Park Station. Alighting there, you can make your way to the ruins of the Old Summer Palace that gave its name to the stop. At its zenith, the Palace was the treasure house of the Qing dynasty. Within its confines were priceless manuscripts and the finest porcelain housed in elegant pavilions, nestled in manicured gardens that would put Versailles to shame. Fifty years after conception, it was looted and destroyed by British troops in retribution for the death of 20 British officials at the hands of Prince Yi. One account of Yuanmingyuan's last day comes from the diary of a British officer, G. J. Woolsey:

When we entered the gardens they reminded one of those magic grounds described in fairy tales; we marched out of them upon the 19th of October, leaving them a dreary waste of ruined nothings.

What precipitated the train of events that ended in a "dreary waste"? The Chinese hunger for silver and the British thirst for tea. The historian Peter Way reminds us:

It came from no other place. India did not then produce any, nor Ceylon, Java, or Formosa; Japan was inaccessible; the world perforce drank China teas. Above all, the English drank them.

By the 1800s, Britain, in the persona of the East India Company, had become Imperial China's dominant trading partner. From China issued porcelain, silk, and tea. However, little from Europe interested Chinese consumers. Furthermore, the Qing, suspicious of foreign interlopers, limited both the number and movement of European traders under what came to be called the Canton system.

What the Qing would accept was silver. This required Britain, on the gold standard, to go cap in hand to the continentals for silver. Eventually, the East India Company realized that they could substitute opium cultivated in Bengal for silver. To circumvent the Chinese prohibition on opium, the Company auctioned off opium to independent merchants on condition that it would be exported to China. The opium was offloaded at Lintin Island (on the Pearl River between Honking and Guangdong Province) onto waiting fast boats owned by Chinese traders. By 1825, most of the money needed to buy tea in China was financed by illegal opium. The opium trade enriched the English exchequer to the tune of three million sterling annually.

In 1833, the East India Company lost its monopoly over tea and trade with China. This led, inevitably, to an increase in the supply of opium and a drop in the flow of silver into China. By 1838 the amount of smuggled opium entering China was estimated to be 1400 tons a year, accounting for about one-fifth of Indian revenues for the East India Company. By some estimates, sufficient to supply 10 million addicts.

Starved of the silver needed to finance government and facing a growing problem of widespread addiction, it fell to the Daoguang Emperor to deal with the scourge. His advisors were divided between prohibitionists and those who advocated legalization and taxation. The prohibitionists won, and Lin Zexu, a man with a reputation for probity and unyielding rectitude, was given the task. He ordered a halt to foreign trade and required foreign merchants to forfeit their opium stocks. When they demurred, Lin threatened them with death and immured them within Canton; 3.5 million pounds of opium was seized and dumped into the sea after a ceremony in which Lin Zexu apologized to the sea for polluting it.

In Britain, Lin's actions were framed as an affront to free trade and imperial honor. A view endorsed by John Quincy Adams and Karl Marx, perhaps the first and only time Marx and an American president have been in agreement. Lin, with his Emperor's approval, conveyed a letter to Queen Victoria summarizing China's position. A portion of the letter is telling as it argues that the opium trade imposes a negative externality. It is reproduced below:

But, during the commercial intercourse which has existed so long, among the numerous foreign merchants resorting hither, are wheat and tares, good and bad; and of these latter are some, who, by means of introducing opium by stealth, have seduced our Chinese people, and caused every province of the land to overflow with that poison. These then know merely to advantage themselves, they care not about injuring others! This is a principle which heaven's Providence repugnates; and which mankind conjointly look upon with abhorrence!

The traders in opium did not account for the social cost they imposed on China in counting their profits.

Two years after Lin had poured a fortune into the seas, the British dispatched a fleet of steamers and gunboats up the Yangtze River. End to end it stretched for 3 miles. They returned with trading posts in Amoy, Foochow, Ningpo, and Shanghai, control of Hong Kong, the resumption of trade in opium, and the banishment of Lin Zexu to Turkestan. For the British, this was a sideshow. The cynosure of their eyes was Afghanistan, where an army of retribution was advancing on Kabul to avenge the extirpation of a British expedition earlier that year.

Successive Chinese rulers failed to block the flood of opium. By 1900 it was estimated that China was home to 40 million addicts. The scourge of opium eventually tainted the Imperial family. Short of silver, and saddled with huge trade imbalances with the rest of the world, China gave up the ghost. Opium was legalized and cultivation encouraged. The local competition cut into British profits.[9] Eventually, opium became a major revenue source for the Chinese government.[10] Chiang Kai Shek, for example, used it to fund his regime. By 1937 it was estimated that 10% of the Chinese population was addicted to opium (30% in Hong Kong). Under Japanese occupation, opium consumption was encouraged to ensure a more compliant population. It was not until 1949, when Mao seized power, that opium consumption was brought to heel. Addicts were mewed up and the gates of mercy closed to their suppliers. Opium consumption was effectively eliminated by 1960.

7.2 Coase Theorem

The Nobel Laureate Ronald Coase (1910–2013) suggested that externalities be dealt with in the same way one treats apples, oranges, and coffee. Allow individuals to buy and sell them. Coase went further. He argued that in those cases where government action is necessary, the idea of holding the person responsible for the externality liability is not necessarily correct. We illustrate each idea with a fable that Coase himself used to make these points.

7.2.1 Fable #1

Aubrey makes sweets for sale in the kitchen of his home. Maturin, his neighbor, is a doctor. One day, Maturin decided to build a consulting room in his garden adjacent to Aubrey's kitchen. Upon completion, Maturin discovered that the noise generated by Aubrey in the production of sweets made the consulting room unusable. Maturin brought suit to close down Aubrey's business.

If the law ruled for Maturin, more patients could be treated and production of Aubrey's sweets would be halted. If the law ruled for Aubrey, his sweets would survive while Maturin's medical services would be curtailed. What is the correct ruling? In terms of total surplus, it does not matter. What matters is that the law decides in favor of one of them.

[9] This moved one British official to suggest flooding China with cut-price opium to drive the Chinese producers out.
[10] The other being remittances from Chinese migrant labor and merchants from the sugar plantations of Cuba and Hawaii, as well as the California gold rush.

Fix the status quo to be where neither Aubrey nor Maturin is in business. Suppose Aubrey earns $1000 a month from the sweet business, while Maturin would earn an extra $2000 a month by operating his new consulting room. If the judge rules in Maturin's favor, we (the community) lose sweets but get more medical services. Other things being equal, total surplus increases by $2000 a month. If the judge finds in favor of Aubrey, the outcome is the same. Maturin only has to offer Aubrey $1500 a month[11] (from the $2000 he could make), say, to close down his sweet operation and use his consulting room. He makes $500 a month, but that's better than nothing. The total surplus of society is still increased by $2000. So, the judge's ruling is irrelevant because it does not affect the total surplus of society.[12] The lesson of this example can be summarized as follows: **The initial allocation of legal entitlements does not matter from an efficiency standpoint so long as the transaction costs of their exchange are zero**. The transaction costs of an exchange are the costs associated with negotiating the exchange, monitoring compliance with the terms of the agreement, and so on.

The fable has two implications.

1. In the absence of transaction costs it does not matter how legal entitlements are allocated. An inefficient misallocation of legal entitlements will be corrected by a perfectly competitive marketplace.[13]
2. Ensuring efficiency is a matter of facilitating the trade in these rights. Here is what is required.
   • Legal entitlements must be precisely defined and assigned.
   • Contracts for the exchange of legal entitlements must be enforceable.
   • The transaction costs associated with the exchange of such entitlements should be minimized.
   • There should be a competitive market for the exchange of such entitlements.

Coase's observation applies more generally. Anything can be turned into a legal entitlement, not just the right to pollute. As an illustration, consider how a country might go about privatizing previously nationalized industries. One could, as so often happens, set up an auction and an arduous screening process for bidders to ensure that the industry in question ends up in the hands of the person who will run it in the most efficient way. Coase would suggest something very different. Give the legal entitlement to operate the industry and ownership of the resulting profits to anyone on the street. Hold a lottery. Where effort should be expended instead is on ensuring that the legal entitlement is precisely defined and that it can be freely exchanged. If the winner of the lottery is not the most efficient manager of the enterprise, s/he will be bought out by a more efficient manager.

---

[11] Assume Aubrey accepts.

[12] The ruling does matter to the parties concerned, because their individual incomes are affected.

[13] Thus, the question of who gets what has to be settled on other grounds.

Mispriced Externality Revisited

We examine Coase's proposal in the context of our earlier example of two farms. Trade in Dicamba drift will result in a price, and the question is whether that price will produce the central planner's solution.

Suppose, to begin with, that we give to farm 2 the right to be Dicamba free. Furthermore, if farm 2 wishes, it can sell this right to farm 1 for a price of t per unit of Dicamba discharged.

If farm 2 posts a price of t per unit of Dicamba used, farm 1 will choose x_1 and z to solve

$$\max_{x_1 \geq 0, z \geq 0} p_1 x_1 - C_1(x_1, z) - tz.$$

Observe that this is exactly the same optimization problem that farm 1 faces when Dicamba is taxed. The first-order conditions for optimality are

$$\frac{\partial C_1}{\partial x_1} = p_1, \quad \frac{\partial C_1}{\partial z} + t = 0.$$

Given t and the value of z chosen by farm 1, farm 2 will choose x_2 to maximize its profit:

$$\max_{x_2 \geq 0} p_2 x_2 - C_2(x_2, z) + tz.$$

The first-order optimality conditions for firm 2's problem are

$$\frac{\partial C_2}{\partial x_2} = p_2.$$

There is a choice of t that will mimic the central planner's solution. However, will farm 2 choose that particular value of t? Farm 2 will choose t to maximize *its* profit. It is not obvious that this selection will coincide with that of the central planner. Furthermore, even if it did, farm 2 would have to know farm 1's costs to determine the right choice for t.

Why should farm 2 have the right to be Dicamba free? Perhaps farm 1 should have the right to use Dicamba. Suppose farm 1 has the right to use up to K units of Dicamba. If it wishes, it can yield that right to farm 2 for a price of t per unit. Thus, if farm 1 uses $z \leq K$ units of Dicamba, it has chosen *not* to use $K - z$ units of Dicamba. We can think of these "missing" $K - z$ units being sold to farm 2 for a price of t per unit.

Given t, farm 2 will choose x_2 and z to maximize

$$\max_{x_2 \geq 0, K \geq z \geq 0} p_2 x_2 - C_2(x_2, z) - t(K - z).$$

Notice that farm 2 is controlling the amount of Dicamba used by farm 1. The first-order conditions for optimality are

$$\frac{\partial C_2}{\partial x_2} = p_2, \quad \frac{\partial C_2}{\partial z} - t = 0.$$

For a fixed t, farm 1 will take farm 2's choice of z as given and choose x_1 to solve

$$\max_{x_1 \geq 0} p_1 x_1 - C_1(x_1, z) + t(K - z).$$

The first-order conditions for optimality are

$$\frac{\partial C_1}{\partial x_1} = p_1.$$

Once again, we see that an appropriate choice of t will mimic the central planner's solution.

7.2.2   Fable #2

Coase went on to consider what happens when transaction costs are sufficiently large to prevent trade from producing the efficient outcome. In these cases, there is a role for government intervention, usually in the form of the courts. In these cases, how should the courts decide? Once again, an example.

Consider a railway track through a stretch of land, portions of which are owned by different farmers. The railway company runs a coal-burning locomotive along the tracks which emits sparks that, on occasion, set fire to farmers' crops. The railway company and the farmers (because there are so many of them) cannot settle in the manner of Aubrey and Maturin (i.e. the transaction costs of the negotiation are very high). The courts step in.

If the railroad is made liable for the damage caused by the sparks, it will respond by running fewer trains or installing spark-control equipment. If the railroad is not made liable, the farmers will respond by shifting their crops away from the tracks, say. Which should it be?

Suppose running the train yields $1000 worth of profit but causes $2000 worth of crop damage. Hence, running the train reduces total wealth. To prevent this, we need to have the railway company internalize the cost of the damage inflicted by making them liable.

On the contrary, is it not reasonable to blame the farmers for their foolishness in leaving their crops by the railway track. If you think this strange, suppose that it only costs the farmers $100 to ensure the safety of their crops. If we make the railroad liable, what happens? The railroad stops running, and the farmers do not take precautions to secure their crops. Let us assign this state a total wealth of W. Now suppose we make the farmers liable. The train runs, increasing wealth by $1000. The farmers will now pay $100 to safeguard their crops, so total wealth decreases by $100. In sum, the total wealth under the second regime is $W + \$900$. So, we are better off making the farmers liable.

Were the numbers reversed, we would have made the railroad liable. That's the point. Cause of damage is irrelevant. It's who has the lower cost of avoiding the damage that's important. Steven Landsburg puts it very well:

And so we come to the flip side of the Coase Theorem. When circumstances prevent negotiations, entitlements – liability rules, property rights, and so forth – do matter. Moreover, the traditional economist's prescription for efficiency – making each individual fully responsible for the costs he imposes on others – is meaningless. It is meaningless because the costs in question result from conflicts between two activities, not from either activity in isolation. The traditional prescription blinds us to the fact that either party to a conflict might be in possession of the efficient solution, and that the wrong liability rule can eliminate the incentive to implement that solution.

In the story of the railroad and the farmers, we compared only two possibilities; the railroad pays or the farmers pay. A third possibility is to have the farmers and the railroad share the costs of avoiding the damage. If the least cost of avoiding the damage was known to all, the only issue would be how to divide it between the two parties. The appropriate division is a matter of equity, not economics. Suppose now that the courts knew who had the lower cost of avoiding the damage, but not its actual value. In this case dividing up the cost becomes difficult and it is easier to assign liability exclusively to one party. See Section 7.3 for a more extensive discussion.

7.2.3   Transaction Costs

The most startling implication of Coase's argument is that in a world with no transaction costs it matters not at all how we choose to organize the production and exchange of goods and services.[14] For example, in our world, when one wants a new car, one goes to a car dealership and picks from the models available. An alternative arrangement would be to contract with an automotive designer to design the car. Next one would contract with a steel manufacturer, a tire manufacturer, a plastic manufacturer, an electrician, a mechanic, and so on to get the parts to actually build the car. Why don't we see such an arrangement? Coase tells us why: transaction costs. The costs associated with negotiating all these separate contracts and then monitoring compliance become prohibitive for one person. If one wishes to explain why economic activity is organized one way rather than another, follow the transaction costs.

As an example, let us list some of the transaction costs associated with the purchase of a secondhand car:

- Identifying a seller of the type of car one is interested in.
- The cost of verifying that the car is in the condition the buyer expects.
- The cost of ensuring the buyer will pay the agreed amount.

If these costs are higher than what each of us could gain from the trade, there will be no exchange. Since the sale of cars is a common occurrence, how does society organize itself so as to reduce these transaction costs. Casual observation suggests the answer. Classified advertisements, having a mechanic check the car, requiring a certified check, and so on. In summary, Coase provides an explanation, in terms of transaction costs, for the existence of particular institutional arrangements.

---

[14] How legal entitlements to property and so on are assigned determines how the economy is organized.

7.3   Public Goods

If one accepts that externalities should be handled by defining appropriate property rights and letting the market trade them, is it always possible to set up a perfectly competitive market to do so? No. An important instance is the provision of a public good. A public good is not simply a good or service that generates a positive externality. This bears repeating:

1. Public goods are not goods supplied to the public.
2. Public goods are not goods the public would like to consume.
3. Public goods are not goods that it would be good for the public to have.

A **pure public good** must generate a positive externality, be **non-rivalrous** *and* **non-excludable**. Non-rivalrous means consumption by one does not materially reduce availability of the good or service to others. Non-excludable means that it is impossible to exclude anyone from enjoying the benefits of the good.

Perfect examples of pure public goods are hard to find, but there are many that come close. First up, the quadratic formula. If I need to explain why it generates a positive externality, you should not be reading this book. It is non-rivalrous, because one person using it does not prevent another from using it. Is it non-excludable? Technically, yes. If I know the formula and you don't, I can keep it secret from you. This is not as outlandish as it seems. In sixteenth-century Italy it was not unusual for mathematicians to challenge each other to duels. Each gave the other an equation to solve. Whichever solved his rival's problem in the set time (usually 30 days) won. To the winner, fortune and glory.

Scipione del Ferro, a leading mathematician of the day, was frequently challenged. The "ace up his sleeve" was a formula for the solution of a certain type of cubic called the "depressed cubic." He did not publish the solution, but did share it with a small circle of his students, among them one Antonio Fiore. Enter, stage left, Nicholas Tartaglia, who had discovered a formula to solve *all* cubic equations. del Ferro, now dead, could not be challenged. So Tartaglia trained his sights on the student, Fiore. Tartaglia won.

Tartaglia was subsequently approached by Gerolamo Cardano, who wished to publish Tartaglia's secret in his textbook. Tartaglia declined. Cardano, undeterred, scoured the available mathematical literature of the day and found Scipione del Ferro's notebooks. In them, Cardano discovered that del Ferro had had all the ingredients to find a formula to solve all cubic equations. He, del Ferro, had not put them together. Cardano published his discovery, to the consternation of Tartaglia. In response, Tartaglia challenged Cardano to a duel. Cardano deflected the challenge onto his student Lodovico Ferrari. Ferrari possessed the solution to the quartic! Tartaglia lost and died penniless. Ferrari went on to fortune and glory, retiring as a professor at the University of Bologna.

Thus, the quadratic formula, and the scientific ideas, are excludable in the short run, but in the long run the secret leaks out or is discovered by others.[15]

The next candidate for consideration is breathable air. Assuming the earth can renew the oxygen we need fast enough, my breathing does not prevent you from breathing. So, the non-rivalrous condition is met. I cannot exclude you from breathing, except by force, which we rule out. Thus, the non-excludability condition is met. However, were humans to live upon an airless planet, they might rely on breathable air that is sold in bottles. In that case, breathable air would be rivalrous and excludable.

The third candidate is national defense. My enjoyment of the benefits conferred by national security does not diminish the enjoyment of my fellow citizens of the same. Thus, it is non-rivalrous. Is it excludable? Certainly those who live beyond the nation's boundaries are excluded. One might even exclude those living within the nation's borders by exile.

While we may never find a perfect example of a public good, the illustrations above suggest that we can come close. Thus, it is more useful to think about what constitutes a pure public good in terms of three questions:

1. What is the positive externality and who benefits from it?
2. Who can reasonably be excluded from enjoying the externality?
3. Is there a perceptible decline in the benefit with an increase in the number of people who enjoy it?

Let us apply these questions to the decision to vaccinate one's children against, say, smallpox. There is an immediate benefit to the child from dramatically reducing the risk of infection by smallpox. The positive externality is that it reduces the chance of infection for those who come into contact with the child. Could one exclude others from enjoying this externality? Yes, by denying them access to the child. However, this is the same as denying the child access to others. In principle possible, but practically impossible. One cannot, for example, approach the child's school and dictate who will or will not be a classmate. So, the assumption of non-excludability seems reasonable here. Is it non-rivalrous? It is important to distinguish between the vaccine and the externality. The vaccine is rivalrous. The child's consumption of the vaccine prevents another from consuming it. The externality, however, is non-rivalrous. Why? The fact that one classmate sees a reduction in the risk of infection does not prevent another from enjoying the same reduction.[16]

In the next two subsections of this chapter we examine the difficulties associated with relying on a market to provide a public good. The first example considers the problems that a monopolist faces when providing a public good. The second considers the possibility of a perfectly competitive market providing the public good.

---

[15] And, as noted by Spock, "Military secrets are the most fleeting of all."

[16] There is a caveat. The probability of infection is density dependent. Thus more people interacting simultaneously with the vaccinated child increases the risk of infection.

7.3.1   News

Does the news generate a universal positive externality? Those who suspect that the news may reveal something they would rather remain secret would say no. Others are indifferent to the news altogether. Nevertheless, a sufficient number appear to value the news, so let's limit attention to them.

Modern technology and web services like the Huffington Post and Google have made news non-excludable. The media baron Rupert Murdoch, for instance, called Google and other search engines content kleptomaniacs. Consumption of the news is clearly non-rivalrous. Under these conditions can one make money from running a newspaper?

Suppose that it costs C to produce a newspaper of a particular type. The cost C is not the cost of distribution, anyone can open a news site and distribute stories these days. Think of C as the cost of research and investigation. There are n potential readers of the newspaper. Let v_i be the RP of reader i for access to that type of newspaper. The question that concerns us is, how should the newspaper price its product?

Let's formalize this as a game with the following steps:

1. The newspaper announces a pricing schedule.
2. Each reader makes a decision to accept the price or not.
3. If total revenue raised is at least C, the newspaper is produced, otherwise not.

Suppose the newspaper had the power to charge each reader i a price of v_i (i.e. engage in perfect price discrimination). If $\sum_{i=1}^{n} v_i > C$, the newspaper would generate sufficient revenue to cover the cost and have some left over. Suppose each reader is offered a newspaper at a price equal to their RP. Is there a Nash equilibrium in which sufficient revenue from readers alone can be collected to support the newspaper?

Suppose everyone buys the newspaper. The surplus of each reader will be zero. Consider reader #1, say. If she chooses not to buy the newspaper, she continues to enjoy the benefits of the newspaper as long as the revenue from the remaining paying readers covers C. This is because the news is non-excludable and non-rivalrous. Her surplus from dropping out will be v_1, which is clearly larger than zero. However, if her dropping out would cause the newspaper to fold, her surplus would remain the same (i.e. zero). Hence, if there is an equilibrium where the newspaper is provided, it must be the case that all those choosing to buy the newspaper collectively pay *exactly* C. Furthermore, they are exactly indifferent between buying and not. At best the newspaper can only break even! If $v_i \leq C$ for all i, no reader by themselves has an incentive to support the paper, so there is another Nash equilibrium: no reader choosing to buy the newspaper.

This is rather bleak and one might wonder if it is caused by charging every reader their RP. Let's consider another possibility, where the newspaper announces a uniform price p. Let $D(p)$ be the number of readers with an RP of at least p (i.e. the demand curve for news). The newspaper will be in business provided there is a value of p such that $pD(p) \geq C$. To ensure that no reader with an RP of at least p chooses to opt out, we need $(D(p) - 1)p < C$. In words, if this reader chooses not to purchase, the remaining readers are insufficient to support the paper and so it folds. In other words, the newspaper is within one paying reader of breaking even. A precarious situation.

We have a service whose collective value exceeds the cost of providing it, yet those who benefit from it don't have a compelling incentive to pay for it. It is a manifestation of the phenomenon called **free riding** that always arises with the provision of a public good. Because none can be excluded from enjoying the benefits, each has an incentive to avoid paying their share of the cost of provision. If I know you will pay for the provision of the good, I am better off sitting on my hands. I get the benefit and pay nothing!

How does a newspaper looking to survive overcome this?

1. Rely on a benefactor to subsidize the paper. Such an individual may be strongly tempted to "distort" the news reported.[17] They are entitled to do this, but it will diminish the benefits enjoyed by readers. This lowers the revenue that can be collected from them, in turn pushing up the need for cash injections from the benefactor.
2. Rely on advertising (i.e. multiple benefactors). As long as no one benefactor is dominant, it diminishes the ability of any one of them to distort the news.
3. Making the news an excludable good through the use of pay walls. However, once I read a "man bites dog" story, nothing prevents me or CNN from sharing the details with millions of others via social media or TV.
4. Cut costs. For example, reduce investments in research and reporting.
5. Bundling the news with the delivery mechanism (i.e. internet access). A firm that both controls internet access and provides news would be able to make news excludable.

The second strategy has been the one that newspapers have relied on, but no longer. The decline in print advertising has not been offset by revenue from on-line ads. In 2011 newspaper advertising globally amounted to $76 billion, down 41% since 2007. Only 2.2% of newspapers' advertising revenues in 2012 came from on-line platforms.[18]

7.3.2 Vaccination

In many countries vaccinations for certain diseases are mandated rather than voluntary. Why might this be the case? Suppose the cost (both actual and psychic) of vaccination to a family is $1 and the benefit to the child and family from vaccination is $0.75. Let $2 denote the value of the positive externality (from reducing the risk of infection via contagion) enjoyed by others from one's child being vaccinated.

---

[17] In 2016, billionaire Sheldon Adelson bought the *Las Vegas Review-Journal*. After Adelson failed to have a judge removed from a contentious lawsuit that threatened his business, journalists were told they must monitor the courtroom actions of the judge and two others in the city. Billionaire Jeff Bezos bought the *Washington Post* in 2013. He suggested creating a premium feature that would allow readers to remove all the vowels from a story they didn't like.

[18] These figures are from the World Association of Newspapers.

Then, the efficient outcome is for the child to be vaccinated because total surplus is $2 + 0.75 - 1 > 0$, which exceeds the total surplus from not being vaccinated, which is normalized to zero. However, if we leave the decision in the parent's hands, they will choose not to vaccinate because $0.75 < 1$ (i.e. the personal cost exceeds the individual benefit). Recall that the family does not enjoy the benefit of $2. This goes to others, outside the family. Thus, the presence of the unpriced externality leads to an inefficient outcome.

Compulsory vaccination is a solution, but is it the only one? One could define a property right that could be traded. Perhaps a right not to be vaccinated, formalized in the form of a permit with the child's name. Either one shows the child has been vaccinated, or one exhibits the permit with that child's name. If the family keeps the permit, they choose not to vaccinate their child. If the family sells the permit to another, they receive a payment and in turn must vaccinate the child. So, the parent of another child who attends school with yours could pay you to have your child vaccinated. Will a market for permits produce the surplus-maximizing outcome?

Suppose there are n families and each incurs a cost of c from being vaccinated.[19] Vaccination does not provide 100% protection against infection, but the more who are vaccinated, the better off each family is (vaccinated or not). Let $B(k)$ denote the benefit enjoyed by each family (vaccinated or not) when exactly k families receive the vaccination. We will suppose that $B(k)$ is increasing in k. Furthermore, for all $k < n$ we want

$$nB(n) - nc > kB(k) - kc.$$

In words, the net benefit of everyone being vaccinated exceeds the net benefit of fewer than n families being vaccinated.

We will make two important assumptions about the benefit function B. First, there are diminishing marginal benefits as the number of families who get vaccinated increases. This can be formalized as follows:

$$B(n) - B(n-1) \le B(n-1) - B(n-2) \le \cdots \le B(1) - B(0).$$

In words, the marginal benefit of going from zero to one family vaccinated is greater than the benefit of going from two to three, and so on. In particular, we are going to assume that

$$B(n) - B(n-1) < c. \tag{7.5}$$

That is, the incremental benefit to the last family to be vaccinated is less than the cost of vaccination. Our second assumption is

$$n[B(n) - B(n-1)] > c. \tag{7.6}$$

To interpret inequality (7.6), observe that $nB(n)$ is the total benefit if all families get vaccinated, while $nB(n-1)$ is the total benefit if only $n-1$ families are vaccinated.

---

[19] This cost can be purely psychic.

Therefore, inequality (7.6) says that the increase in *total* benefits from the last family being vaccinated exceeds the cost of vaccination c. Taken together, these assumptions say that the last family to get vaccinated does not get much of a benefit relative to the cost of vaccination, but confers a huge benefit on everyone else.

Suppose we make the decision to be vaccinated entirely voluntarily, what will the outcome be? We can answer this question by modeling the decision to get vaccinated or not as a simultaneous-move game. Each family simultaneously and independently decides whether to get vaccinated. Thus, each family has two strategies: vaccinate (V) or not (N). We ask if there is a Nash equilibrium of this game where everyone chooses V.

If every family chooses V, then family #1, say, enjoys a surplus of $B(n) - c$. Holding the choices of the other families fixed, would family #1 benefit from choosing N instead? It would be $B(n-1)$. Notice, by (7.5), $B(n-1) > B(n) - c$. Therefore, its payoff is higher from choosing N. Given that the other families have chosen V, family #1 is better off choosing N instead. Hence, the surplus-maximizing outcome cannot arise as a Nash equilibrium. This is because no family takes into account the benefit they confer on the other families when they choose to get vaccinated. It suggests that making the vaccination decision voluntary is unlikely to result in the surplus-maximizing outcome.

Let us examine whether trade in the permits will "solve the problem." Suppose the price to buy or sell a permit is set at p. If a family buys one permit but does not sell its permit, it must pay p but does not have to vaccinate. In return, the family that sells its permit must vaccinate.

Is there a price p where we achieve the surplus-maximizing outcome where everyone gets vaccinated? If there is such a price, everyone must sell their permit. In order to clear the market, the permits sold must all be bought. Consider family #1. Suppose it sold its permit and bought some number d from other families. Its benefit is

$$B(n) + p - c - dp.$$

Among all the purchase decisions it could make, this should maximize its benefit. In particular, what if it decided to sell its permit but only buy $(d-1)$ permits from others. Then it would enjoy

$$B(n-1) + p - c - (d-1)p.$$

As buying d permits was supposed to maximize the benefit of family #1, it must be that

$$B(n) + p - c - dp \geq B(n-1) + p - c - (d-1)p \implies B(n) - B(n-1) \geq c.$$

However, this contradicts (7.6).

Is there another scheme that might work? What if the government were to auction off such permits to the highest bidder? The first challenge is to decide on the number of permits that will be made available. If the number of permits equals or exceeds the number of children, they will sell for zero. If the number of permits is less than the number of children, how much less should it be? It should be set at the level where the marginal benefit of vaccinating one more child equals the marginal cost (these include the psychic elements associated with the fear of vaccination) of one more vaccination. It is unclear how one would determine this. Also, what would happen to the money raised by the auction? In the next section we will argue that the difficulties raised here are not unique to vaccines but are more widespread.

7.4   The Public Goods Problem

> *Out of the crooked timber of humanity, no straight thing was ever made.*
>   Immanuel Kant

It will be useful to summarize where we are. Under the price-taking assumption and in the absence of externalities, competitive markets deliver outcomes that in a sense cannot be improved upon (Pareto optimal and cost minimizing). If externalities are present, they can be "priced in" by defining a property right and setting up a competitive market for the exchange of that right. We have seen with the vaccine example that a perfectly competitive market is not guaranteed to provide a public good even if it is efficient to do so. The newspaper example shows that a monopolist cannot do so either. If the market (imperfect or otherwise) cannot provide the public good, can government? Of course it can, but as will be argued here, it faces the same difficulties that the market does.

Suppose C is the cost of providing a public good that will benefit two agents, $i = 1, 2$. Let b_i be the benefit enjoyed by citizen i from the public good for $i = 1, 2$.

A government focused on efficiency should provide the good if $b_1 + b_2 \geq C$ and not otherwise. This requires that the government determine the b_is, verify that their total exceeds the cost of provision, and if so decide who should pay how much for the public good.

At minimum there are three desirable features we might want of any scheme for government provision of the public good. These are listed below:

1. Efficiency: only build if $b_1 + b_2 \geq C$.
2. Budget balance: if the good is to be provided, the government should raise exactly enough money to cover the cost of provision.
3. Individual rationality: if built, no agent should be charged more than the benefit they enjoy.

We shall argue that satisfying all three in *every* instance is impossible. This means that if the government chooses to provide a public good, there will be occasions when it will spend more than the benefit provided, spend more than the cost of provision, or charge some agents more than the benefit they enjoy. This is the public goods problem.

To see why it is impossible for the government (or indeed anyone) to come up with a scheme that *always* satisfies the three conditions above, suppose, for a contradiction, that there is such a scheme. Suppose also that the benefits are such that $b_1 + b_2 > C$.

As the conjectured scheme satisfies efficiency, it must provide the public good in this instance. As the conjectured scheme satisfies individual rationality, each agent must be charged a price that does not exceed his or her benefit. In particular, agent i must be charged a price $p_i \leq b_i$ for $i = 1, 2$. As the conjectured scheme satisfies budget balance, $p_1 + p_2 = C$. As $C < b_1 + b_2$, it means that either $p_1 < b_1$ or $p_2 < b_2$, or both. So, suppose $p_2 < b_2$.

Now consider how the conjectured scheme will operate if agent 1's benefit is not b_1 but $p_1 - \epsilon$ instead, where $\epsilon = b_2 - p_2$. In this instance, the total benefit would be

$$p_1 - \epsilon + b_2 = C - p_2 - \epsilon + b_2 = C - p_2 - b_2 + p_2 + b_2 = C.$$

Hence, according to efficiency, the public good will be provided. In this case, by individual rationality, agent 1 must be charged no more than $p_2 - \epsilon$.

Return to the original instance where agent 1 enjoys a benefit of b_1. Agent 1 can anticipate that if she reports her benefit as $p_1 - \epsilon$ instead, the public good will still be provided and she will be charged less than she would in the original instance. Hence, agent 1 has an incentive to shade her reported benefit down from its actual value. In fact, agent 1 has an incentive to report that her benefit is $C - b_2$. As the total *reported* benefit will exactly match the cost of provision, the public good will be provided. By individual rationality, agent 1 cannot be charged more than $C - b_2$. Agent 2 is subject to the same temptation. She will report a benefit of $C - b_1$. But this means that the total amount charged to the agents cannot exceed

$$C - b_1 + C - b_2 < C.$$

In other words, budget balance is violated!

We can formalize the argument above in the following way. The conjectured scheme sets up a game between the two agents in which a strategy consists of reporting one's benefit. In this game we ask if there is a (Nash) equilibrium where each of the agents truthfully reports their benefits. Unfortunately, as shown above, there is not.

Appendix A: Optimization

This is not a comprehensive account, but an *aide memoire*. The reader is expected to have covered this material in depth in a calculus class.

A.1   Single Variable Unconstrained

We are interested in solving the following optimization problem: $\max_x f(x)$. In words, find the value of x that maximizes $f(x)$. If f is differentiable, we identify a candidate optimal by first differentiating f with respect to x and setting the derivative to zero:

$$\frac{df}{dx} = 0. \tag{A.1}$$

Let x^* be a solution to equation (A.1) (there might be more than one). If there is no solution to (A.1), then there is no solution to our initial optimization problem. Note that equation (A.1) is called a first-order condition (FOC). The FOC is a necessary condition for optimality but not a sufficient one.

Now, x^* is a *possible* solution to our optimization problem. To verify that it is, we must check the sign of the second derivative of f. If the second derivative of f is at most zero for all possible values of x, then x^* is an optimal solution to our optimization problem. This step is called the second derivative test, or second-order condition (SOC).

A.2   Single Variable Constrained

We are interested in solving the following optimization problem:

$$\max f(x)$$

$$\text{s.t. } a \leq x \leq b.$$

First, we ignore the constraints $a \leq x \leq b$ and solve the unconstrained problem. If the solution to the unconstrained problem, x^* say, satisfies $a \leq x^* \leq b$, we have found the optimal solution to the constrained problem.

If the solution to the unconstrained problem does not lie between a and b, and there is no solution to the FOC in the interval $[a, b]$, the problem becomes more difficult. In many economic applications the function f will be non-decreasing. We can check to see if f is non-decreasing by examining the sign of its derivative in the interval $[a, b]$. It should of course be non-negative. By the fact that f is non-decreasing, we deduce that $x = b$ must solve our problem. This is sometimes called a "corner" or "boundary" solution.

Example 55 *Solve*

$$\max \ln x^2$$

$$\text{s.t. } 2 \leq x \leq 5.$$

Answer: *The optimal solution is $x = 5$.*

Justification: *Observe that $\frac{df}{dx} = 1/x^2 \cdot 2x = 2/x$. This can never have value zero in the interval $[2, 5]$. In fact, for all $x \in [2, 5]$, $\frac{df}{dx} > 0$. Thus, $f(x)$ is strictly increasing on $[2, 5]$. Hence, the maximum of f is achieved when $x = 5$.* □

A.3   Two Variables Unconstrained

We are interested in solving the following optimization problem: $\max_{x,y} f(x, y)$. We first use the FOCs to identify a candidate solution. Specifically, we look for (x^*, y^*) that solve

$$\frac{\partial f}{\partial x} = 0 = \frac{\partial f}{\partial y}.$$

Once again, this is only a necessary condition for optimality. To verify whether (x^*, y^*) are indeed optimal, we must check the SOCs. For local optima this reduces to checking (1) whether diagonal entries of the following matrix (called the Hessian) evaluated at the critical point (x^*, y^*) are negative for maximization problems (or positive for minimization problems) and (2) whether the determinant of the Hessian evaluated at the critical point (x^*, y^*) is positive. For global optima the previous two conditions must be satisfied in all the domain of the function [i.e. $\forall (x, y) \in \mathbb{R}^2$]. Let

$$H = \begin{bmatrix} f_{xx} & f_{xy} \\ f_{yx} & f_{yy} \end{bmatrix}.$$

Here $f_{xx} = \frac{\partial^2 f}{\partial x^2}, f_{yy} = \frac{\partial^2 f}{\partial y^2}, f_{yx} = \frac{\partial^2 f}{\partial x \partial y}, f_{xy} = \frac{\partial^2 f}{\partial y \partial x}$. The determinant of H is $f_{xx}f_{yy} - f_{xy}f_{yx}$. To summarize:

1. Local maximum

$$f_{xx}\big|_{x=x^*, y=y^*} < 0,$$

$$f_{yy}\big|_{x=x^*, y=y^*} < 0,$$

$$\left[f_{xx}f_{yy} - f_{xy}f_{yx}\right]\big|_{x=x^*, y=y^*} > 0.$$

2. Global maximum

$$f_{xx}|_{x,y} < 0 \quad \forall (x, y) \in \mathbb{R}^2,$$
$$f_{yy}|_{x,y} < 0 \quad \forall (x, y) \in \mathbb{R}^2,$$
$$[f_{xx}f_{yy} - f_{xy}f_{yx}]|_{x,y} > 0 \quad \forall (x, y) \in \mathbb{R}^2.$$

3. Local minimum

$$f_{xx}|_{x=x^*, y=y^*} > 0,$$
$$f_{yy}|_{x=x^*, y=y^*} > 0,$$
$$[f_{xx}f_{yy} - f_{xy}f_{yx}]|_{x=x^*, y=y^*} > 0.$$

4. Global minimum

$$f_{xx}|_{x,y} > 0 \quad \forall (x, y) \in \mathbb{R}^2,$$
$$f_{yy}|_{x,y} > 0 \quad \forall (x, y) \in \mathbb{R}^2,$$
$$[f_{xx}f_{yy} - f_{xy}f_{yx}]|_{x,y} > 0 \quad \forall (x, y) \in \mathbb{R}^2.$$

5. Saddle point

$$[f_{xx}f_{yy} - f_{xy}f_{yx}]|_{x=x^*, y=y^*} < 0.$$

6. Inconclusive

$$[f_{xx}f_{yy} - f_{xy}f_{yx}]|_{x=x^*, y=y^*} = 0.$$

Example 56 *Find the minima of the following function:* $f(x, y) = 3x^2 + y^2 - 2xy - 4y$.

Answer: *There is a unique global minimum at* $(1, 3)$.

Justification: *First, use first-order conditions to find the critical points:*

$$\frac{\partial f}{\partial x} = 6x - 2y = 0,$$
$$\frac{\partial f}{\partial y} = 2y - 2x - 4 = 0,$$
$$\Rightarrow (1, 3) \text{ is the only critical point.}$$

Second, calculate the Hessian matrix:

$$H = \begin{bmatrix} 6 & -2 \\ -2 & 2 \end{bmatrix}, \quad \forall (x, y).$$

Its determinant is positive everywhere, and both diagonal entries are positive. Therefore, (1,3) is a global minimum. □

A.4   Two-Variable Equality Constraint

We are interested in solving the following optimization problem:

$$\max f(x, y)$$

$$\text{s.t. } ax + by = c.$$

There are two approaches that can be used.

A.4.1   Method of Elimination

Take one of the variables, y say, and use the equality constraint to write it in terms of the other: $y = \frac{c-ax}{b}$. Then, substitute it into the function whose value we are trying to maximize. The optimization problem becomes

$$\max f\left(x, \frac{c-ax}{b}\right).$$

This is an unconstrained optimization problem in a single variable.

Example 57 *Find the values of x and y that solve the following maximization problem:*

$$\max f(x, y) = (9x + 2y)^3$$

$$\text{s.t. } 4x + y = 1.$$

Answer: *This problem does not have a solution.*

Justification: *Solve for y as a function of x using the constraint*

$$y = 1 - 4x.$$

Substitute it into the objective function:

$$\max(9x + 2(1 - 4x))^3 = \max(2 + x)^3.$$

This is increasing in x. As x is unrestricted in sign, we would just set $x = \infty$.   □

A.4.2   Method of Lagrange Multipliers

Write down the Lagrangian

$$L(x, y, \lambda) = f(x, y) + \lambda(c - ax - by).$$

Find the values of x, y, and λ that solve this unconstrained problem. The FOCs are

$$\frac{\partial f}{\partial x} - \lambda a = 0,$$

$$\frac{\partial f}{\partial y} - \lambda b = 0,$$

$$c - ax - by = 0.$$

Any candidate for an optimal solution must be a solution to this system of equations. Let (x^*, y^*, λ^*) be a solution to the FOCs; there can be more than one. Therefore, we must check the SOC. This will involve checking the sign of the determinant of a matrix called the bordered Hessian. In general, it takes the following form:

$$\begin{bmatrix} L_{x^*x^*} & L_{x^*y^*} & L_{x^*\lambda^*} \\ L_{y^*x^*} & L_{y^*y}^* & L_{y^*\lambda^*} \\ L_{\lambda^*x^*} & L_{\lambda^*y^*} & L_{\lambda^*\lambda^*} \end{bmatrix}.$$

For the particular version of the problem we are interested in, it simplifies to

$$\begin{bmatrix} L_{x^*x^*} & L_{x^*y^*} & -a \\ L_{y^*x^*} & L_{y^*y}^* & -b \\ -a & -b & 0 \end{bmatrix}.$$

One computes the determinant of the bordered Hessian at the critical point (x^*, y^*, λ^*). If the sign of the determinant is positive (negative), then the critical point is a local maximum (local minimum).

If there is more than one critical point where the sign of the determinant of the bordered Hessian is positive, the critical point with the highest value of $f(\cdot, \cdot)$ is the maximizer.

If the function $f(x, y)$ being maximized satisfies an additional condition called quasi-concavity (convexity), then any local maximum (minimum) is in fact a global maximum (minimum). This condition is discussed in detail in Chapter 6.

Example 58 *Find the values of x and y that solve*

$$\max xy^4$$

$$\text{s.t. } x + 5y = 10.$$

Answer: $(x^*, y^*) = (2, 1.6).$

Justification *Set up the Lagrangian*

$$L = xy^4 + \lambda(10 - x - 5y).$$

Differentiate w.r.t. x, y, and λ:

$$\partial L/\partial x : y^4 - \lambda = 0, \tag{A.2}$$

$$\partial L/\partial y : 4xy^3 - 5\lambda = 0, \tag{A.3}$$

$$\partial L/\partial \lambda : x + 5y = 10. \tag{A.4}$$

Examining (A.2)–(A.4) we see that there cannot be a solution where at least one of the three variables x, y, λ is zero. Hence, in any solution x, y, λ > 0. This allows us to divide (A.3) by (A.2) to obtain

$$\frac{4xy^3}{y^4} = \frac{5\lambda}{\lambda} \Rightarrow y = 0.8x.$$

If we substitute this into (A.4), we deduce that $x^* = 2, y^* = 1.6, \lambda^* = 6.55$.
Therefore, there is just one critical point. If we determine that it is a local maximum,
we know that it will be a global maximum.

To determine if our critical point is a local maximum, we must verify the SOC.
That requires the bordered Hessian

$$\begin{bmatrix} 0 & 4y^3 & -1 \\ 4y^3 & 12xy^2 & -5 \\ -1 & -5 & 0 \end{bmatrix}.$$

When evaluated at $x^* = 2, y^* = 1.6, \lambda^* = 6.55$, this becomes

$$\begin{bmatrix} 0 & 16.384 & -1 \\ 16.384 & 61.44 & -5 \\ -1 & -5 & 0 \end{bmatrix}.$$

The determinant of this matrix is 102.40 (i.e. positive). Hence, $x^* = 2, y^* = 1.6$ is a
global maximum.   □

Example 59 *Find the values of x and y that solve the following:*

$$\max x^2 + y^2$$

$$\text{s.t. } x + y = 4.$$

Answer: *There is no solution.*

Justification: *The FOC gives us $x^* = y^* = 2$ and $\lambda^* = 4$. The bordered Hessian is*

$$\begin{bmatrix} 2 & 0 & -1 \\ 0 & 2 & -1 \\ -1 & -1 & 0 \end{bmatrix}.$$

It is straightforward to verify that the determinant has the wrong sign, so $(2,2)$ is not
a solution. In fact, the optimization problem has no solution! One can see this by
making x very large and y very negative (but ensuring that $y = x - 4$).   □

A.5   Two-Variable Equality Constraint with Non-negativity

We are interested in solving the following optimization problem:

$$\max f(x, y)$$

$$\text{s.t. } ax + by = c$$

$$x, y \geq 0.$$

There are two approaches that can be used.

A.5.1 Method of Elimination

Take one of the variables, y say, and use the equality constraint to write it in terms of the other: $y = \frac{c-ax}{b}$. Assume $b > 0$. However, we must not forget that $y \geq 0$, so

$$y = \frac{c-ax}{b} \geq 0 \Rightarrow x \leq \frac{c}{a}.$$

Then, substitute the expression for y in terms of x into the function whose value we are trying to maximize. The optimization problem becomes

$$\max f\left(x, \frac{c-ax}{b}\right)$$

$$\text{s.t. } 0 \leq x \leq \frac{c}{a}.$$

This is a constrained optimization problem with a single variable.

Example 60 *Find the values of x and y that solve the following maximization problem:*

$$\max(3.5x + y)^3$$

$$\text{s.t. } x + 2y = 1$$

$$x \geq 0, y \geq 0.$$

Answer: $(x^*, y^*) = (1, 0)$.

Justification: *Solve for y as a function of x using the constraint*

$$y = 1/2(1 - x).$$

Substitute it into the objective function:

$$\max(3.5x + (1/2)(1 - x))^3 = \max(1/2 + 3x)^3$$

which is increasing in x.
   x is bounded above because

$$y = (1/2)(1 - x) \geq 0 \Rightarrow x \leq 1.$$

Therefore, the maximum is well-defined, and is attained when x takes the highest value possible:

$$(x^*, y^*) = (1, 0). \qquad \square$$

A.5.2   Method of Lagrange Multipliers

Ignore the non-negativity restriction: $x, y \geq 0$. Then solve using the method of Lagrange multipliers. If the optimal solution (x^*, y^*) satisfies the omitted non-negativity constraints, we are done. If not, we deduce that the optimal solution must have $x = 0$ or $y = 0$, or both.

A.6   Two-Variable Inequality Constraint

We are interested in solving the following optimization problem:

$$\max f(x, y)$$

$$\text{s.t. } ax + by \leq c.$$

In economic settings $f(x, y)$ is usually monotone in x and y, and $a, b \geq 0$. This is what is assumed here. This allows us to conclude that an optimal solution (x^*, y^*) satisfies $ax^* + by^* = c$. Hence, we can assume that the inequality constraint holds at equality and apply the methods of the previous section.

A.7   Two-Variable Inequality Constraint with Non-negativity

We are interested in solving the following optimization problem:

$$\max f(x, y)$$

$$\text{s.t. } ax + by \leq c$$

$$x, y \geq 0.$$

If $f(x, y)$ is usually monotone in x and y, and $a, b \geq 0$, then, in any optimal solution (x^*, y^*), we have $x^* \geq 0$ and $y^* \geq 0$. Hence, the non-negativity constraints are redundant and can be ignored. This allows us to solve the problem as above.

Example 61 *Find the values of x and y that solve the following maximization problem:*

$$\max 2x + 3y$$

$$\text{s.t. } 4x + 2y \leq 8$$

$$x \geq 0, y \geq 0.$$

Answer: $(x^*, y^*) = (0, 4)$.

Justification: *First, ignore all constraints and solve* max $2x + 3y$. *The solution will be* $x = y = \infty$. *Thus, the omitted non-negativity constraints* $(x, y \geq 0)$ *are satisfied but not the inequality constraints* $4x + 2y \leq 8$. *Hence, we know that the inequality constraint must hold at equality. So we solve*

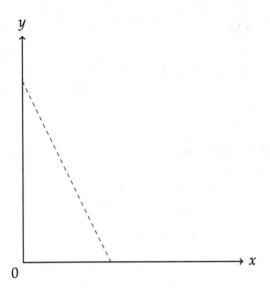

Figure A.1 Portion of line

$$\max 2x + 3y$$

$$\text{s.t. } 4x + 2y = 8$$

$$x \geq 0, y \geq 0.$$

This can be done via substitution or Lagrange multipliers. Let's do the second. The Lagrangian will be $L(x, y, \lambda) = 2x + 3y + \lambda(8 - 4x - 2y)$. The FOCs will be

$$\frac{\partial L}{\partial x} = 2 - 4\lambda = 0,$$

$$\frac{\partial L}{\partial y} = 3 - 2\lambda = 0.$$

$$\frac{\partial L}{\partial \lambda} = 8 - 4x - 2y = 0.$$

There is clearly no solution to the FOCs.

Figure A.1 shows a portion of the graph of the line $4x + 2y = 8$ (the dashed line). This is the portion of the line for which x and y are non-negative. The analysis above tells us that the optimal solution must lie on this dashed line. Furthermore, the absence of a solution to the FOC tells us that the optimal solution we seek is not in the interior of the dashed line. Hence, it must be at the two ends (corners): $(2, 0), (0, 4)$. Clearly, $x^* = 0, y^* = 4$ has the largest objective function value and this is the solution. □

Index

Printed in the United States
by Baker & Taylor Publisher Services